Integrating Theory and Practice
in Social Work Education

Integrating Theory and Practice in Social Work Education

Florence Watson, Helen Burrows and Chris Player

Jessica Kingsley Publishers
London and Philadelphia

The right of the contributors to be identified as authors of this work has been asserted by them in accordance with the Copyright, Designs and Patents Act 1988.

First published in the United Kingdom in 2002 by
Jessica Kingsley Publishers Ltd,
116 Pentonville Road, London
N1 9JB, England
and
325 Chestnut Street,
Philadelphia, PA 19106, USA.

www.jkp.com

© Copyright 2002 Jessica Kingsley Publishers Ltd

Library of Congress Cataloging in Publication Data
A CIP catalog record for this book is available from the Library of Congress

British Library Cataloguing in Publication Data
A CIP catalogue record for this book is available from the British Library

ISBN 1 85302 981 5

Printed and Bound in Great Britain by
Athenaeum Press, Gateshead, Tyne and Wear

Contents

List of figures and tables

Acknowledgements

We would like to thank David Chandler, External Assessor to the Norfolk Diploma in Social Work Programme, for his suggestions about guidance provided to students for integrated assignments and his support for this project. We are also very appreciative of the assistance given by Lorraine Agu, Lee Durrant and Simon Shreeve, who contributed chapters to the book. Thanks are also due to the college's programme partners, Norfolk County Council Department of Social Services, and in particular the many practice teachers whose interest in this guidance has helped it along. Thanks are due to Kris Morris for her suggestion about ideas and information. We would like to acknowledge the support of our centre director, Jim Smyth, who helped us to find time in our busy teaching schedules to write. Thanks are also due to our families and friends, who kept encouraging us to write whenever our energy failed us. Special thanks go to George, who helped with the *Star Wars* references. Last, but not least, we owe many thanks to our wonderful social work students, who acted as unwitting guinea pigs as we developed this book and who gave us many excellent suggestions that we only hope we have done justice to. Particular and special thanks are due to Denise Cioban, Jan Clarke, Susan Fernandez, Damaris Harrison, Tracey Hawke, Sharon Jones, Daniel Knight, Tracey Whittaker and Frankie Winrow-Giffin for their unstinting support and practical help with this book. Without their generosity and kindness it would not have been possible.

CHAPTER ONE

Introduction

Theory and a foundation academic knowledge of a given occupation and its sphere of work has traditionally been used as one of the bases on which occupations lay claim to being professional. The extent to which this actually assists an occupation to achieve professional status is highly contested (MacDonald 1995). Nonetheless, professional expert knowledge, discretion and judgement rest at the interface between the work or tasks involved and the skill achieved through on-the-job training and practice and the abstract knowledge or theory that underpin this (Abbott 1988). The tension between theory and practice is thus ever present in professions and in education for professions. Usually the need for formal training in both theory and practice skills is achieved through a combination of academic college or university based teaching and work-based experiential learning achieved through some form of apprenticeship – or in the case of the Diploma in Social Work (DipSW) supervised practice placements (Central Council for Education and Training in Social Work (CCETSW) 1996a). This pattern of professional education, in turn, is closely linked to the ongoing debate about whether education and training for a practical occupation are better done within an academic institution or through work-based training (which is resurfacing as discussions about the future shape of social work education continue).

This debate is not unique to social work, but is peculiarly acute within this occupation because within the profession there remains a vocal anti-professionalism ethical stance which leaves some of its members ambivalent about the supposed benefits of professional status (Hugman

1998a). Moreover many social work educators themselves experience dissonance at trying to be both academics and practitioners at one and the same time (Lyons 1999). Within qualifying social work professional training, the resolution of this tension is expressed through the requirement that in order to achieve professional accreditation, social work students must be able to 'take a rigorous approach to the acquisition of knowledge, and be able to select and apply it in practice' (CCETSW 1996a, p.19).

All this sounds impressive in academic conferences and professional meetings, and looks good on paper in the form of academic publications and policy documents. Many people would agree that it is important to achieve a rigorous approach and no one wants to undermine the importance of this synthesis of knowledge and professional judgement. As one colleague put it to us: no one wants to see a social worker walk up the path to complete a care assessment who is 'full to the gills of book learning but cannot do the job'. Equally, no one wants to see someone who has learned all the rules by rote and dogmatically undertakes all the steps in an assessment by rote without appreciating the overall impact of the work he/she is doing and the way it might affect people. As Howe so eloquently puts it: '…not only is theory in social work unavoidably integral to any practice, but also its relegation to an implicit, unarticulated status leads to poor, indeed dishonest practice' (Howe 1987, p.1).

However important it may be to achieve, the harsh reality of educating budding professional social workers about the importance of theory to their practice is not easy. One of the standard theory texts used on many social work courses acknowledges this:

> When, not for the first time, I found myself saying to a student social worker that there is more than one way to skin a cat, I realized that there was much to be said about different ways of explaining the world… The mention of theory and skinning cats does not, however, bring about instant joy in the hearts of many social workers. For them, the relationship between theory and their practice remains something of a mystery. (Howe 1987, p.1)

If already qualified and very experienced practitioners struggle to identify the ways they use theory in their everyday working life, what hope have inexperienced students? Yet they are required to do just this, and their practice teachers are required to support and assist them in this process whilst students are on placement: 'Practice teachers need to reinforce the understanding and application of knowledge and theory in practice' (Lishman 1991, p.7).

Often the interface between theory and practice is achieved through formal written assignments and every year DipSW students struggle with assignments where they are required to demonstrate their use of theory, ethics and values, law and research in their day-to-day work as practitioners. All professional qualifying courses, whether non-graduate or Master's level degree courses, require students to write at least one (often more than one) assignment which attempts to integrate theory and practice together. Although an academic assignment, the students base it on work done while on placement. Nonetheless there is considerable academic content to these assignments, evidenced through extensive library research about theories, policy, legal cases, etc., the formal referencing and bibliography, and the academic style of language and complexity of argument and analysis.

These assignments are called by various titles – case studies, integrated assignments, practice analysis. They may come at differing stages of the programme: some may be a part of (or come soon after) completing the first placement, more often they are due at the end of the second supervised placement. Nonetheless, regardless of title, the core components of these assignments all include *both* the student's own work on placement *and* analysis about the theory (etc.) which underpinned this practice. In addition, usually these assignments include a requirement for students to reflect on and evaluate their own work, in accordance with CCETSW's requirement (under point 3.5) to 'provide evidence of their capacity to reflect on their practice; transfer knowledge, skills and values in practice; and, understand their responses to change, including their personal learning styles' (CCETSW 1996a, p.38). Evidence of this skill is required both in practice while on placement and through written work – hence these integrated assignments.

Integrated assignments are usually intended to demonstrate that students are *integrating* what they have learned on a number of academic modules with what they have learned on practice placement. In other words, it draws together, usually towards the end of the course, in an holistic way, evidence of social work competencies. Assignments should therefore demonstrate that students are ethical and reflective workers who are able to integrate theory with practice (including practising in anti-discriminatory and antiracist ways).

This is not an easy task to achieve. Before most students write their integrated assignments, considerable planning and research are required. This is not an assignment which students can expect to complete quickly, without a great deal of preparation, or at the last moment. Sometimes students have commented that they feel isolated from the colleges or universities at which they are studying when completing these assignments, particularly since these assignments are typically completed while a student is on placement. Students spend the majority of their time on practice placement whilst undertaking their integrative assignment. While they may receive a lot of guidance about their practice, in contrast they feel they are just expected to get on with it in relation to the academic assignment, without having a great deal of formal guidance or support about how to complete the work, or explanation about what they need to do to pass or what standard is required. Clearly we remember vividly our own experiences of doing these assignments for our various courses (Coventry, Exeter, Leicester) while we were all on our final placements. We all independently experienced this sense of isolation and confusion about 'What do they *really* want?', and felt frustrated about the seeming lack of clear guidance ('Well it depends on the nature of your practice and that is individual') about how to tackle this type of assignment.

This book has been written as one means of addressing this issue, so that students have a guide to refer to as needed. It is not meant to substitute for tutorial or other support or guidance for these kinds of integrated assignments, but to supplement them. Each college or university DipSW programme will have its own specific requirements and marking criteria for these assignments – differing word limits, differing emphases on the proportion of theory versus law versus self-reflection, slightly differing academic requirements about referencing, etc. This book cannot possibly substitute for the specific guidance students receive through their courses nor through individual tutorials with practice teacher or tutor. It is, however, intended to help students understand the context in which specific guidance from their courses has been set.

Every year some students fail these integrated assignments for a variety of reasons. Failure in the integrated assignment can sometimes occur because students substantially misunderstand how to evidence theory, research, ethics, etc. in their practice through academic writing. These students may have passed all other previous academic assignments with flying colours and may have received glowing praise for their practice while on placement. However, when required to marry together theory and practice into one written assignment they stumble at the first hurdle. Essentially, they misunderstand how to fulfil the expectations of markers and external assessors.

Academically weaker students also are more likely to struggle with these assignments because, although sound practitioners, they often feel they practise on instinct or follow procedures. How often have tutors heard students say: 'I have always struggled with the theory side of things but I know I can do it in the real world and I'm good with people'? Often these are the students who have difficulty providing evidence of how they actually use theory in the real world of practice. These are the students who need the clearest guidance of all, but who can and do achieve respectable marks in their coursework if provided with insightful academic support. Yet the best way of providing this support can puzzle tutors – particularly when students have relatively little contact with tutors whilst on place-ment, and when social work tutors (like many other teaching staff) are increasingly stretched to their limits and find it difficult to find the time to provide additional one-to-one support to students.

This book arose as a result of our experiences as academic tutors at Norwich City College in teaching a non-graduate DipSW course which accepts students with a wide variety of academic backgrounds. Being located in a college of further and higher education, we all have a strong commitment to inclusive education and to widening the participation in DipSW programme to students who might not have the formal academic qualifications usually required for entry. A nice principle to talk about at parties or social work conferences, this places considerable demands on tutors to support students in learning how to understand and meet academic requirements, probably more so than would be needed by tutors for a highly academic and highly selective Master's level programme that would only accept students with a solid 2:1 average for their first degree. (At this point it should be emphasised that we are in no way disparaging the selection required for Master's programmes, which is as appropriate and right for that type of course as non-selection is for ours. In a nutshell, different horses for different courses. We are simply pointing out that most tutors on Master's level programmes can assume students have some awareness of what is meant by academic referencing, how to use a library catalogue, how to skim read, etc. whilst tutors of non-graduate courses have no such assurance.)

In 1999 the inevitable result of our relatively non-selective academic entry system occurred: 9 out of 24 possible graduates from the DipSW programme failed – 38 per cent of the expected graduating class. Our external assessors supported the course tutors to maintain standards and require those students to resubmit the failed final integrated assignments, rather than lower standards and pass students through as good enough. However, the assessors also suggested that we consider how and why this had happened, and in particular, look at the scant two-page guidance we gave to students about the content requirements for the integrated assignment to see if it could be improved.

Review of the progress of the problematic year group – in particular a look at their academic marks throughout the two years of the programme – reassured tutors that they had been identified as a particularly weak group academically from the very beginning. A substantial proportion of the group had failed one or more modules before attempting the final assignment and a larger than usual percentage of the class had failed several modules (barely passing them on resubmission). Only one of the nine students who failed the final assignment had not failed at least one module earlier in the course. The spread of marks through the academic classifications (bare pass, 3rd, 2:2, 2:1, 1st) for this group of students throughout the two years of their programme showed that while (as with all groups) there were a few students who achieved marks at the higher end of the range, there was a disproportionately high number of students consistently achieving in the low 2:2, 3rd and bare pass range of marks.

These were students who had needed more support from tutors than could be provided on an individual basis (e.g. through extra tutorials), which had hitherto been the way extra help was traditionally offered on our course. All students had access to additional academic tutorial support for assignment writing and the editing of draft assignments through a learner support service available from the college library. However, many students, although they had failed other assignments in the past and had passed on resubmission only after using this service, did not seek help in this way for the integrated assignment. They explained, with some justification, that it was difficult to arrange time away from their placements to come into college to see the tutors at the learner support service and that what they felt they really needed was something they could access whilst in their placements.

Notably, for all the failed assignments, essay plans that the students had developed before submitting their assignments showed they had gone substantially off track with their ideas from the very beginning. Several of these students had been offered advice about their assignments through tutorials or written comments about essay plans, only to reject this advice and subsequently fail. Clearly the ad hoc way of providing support to weaker students, while it might work well with a class of average abilities (or better), was not as effective with a class containing a higher than average number of weaker students – probably due to the inevitable limitations of staff time.

As stated earlier, this book developed from our experiences of helping this group of students (of whom most eventually passed on resubmission). The revised guidance notes that our external assessors suggested we consider writing kept expanding until they comprised several thousand words and formed the core of this book. They were intended as written guidance, specific to the integrated assignment, which our students could take with them onto their placements and refer to as needed. Students, however, pointed out that the guidance was more widely applicable than simply help for the one assignment at Norwich City College. They said it was a shame it could not be more readily available as it was relevant to other kinds of theory-to-practice assignments and they were sure students on other courses would find it equally helpful.

We also revised some of the teaching exercises we had been using in various academic modules (and wrote additional exercises) to improve the connection between theory and practice and specifically heighten students' understanding of how the theory they learned in the college setting would relate to the work they did on placement. The exercises were altered in order to give them further practice about the kind of analysis they would need to complete as a part of their integrated assignments. Student comments as part of the evaluations completed routinely at the end of teaching each module were very complimentary about the high value they placed on these teaching exercises (they have been incorporated into this book in Chapter 13). They serve to emphasise that the integration of theory with practice in social work education does not rely on one or two assignments at the end of a course, but is an integral part of the teaching throughout a good professional course.

This book has been organised so that readers are provided with information about different aspects of the integrated assignment, in the order (more or less) in which the various tasks associated with preparing an integrated assignment have to be completed. As much as possible, simple straightforward (and sometimes non-academic) language has been used. We have tried to make this book easy to understand and user friendly, since we all agreed what *is* the point of guidance which readers have to puzzle over to make sense of. Clarity – not complexity – is the key to good guidance. Examples are given wherever appropriate (although readers need to remember these examples do not include every possible permutation), many of them drawn from assignments submitted by students of the Norfolk DipSW. (All examples have been anonymised to protect confidentiality; the pronoun 'she' has been used, regardless of the real sex of the student.)

Teaching exercises which help people to understand the relationship of theory to practice are included in Chapter 2. These may be used by lecturers in a classroom setting or alternatively as self-study exercises. However, regardless of how they are used, it is usually helpful for students completing an exercise on their own to debrief to another person (fellow student, academic tutor, practice teacher) about what they did. This will spark discussion and new analysis as other people will notice other aspects of theory and practice than the individual who did the exercise alone. This should not automatically suggest the first person was wrong, merely that two heads are better than one. Individual differences in styles of learning inevitably mean people view the same event in different and unique ways. This diversity strengthens understanding about the intricate relationship that theory has with practice and enhances education and understanding.

Once students are at the point in their programme of having to write an integrated assignment, the first step is to ensure that they understand the content and focus of the paper and appreciate the amount of work it will involve so that they allocate sufficient time and attention to write a good assignment. This is no different from what is required for all academic assignments. In the past, when students started a module they were given the question or assignment topic well in advance and began thinking about what it really meant several weeks before they started writing their actual papers. They looked at the word length and complexity of the topic to consider approximately how long it would take to complete the library research and background reading and then write the essay. This process of understanding what is really meant is discussed in Chapter 3. It also provides some guidance about how to choose a topic to write about and complete a plan to assist a student in developing an assignment. It is important to develop a good working plan since this will set people on the right track from the very beginning.

Chapter 4 provides some guidance about the tutorial and practice teachers' roles in supporting students who are writing their integrated assignments. How can tutors most effectively help students? How can practice teachers fit the time to help students into their already overworked days and rushed schedules? How can students make the most effective use of the limited one-to-one support available to them? The process of researching the integrated assignment, the scope of this process and how to obtain all the material which is needed is discussed in Chapter 5.

The final stages of completing an integrated assignment – that of actually writing it – are discussed in Chapters 6 to 10. It is extremely important that students take care to ensure their integrated assignments include the kind of high quality work which the content and focus of this assignment demand. Therefore considerable guidance about the standard of work which is expected is provided in these chapters. Clearly this information is crucial to appreciate at the writing stage. However, anyone completing a theory-to-practice assignment would be well advised to consider this at *all stages* of the assignment, even in the very earliest stage of preparation, since without good preparation designed to achieve this kind of high quality information and evidence, it will not be possible to produce good quality work.

Chapter 11 has been written from two students' perspectives. The two contributing authors are graduates of the DipSW at Norwich City College. Both were extremely able students who obtained high marks during their course. Nonetheless one failed his final integrated assignment the first time around because, no matter how high his academic abilities, he substantially failed to meet the required focus of the assignment and wrote off topic. Students most want to hear what it's really like from other students, and this chapter offers that opportunity.

Chapter 12 has been contributed by an experienced social worker and educator. Lorraine Agu was external assessor for the Norfolk DipSW programme at Norwich City College for four years, and was one of the CCETSW external assessors who suggested revising guidance to students in the wake of the high percentage of failed assignments in 1999. She was instrumental in suggesting this book and so, after her appointment as external assessor ended, was approached to contribute to it. Her contribution provides a unique perspective not only as an external assessor but also as a Black woman involved in professional education and committed to the widening of participation to people from more diverse backgrounds than those who traditionally access higher education.

In these days of scepticism about effectiveness and programme evaluation, no conclusion would be complete without some mention of achievement. 'Yes, but does it work?' people ask – hence the subtitle of Chapter 13, 'The Proof of the Pudding…'. Some results of student achievement from before the guidance was developed, through 1999 and beyond, are presented, along with the consumer perspective – comments from students who received the first version of the guidance booklet, from which this book was developed.

Finally, we make no claims that this book is stunningly new, the exciting answer to all students', tutors' and practice teachers' problems, nor an easy fix to the knotty problem of evidencing theory in practice-oriented assignments. These assignments are not easy and a good assignment results only from a lot of hard work. We merely hope that this guidance will help students (and the tutors and practice teachers helping them) to focus their hard work in ways which achieve the intended result – a good pass and a professional social work qualification. In addition, we believe that the process of writing an integrated assignment can only support the continued development of theory and skills of reflection. This process in itself contributes to the maintenance of high professional standards in social work and a continuing commitment to empowering practice.

CHAPTER TWO

Formal Teaching Preparation for Placement

In one sense all teaching throughout the two years of the DipSW is preparation for academic assignments completed about the final placement. However, students do not always view it this way. To some students, the contents of the various academic modules are separate from one another and from practice requirements. CCETSW clearly does not agree with this, as witnessed in its guidance to programme providers:

> Students must be assessed on their understanding of relevant knowledge and theory in the context of its application to social work practice and their ability to apply it. Therefore, for the award of the DipSW, academic disciplines should only be assessed with relevance to social work practice. (CCETSW 1996a, p.37)

Nonetheless, some students do not always recognise quite so readily the applicability of what they learn in the classroom with what they do in the real world of social work. In order to combat this tendency to view academic modules as somehow separate, the following teaching exercises can be used. These exercises are designed specifically to enable students to understand the connection between theory and practice. They can be used as classroom-based exercises, in which students work together in small groups. Alternatively they can be used as home study exercises. Usually they work extremely well once students have completed their 50-day practice placement since this gives them a basis for applying theory to their own work. Part-time students who are currently employed in a social work setting can apply these exercises to their current practice as social work assistants. (In this book we have used a variety of terms to refer to the people with whom social workers practise: service users, clients, cases, carers, families etc. We recognise that some of these terms are more acceptable in some services than in others and that individuals' choice of which terms they use can reflect their values perspective. However, we have chosen to use the terms as appropriate in different situations.)

Ground rules

The process of reflection on practice and experiential learning requires a level of self-analysis. Many of these exercises require some self-disclosure: prior to undertaking any of these activities in teaching groups, we would recommend strongly that the lecturer undertakes some preparatory work with the student group. This work should maximise group processes to provide a safe learning environment which in turn supports the process of self-disclosure. To facilitate this we propose that ground rules are drawn up with the class to help maintain a safe and anti-discriminatory approach. We adopt those of Thompson *et al.* (1998):

> *Communication*: Feel free to give your opinion and to disagree with the opinion of others, without putting them or their opinion down.

> *Commitment*: Be here and work hard for the duration of the course. You are responsible for your own learning.

> *Contribution*: Be aware of how much or how little you are contributing. If you normally say little, try to give more. If you are saying too much, try to give a little less in order to give other people a chance.

> *Confidentiality*: It is a good idea to share the general issues that arise with colleagues outside the group. However, any individual or personal information about real people will remain within the group. The only limit to this convention is if the trainers believe that there is a serious danger to the course participant or their clients, in which case confidentiality will be broken after informing the participant.

> *Care*: Take care of yourself and the other people in the group. The trainers will agree to look after the whole group to try to ensure a positive experience, but they need you to help care for yourselves.

Person-centred: In this [exercise] it is acceptable not to be client- or child-centred, but instead to be person-centred. This [exercise] is largely about how you as a person, are dealing with the professional and personal pressures in your life [appropriate for the more self-reflective exercises].

Culture: In our society whole groups of people are devalued and given less status than others. This can be because of their race, gender, age, disability or sexuality. On this course we will attempt not to devalue, by what we say or do, any of these groups of people. (Thompson *et al.* 1998, p.70)

Exercise 1: Practice logs and reflective practice

This exercise helps students to understand how they have learned throughout their placements. It also helps students to develop skills at reflecting back on their work and examining how it changed over time. It facilitates students recognising how they can use reflection to develop and improve their practice and identify transferable theory-based skills. The exercise is ideally suited soon after the 50-day placement has been completed. Alternatively it may be used while the placement is ongoing. If students are not formally required to complete practice logs whilst on placement, the exercise can still be completed while the placement is ongoing. In this case a practice teacher would need to ask the student to complete a daily record of work and thoughts about how or why the student made these decisions or worked in this way for one or two weeks (possibly with a gap between the two weeks). At the end of this, the exercise could be used as pre-supervision preparation by the student for a meeting with the practice teacher.

Pre-exercise preparation

This exercise is based on the following background reading:

Best, D. (1998) 'On the Experience of Keeping a Reflective Journal while Training.' In A. Ward and L. MacMahon (eds) *Intuition is Not Enough: Matching Learning with Practice in Therapeutic Child Care.* London: Routledge.

Schon, D. (1983) *The Reflective Practitioner: How Professionals Think in Action.* New York: Basic Books.

Tait, M. (1999) 'Using a Reflective Diary in Student Supervision.' In V. Cree and C. Macauley (eds) *Transfer of Learning in Professional and Vocational Education.* London: Routledge.

Students should read a chapter from Schon and at least one of the other articles. They will also need to use the practice logs they kept while on supervised placement.

Written exercise

Look at your practice log from your 50-day practice placement and try to answer the following questions:

1. Is there a difference between the amount you wrote describing what you did compared to how much you wrote about *how* or *why* you worked in that way as the log progresses? Do a rough word count of how much was devoted to describing what happened versus how much was devoted to discussing why and how it happened, if that helps you to answer this question.

    Probably at the beginning you spent more time describing what happened since you were spending much of your time and energy learning the ropes – the details of what forms to fill in, how to use procedures, the facts about each person you met. By the end of placement, however, you were concentrating more on discussing how you felt about completing a piece of work (e.g. 'I felt it had all been a waste of time because she refused the service and had to remind myself it was still good work because she made the choice knowing all her options and that is something I feel is very important as a social worker and different from what the doctor and nurses feel') or why you did something one way rather than another (e.g. 'I was very aware of the physical space between Mr T and me and tried to remember my body language – remembered to try to phrase things so he would agree with me and feel I was listening to him' – techniques from Leadbetter and Trewartha 1996).

This shift from describing what to discussing how and why shows that what *you* were learning changed as the placement progressed. Identifying how and why also links the facts of what you were doing to the theory behind it.

2. Is there a case or piece of practice you worked on over the course of several weeks while on placement? This might be, for example, keywork with a young person in a children's home, or assessment of need of a vulnerable older person whose needs changed over time so that at the beginning of your work you were developing a package of care in the community but by the end of placement you were completing the paperwork for the person's admission to a nursing home.

    If you worked in a placement where this kind of longer-term social work intervention was not done, but where you had a number of short-term pieces of work (e.g. intake or reception team, hospital social work), choose two or more pieces of practice from beginning, middle and end of placement in which you completed the same task. This could include, for example, completion of initial intake assessment records for referrals from the general practitioner (GP) for disabled people or provided information to relatives or carers of people suffering from dementia who had been admitted to hospital.

    Now consider the differences between the practice you were doing at different stages of the placement. At any point did you note down how you did something differently later on from the way you did it at the beginning because you had learned from what happened earlier? For example: 'Made sure K was sitting where he could see the paperwork while I was writing this down this time since he'd said last time how he hated the way professionals hide away their notes and won't let you see things unless you ask'; 'Made sure I had collected all the forms before going round to see Mrs W so I wouldn't waste time having to go back again the way I did with Mr Y!'

This review of your practice log should have assisted you to identify how much you have learned and how skills developed over time, often as a result of incremental knowledge about a given individual client or situation or through altering behaviour so you avoided making the same mistake twice or did the same task more efficiently and effectively the second time around.

Exercise 2: Learning how to reflect on practice

This classroom-based exercise is designed to last for approximately three hours. It is designed to help students understand *how* to reflect on their practice and to turn experience into reflective learning.

Pre-exercise preparation

The following background reading should be completed by students before coming to class:

> Nash, C. (2000) 'Applying Reflective Practice.' In C. Davies, L. Finlay and A. Bullman (eds) *Changing Practice in Health and Social Care.* London: Sage.

> Quinn, F.M. (2000) 'Reflection and Reflective Practice.' In C. Davies, L. Finlay and A. Bullman (eds) *Changing Practice in Health and Social Care.* London: Sage.

Part 1 of the exercise

Work in pairs. Each of you needs to discuss *briefly*, within your pairs, a piece of social work practice you completed on your first placement (or, if you are currently in practice, completed *at least one year ago*). This needs to be a piece of practice where you held strong feelings (good or bad) about the outcome of the work. Analyse and reflect on your past practice applying the Gibbs reflective cycle (Quinn 2000, p.84) as a model to assist you in understanding the emotional and practice skills you learned from this situation.

Tip for teachers

This exercise should take approximately 20 minutes to complete and can be followed up by a debriefing session with the whole class. This offers an opportunity to discuss the strengths and limitations of reflection and debriefing as a tool for professionals to learn and develop competence.

Part 2 of the exercise

Work in small groups of four or five. Each of you needs to discuss with the rest of the group a piece of social work practice you completed on your first placement (or, if you are currently in practice, completed recently in your workplace). This needs to be a different piece of practice from the one you chose to discuss in Part 1. The practice example needs to be one where someone raised questions about your decision or judgement around you (e.g. practice teacher, co-worker or professional from another agency) so that you had to explain more completely *how* and *why* you did the work or made those decisions. Note that this does not necessarily mean you were being accused of malpractice, simply that unlike other parts of your work where people accepted without question what you did, this time you were asked to explain or discuss it a bit more in-depth. Once you have shared your experiences choose *one* example from the group to analyse and use as a basis of this exercise. As a group, apply Johns's model of structured reflection (Quinn 2000, p.85). In your analysis, concentrate on points 3.1 to 5.3.

Tip for teachers

This exercise should take approximately 20–25 minutes. Note the key points on flipchart paper and choose a member of the group to present this to the rest of the class when all the groups will be expected to feed back to each other.

Exercise 3: Dealing with feelings through reflection

This exercise is designed to offer students an opportunity to reflect on work they have done in the past which left them with strong feelings. It facilitates students' understanding of the emotional elements of practice and the use of reflection in processing them.

Pre-exercise preparation

The following background reading should be completed by students before coming to class:

Best, D. (1998) 'On the Experience of Keeping a Reflective Journal while Training.' In A. Ward and L. MacMahon (eds) *Intuition is Not Enough: Matching Learning with Practice in Therapeutic Child Care*. London: Routledge.

Derezotes, D. (2000) 'Affective Development.' In D. Derezotes, *Advanced Generalist Social Work Practice*. Thousand Oaks, CA: Sage.

Classroom-based exercise

Work in small groups of four or five. Each of you needs to identify a practice situation which developed on the 50-day practice placement where you felt strong emotions about the piece of practice, emotions related to the boundaries of personal or professional roles. Perhaps this was a situation which held associations or reminders of past painful personal experiences – for example, working with a person who was being admitted to hospital under Section 3 of the Mental Health Act 1983 might bring back memories for you if you had experienced mental health problems some years ago. Perhaps this was a situation which brought back happy memories – for example, where you felt joy and pride through helping young people decorate, furnish and move into their own flat and start at college, feelings which perhaps reflected back to the joy you yourself felt years ago as you set up your first home.

Tip for teachers

Students should be reminded to discuss only situations or experiences that they feel comfortable about sharing with the group. As a group they should then discuss these situations and the feelings they engendered in the context of the following questions:

1. What are the appropriate boundaries of personal versus professional roles?

2. How could writing in a learning log or practice journal assist in identifying these boundaries, reflecting on them and developing appropriate methods for dealing with the feelings in positive ways?

It is clear from the personal nature of the issues being discussed that any feedback would need to be handled sensitively and the establishment of ground rules will support this process.

Exercise 4: Integrating theory to practice

This exercise is useful in helping students to integrate theory they have learned over the course of several modules for the DipSW so that they can see how every piece of social work practice is imbued with a variety of theories.

Pre-exercise preparation

This exercise is based on the following background reading:

> Prince, K. (1996) 'Discussion of the Action Research Theoretical Perspectives.' In K. Prince, *Boring Records?* London: Jessica Kingsley.

In order to complete this exercise, students will also need to draw on their own past and/or current practice experience and what they have already learned through other modules completed for the DipSW.

Part 1 of the exercise

Choose one record you have written as a part of practice. Examples of the kinds of items you may wish to choose include: pieces from your practice log from the 50-day practice placement, a letter you sent to a client, a letter you sent to another professional, a note you shoved through the door of a client's house when you went for a visit and she was not there, a pre-sentence report, a brief file recording about a home visit, a form you filled in to get Sec. 17 funds, a core assessment, initial referral information entered into the agency's computer database etc. (use your imagination!). You do not need to have a copy of the record in your possession *provided you still remember clearly what you said, how you said it, and how it looked.*

Once you have chosen your one record, try to answer the following questions:

1. When you wrote this record did you consciously think about whether or not you would be showing it (or should show it) to the client?

2. When you were writing this record did you consider how the client would respond to (a) the information it contained, (b) the way you were wording this, (c) the way it looked (e.g. full sheet of A4 versus scrappy bit of paper dug out of the bag you had with you; large font versus small font, etc.)?

3. Did you involve your client in the development or writing of this record (e.g. writing a referral letter with the client's agreement about what it would contain; agreeing a descriptive phrase to use in a report which encapsulated the client's feelings about a situation) or was it written without any consultation with the client?

4. Did you show this record to the client? If so how did the client react?

5. If this record was not shown to the client, how do you think the client would react on seeing it?

Once you have chosen your record and answered the above questions, the next task is to try to identify the theory, policy, research and law which informed or underpinned the record.

Example

Here is a sample we have prepared so that you can see how this is done:

> *Privacy and Social Services* (Thomas 1995) discusses policy and law relating to record-keeping. Some of this underpins the records you wrote. Suppose the example you chose was a report from a social services department (SSD) social worker to the local education authority (LEA) in support of a learning-disabled 5½-year-old boy's statement of educational needs. This report will automatically be copied and provided to the child's parents (who have parental responsibility under the Children Act 1989) as a part of the

statement package, in accordance with regulations and guidance under the Education Act 1981, as well as Department of Health and LEA policy and state legislation relating to access to records. As a minor who is not responsible and too young or disabled to understand fully this report, the child himself will not be given a copy of the report, although you may have discussed some of the contents with him in simple language during your last visit with him (informed by certain case law). So that is some of the policy/law that underpins this – you know it because you read it in Thomas's book.

Theory about communication also informs this practice. A report to the LEA could potentially be an important document which affects special funding for this child. The layout was important. Language was carefully chosen to ensure it conveyed the right message to the readers. It would be difficult to pitch this just right so that both parents (who might not have a particularly high standard of education and would find technical terms difficult) and professionals (who would expect complex and sophisticated language and who potentially might be impressed with the strength of the argument based on this) could all understand the report. Perhaps a separate meeting was held with the parents to discuss a draft before the final version was sent. Think of how communication theory would inform this (e.g. open/closed posture, questions, etc.) and how much a professional would be prepared to redraft the report to fit in with the parents' wishes. Which articles or books have you read on the course which relate to how social workers write records? Which articles or books have you read on the course that discuss how people communicate effectively?

Psychological theory informed what went into the report. Theory about child development (e.g. what a normal 5½-year-old child would be able to do in a mainstream classroom), child's/parents' self-esteem, peer relationships, family interaction, etc., will all have been used as you wrote the content of the report (Daniel, Wassell and Gilligan 1999; Durkin 1995). Thus, when you were writing about how this child's speech was delayed, this recording was informed by the psychological theory about learning and language development. When you were discussing how the parents were very loving and concerned to get all the help possible for their son, your assessment was informed by attachment theory (Howe 1995; Howe *et al.* 1999).

Sociological theory was also incorporated into your record. Remember social interactionism and 'labelling' (Goffman 1967)? Your understanding of how this works, both in terms of how labels which carry certain meanings are attached by others to disabled children and in terms of how this boy might internalise his label, has informed your recommendation in this report. You were concerned not to stigmatise this child as the one child who struggled and was not accepted within a mainstream school so that he developed a 'spoiled identity' (Goffman 1963) and you were equally concerned not to stigmatise him by automatically shunting him off to a special school because 'that's where disabled children go'. You were concerned to ensure the school was given funding to provide adequate services rather than simply remove the child to an inadequately funded special school which was not able to meet his educational needs and which might deepen this problem of labels and stigma.

Sociological theory about the professions and professionalism particularly in relation to the caring professions, and even more crucially to social work, also informed the way you worked with the parents and the fact you had even been asked to complete this report in the first place. Oh yes! You read about this in Abbott and Meerabeau (1998) and Hugman (1998b).

Anti-discriminatory theory (remember that book by Neil Thompson [1997]) was incorporated into this report as well. You chose your language carefully to ensure that negative stereotypes about disabled children were not perpetuated. You also considered carefully the issues of exclusive and inclusive education in terms of what would be the most enabling system for this child. You listened carefully to what both the parents and the child had to say about their experiences and what they want to ensure the voice of the disabled person and voices of his nearest and dearest were not lost and that you were not oppressively pushing your own views onto them.

Core social work ethics and values about respecting each individual, being concerned about confidentiality, and empowering people to make choices were all central to this record (Banks 1995; British Association of Social Work (BASW) 1996). When the report was completed it was put in a sealed envelope, marked 'confidential' and sent to the attention of only those people who were supposed to get it (you did not give it to the next-door neighbour to deliver next week when she went into town to get her shopping). Your file copy went into a file that is kept in a secure place in the building where casual visitors are not allowed. And you have only spoken to those people who 'need to know' (Beauchamp and Childress 1994) about the information in this report. Your report also accurately included the parents' feelings and wishes about what should happen to their son, even though there were times you disagreed with them, and you gave a fair account of the pros and cons of their position even as you discussed alternatives, noting that the choice of school was of central importance to this boy and his parents and that the decisions about the educational statement could have a very detrimental effect on this choice.

Your knowledge of social policy also went into this report. You know it is being read by people who are working within a context of massive change within both the educational system and the system of care for disabled people (Oliver and Barnes 1998). You are aware that 50 years ago there was no such system of statementing for children; indeed, 50 years ago this child's parents would very likely have happily agreed he should go to a residential school miles away from home, where they would have visited him at most once a month. He would have lived there (or in another institution) most of his life, learning few skills. He might never have been taught to read or write. No one would see the need because they believed he might not even grow up to be an adult and would probably never work. If he were taught any skills it would be only the simplest of tasks. No one would have dreamed of asking him what clothes he wanted to wear or what food he wanted to eat. He would have worn bulk-bought clothes just like every other boy at this school and he would have eaten what was put in front of him. You know this because you read about it in Whitehead (1992).

However, that has changed, and the system is still changing. You are aware of the political issues about the state education system, funding problems and a budget crisis. You are aware of the professional controversy about special schools versus inclusive education and how funding and politics (about who should control the way schools are run and the curriculum which is taught) are playing a part in this. You are aware that increasingly the education system is being asked to prove that it provides good value for money and is cost effective, and to evaluate the work it does. League tables were introduced for mainstream schools and this potentially has affected parents' choices about the schools they want to send their children to, as well as having a bearing on schools' willingness to accept students with special needs (Demaine 1999). All this has influenced your recommendation about which school this little boy should attend, and you know all this because you studied social policy.

Now let us look at some of the theories of social work intervention that you have studied on this course. One obvious one is task-centred theory (Doel and Marsh 1992). You were allocated a specific task – to write the report; you went out, saw the family who adopted this goal for themselves and assisted you in working towards it, did the report, and now the file is going to be closed, task completed. Clearly task-centred theory could apply. But perhaps you are not closing the file; perhaps you have been working with this family for almost a year already and will continue to work with them.

Perhaps major issues for them have been personal problems raised with the birth of their disabled son. The father has strong memories about his brother, who was also disabled, and his child's birth has brought up huge issues of guilt and failure about his genetic background, unresolved feelings of rejection and hurt because the father's parents paid more attention to their disabled son than to him, and feelings of jealousy at the loss of his wife's attention. There are also unresolved issues of grieving on the part of the wife/mother about her loss of the normal baby she wanted, as well as anger at her husband that he isn't there for either the child or for her to rely on, just as her father wasn't there for her mother and herself when she was young. Would psychodynamic theories of intervention be applicable?

Perhaps the little boy has dreadful temper tantrums and you have been working with the parents to help them learn better skills for dealing with this problem more effectively to help the child learn appropriate moral and behavioural standards (cognitive-behavioural theories: Cigno and Bourn 1998; Sheldon 1995). Perhaps things reached crisis point last year when the child was sent home from school for hitting another child in the school playground. Father walked out of the family home for five days, mother overdosed (and was admitted to hospital overnight) and the little boy had to be accommodated temporarily in foster care. Crisis intervention theory (Aguilera 1998; Thompson 1991) probably underpinned this work (which was the reason the case was originally opened to you last year).

Probably theories about advocacy (Atkinson 1999; Brandon, Brandon and Brandon 1995) have informed much of the work with this family about the recommendation in your report (as discussed earlier when we were talking about anti-discriminatory practice). And, as you got more involved with this case, and picked up other work with disabled children, you have joined the inter-agency steering group for a new educational consortium. You are on this committee as the SSD representative helping this consortium to develop a National Vocational Qualification (NVQ) programme in connection with the Open College, the LEA and SSD which will train special needs assistants in schools and home care assistants in the SSD for work with learning disabled children. You used your knowledge about the inadequacy of existing training in this area, derived from your radical social work experience of this steering committee (Langan and Lee 1989), to inform your recommendations in the report you wrote about the educational statement.

Part 2 of the exercise

You have seen in the example how we unpicked some of the theory which went into the SSD report written to support a statement of educational needs for a disabled boy. Now you need to choose an example from your own record and go through the same process, applying the theory and deciding how applicable it was to the situation and what you were doing.

You should write approximately 800–1000 words on this. Once you have done that, go on to the next step of this exercise.

Part 3 of the exercise

Now consider what you were originally asked to do: to select a record and to answer certain questions about it. Let us go back to this. You have identified the underpinning theory which went into your record. Some of these theories also, clearly, inform the questions we asked you to complete at the beginning of this exercise, and should also inform your answers. Identify what these theories are.

Part 4 of the exercise

There is a further stage to consider as well: how much was the underpinning theory *explicitly* stated and how much was this only *implicitly* included in the record? For example (going back to the case of the learning disabled child and the report for the statement), in the report you might have *explicitly* referred to the 'good attachment and bonding' between mother and son, thus explicitly referring to psychological theory, but it is more likely your social work values will have been included *implicitly* by the way you chose what to say and how to say it, rather than explicitly referred to (e.g. you would be unlikely to write: 'I am making this recommendation because of my social work values').

Identify in your own record where you explicitly use theory, law and/or policy and where this knowledge is included only implicitly. Probably more things will have been used implicitly and fewer will have been used explicitly, and it is this which is at the heart of why many social work students find it difficult to identify openly the theories they use in practice.

Finally, as you did this exercise, you were also doing some of the tasks involved with reflective practice – looking at what you did in the past, thinking about what you did and why you did this, and the impact this could have on another person. You will learn more about how theory and reflection are intertwined in other exercises.

Exercise 5: Evaluating practice (part 1)

This exercise helps students to learn how to reflect on and formally evaluate their own practice on placement – a core requirement for all students to demonstrate as a part of their training (CCETSW 1996a, p.38). It helps students to identify a framework or structure which they can use to assist self-reflection and self-evaluation. It is an exercise which lends itself to small group work in class (in which students share their ideas with four or five classmates and then present their ideas to the rest of the class) or as a written exercise for students to complete on their own.

Pre-exercise preparation

This exercise is based on the following background reading:

> Trotter, C. (1999) 'What Works and What Doesn't?' and 'Evaluation.' In C. Trotter, *Working with Involuntary Clients*. London: Sage.

Classroom-based or written exercise

Choose a case which you were involved with in your past practice placement. This should be a piece of social work practice which involved a pivotal decision about service provision or decision about intervention and/or professional judgement or assessment which you were involved with making. It should be social work about which you feel very confident that it went well, that any (or most) decisions made were the right ones and that the outcome of this casework was appropriate and good (or the best which could be achieved in the circumstances).

Analyse this piece of social work using the principles suggested by Trotter's discussion about case analysis. Does the piece of work fit this framework for good practice? How much does it differ from this framework?

Exercise 6: Evaluating practice (part 2)

This exercise also helps students to learn how to reflect on and formally evaluate their own practice on placement. Similar to Exercises 2 and 3, it is an exercise which lends itself to small group work in class. When used together in a classroom setting (with students completing each of the exercises in groups, preparing posters with main points and discussing and presenting their analysis to the rest of the class) they take approximately two to three hours to complete. (Tip for teachers: have the students change groups so they are working with different students for each of the exercises.)

Pre-exercise preparation

This exercise is based on the following background reading:

> O'Sullivan, T. (1999) 'Evaluating Decisions.' In T. O'Sullivan, *Decision-Making in Social Work.* London: Macmillan.

Classroom-based exercise

Choose a piece of practice which you were involved with in your past practice placement. This should be a piece of social work practice which involved a pivotal decision about service provision, or decision about intervention and/or professional judgement or assessment which you were involved with making. It should be a piece of practice about which you feel that it did not go well, that the decision was not the right one or that the outcome of this decision was not good.

As a group, analyse this decision or intervention using the principles suggested by O'Sullivan. Which part of Figure 8.1 in O'Sullivan (1999, p.167) would this social work practice or decision fall within? Be prepared to feed back your analysis and discussion to the rest of the class.

Exercise 7: Analysing legal/ethical dilemmas in practice

This exercise involves individual student presentations and is ideally completed as a classroom-based exercise during one of the college or university teaching days that many courses have while students are on placement. Alternatively it could be completed soon after placement. It is intended to give students practice at analysis relating to how law is used in their own practice and practice at evidencing how they made ethically difficult decisions and exercised professional judgement when dilemmas arose in their work.

Pre-exercise preparation

There is no set background reading for this exercise although students will need to have completed the legislation module(s) before attempting this piece of analysis.

Classroom-based exercise

Choose a piece of work you have undertaken as part of your assessed practice to present to the class as a case study. This case study will give you an opportunity to demonstrate your ability to integrate theory, policy and – in particular – law into practice. Within the case study presentation you will be expected to analyse and evaluate your own work with a service user or client, family or group. Because they are based on the practice you are doing on placement, necessarily these will be individual (not group) presentations. They should follow an informal seminar-style format: 50 minutes is allocated for each presentation and within this time you should allow approximately 30 minutes for your own active presentation and approximately 20 minutes for class discussion.

Guidelines on presentation content

Your presentation should include:

1.   a brief thumbnail sketch of an anonymised case in which a legal or ethical dilemma arose and the legal issues that were involved

2.   analysis about how and why the ethical or legal dilemma developed

3.   analysis of the different stages of how you intervened, why this type of intervention was chosen, and of how this implemented statutory legislation, common law principles, procedural guidance, legal guidance and/or case law

4. evaluation of the way in which you resolved the legal or ethical dilemma

5. analysis about the implications of decisions taken (and the way the dilemma was resolved) for:

    (a) the clients

    (b) carers and/or family

    (c) the agency or organisation in which you are placed

    (d) you, as an individual practitioner

    (e) social work as a profession (if appropriate)

    (f) the public (if appropriate).

You should expect to refer in your presentation to:

1. specific legal statutes (and sub-sections, if appropriate) or case law precedents which provide key guidance to your area of work and the specific case example you have chosen

2. social work values, ethical principles and theory as relevant to the specific case situation (including anti-discriminatory and antiracist practice)

3. policy, procedures, research-based knowledge and other theory as relevant to the specific case situation.

You will be expected to provide specific references to the literature which you have drawn upon in your work for the presentation.

Tip for teachers

In the DipSW programme at Norwich City College, this presentation is intended as preparation for one of the formal written assignments that students complete while undertaking their 80-day placements. We always recommend that students choose the same case for the presentation and for the written assignment they submit. Thus the presentation and class discussion which follows have the effect of a group tutorial for the assignment and serve to supplement any individual tutorial support (which is usually limited at this stage due to the pressures students are experiencing on time management through placement requirements). The class interaction serves to support less academically able students to appreciate the legal and ethical ramifications of their practice as they learn from suggestions of the stronger students in the class (and scribble down notes as the class debates how the case proceeded). Equally, academically stronger students who may have a tendency to describe in detail every possible aspect of the law and thus lose focus are brought down to earth quite nicely as other students look puzzled and ask, quite simply, 'Yes, but what was the dilemma and how did you resolve it?'

Exercise 8: Analysing how the care–control and professional accountability debate in academic social work relates to practice

This exercise involves individual student presentations to the class.

Pre-exercise preparation

There is no set or specific background reading for this exercise although students will need to have completed a module in which academic teaching about sociology of the professions, and professional accountability and whistleblowing have been taught. At Norwich City College students are asked to read their choice of case studies in:

Hunt, G. (ed) (1998) *Whistleblowing in the Social Services: Public Accountability and Professional Practice.* London: Arnold.

This helps students to appreciate the complexities of professional and organisational accountability.

Classroom-based exercise

Your presentation is done on an individual basis. Each of you has 30 minutes to give your formal presentation; an additional 15 minutes is then allotted for general class discussion about the issues raised in your presentation.

Guidelines on presentation content

Consider a case which you were personally involved with where you believe individuals and/or the agency took the wrong approach to care versus control and/or lines of accountability (to named clients, their family/friends, the employer, other agencies and/or professional colleagues from other organisations, professional ethics and standards, professional governing body, the courts, the public, etc.) were confused or poor. Write a brief (anonymised) case history, describing what happened, what went wrong, how, why, etc. (a one to two page chronological account using point form which you give to the class may be helpful in doing this).

You will need to analyse the different power dimensions and roles played in the case. Your analysis *must* cover the following points:

1. How were the professionals and their actions and/or decisions viewed by the clients and carers: as caring or controlling?

2. How do you know that the clients and carers held these views?

3. Did the views of the clients and carers about whether actions were caring or controlling change over time? Why (or why not)? In other words, how did clients and carers measure the care or control being exercised?

4. How did the various professionals view their actions – as fulfilling a caring function of social work, or as fulfilling a controlling function?

5. Why did professionals view themselves as caring or controlling? What indicators did professionals use as their measures of the extent of control or care they were using? Did professionals' opinions about the balance between care and control which their work encompassed change over time?

6. To whom were the various professionals and other people involved in this case accountable? Where there were conflicting levels or lines of accountability, which took priority? A diagram showing the different levels of accountability in relation to your chosen case (with arrows showing who was more or less accountable to which person or agency) may assist this analysis.

Present a plan for dealing with this case in a different way – one in which you believe the workers and agencies all strike the right balance between care and control and an ideal of good practice is achieved with appropriate levels of accountability to all parties (or appropriate professional justification for why accountability to one party has been sacrificed in favour of accountability to another) and taking into consideration issues of agency or staff resources.

Discuss what would need to change in the organisation for the ideal to be achieved. Is there a need for different legislation? For different policy (either at a local or national level)? Would empowering clients to sue via the courts assist? Should workers get the union involved? Should workers blow the whistle (and how)?

Relate your analysis to (a) appropriate social work ethics and values, (b) appropriate legislation and policy, and (c) the academic and professional literature about the theory and research which inform the care, control and accountability debate in relation to your chosen case example.

In your presentation you must refer formally to the books and articles which you used in preparing for it. You will be asked questions about this by the class tutor if you fail to discuss the literature during your presentation.

Be prepared to explain to the rest of the class why you have developed your case analysis and plan in this way and to defend or justify your analysis about issues of care, control and accountability and your proposal to your peers. It will be the job of your classmates to ask you questions (either during or at the end of the formal part of the presentation) which examine the casework and plan from a variety of viewpoints to help ensure you have analysed the situation comprehensively, without missing anything obvious. Your job (as presenter) is to try to ensure you have covered all angles so that you feel confident about answering all their questions and no obvious gap in analysis becomes glaringly apparent as the class discusses the case. Remember this is a learning exercise. You won't fail if the questions reveal that these issues could be examined in a different way or that a different plan could have been developed. Also, a different viewpoint and different plan does not necessarily mean your viewpoint is wrong – or that another student's viewpoint is right. The class discussion is intended to help everyone to understand your professional judgement: why you reached the conclusions you did, and why you discarded other ideas in favour of those you chose.

Note that the descriptive element of this presentation (the brief case history) should form only a small part of your work; the bulk of your presentation should focus on analysis about the case, discussion of changes needed, and analysis about ethics, law, policy, theory and research which informed social work practice and your argument.

These presentations are designed to assist you in developing the kind of practice analysis which you will have to do while on your 80-day placement as a part of your integrated assignment. In effect the presentations form a dummy run.

Tip for teachers

This presentation exercise is very effective when done in the second year of the programme, shortly before students start their 80-day placements.

Summary and conclusion

In many respects all of the teaching that students experience throughout their DipSW programmes is imbued with theory and is directly and clearly applicable to their practice. Academic tutors know this. Some students quickly grasp it. They understand how theories and academic material learned through library reading relate to practical aspects of day-to-day social work and show a flair for applying what they read to the tasks of placement. These students effectively teach themselves. They may sometimes thank and praise their teachers for the help they received ('I couldn't have done it without you' or 'I've learned so much from you') which is always nice to hear. Teachers know, however, that while they may have facilitated these naturally gifted students to learn, probably they would have figured it out for themselves anyway sooner or later.

The greater challenge to educators is the problem of how to help average or academically weak students to understand how theory and practice are knitted together, like different coloured strands of wool which form a beautifully and intricately patterned pullover which we wear. We perceive it; it excites *us*. However, *students* do not always perceive this and far from theory stimulating and exciting these students, they approach the entire subject of theory with trepidation and anxiety, feeling deskilled, and hoping just to get it over with as soon as possible (rather like a visit to the doctor for inoculation when one was a child) and put it behind them. Lister notes:

> When introduced to new concepts or challenged on beliefs or assumptions, students can feel de-skilled and find it hard to look at past experience positively. Sometimes this can lead students to be resistant to theory and to be unable to generalise from previous experience. At other times it can create self-doubt. (Lister 1999, p.165)

The value of the exercises we have presented is the way they require students to bring their experiences from the field into the classroom and apply bits out of books to them, thus demonstrating graphically how the book-learning means something in the real world. 'The ability to relate theory to practice is a key factor in the transfer of learning' (Lister 1999, p.164) and these exercises assist students to develop transferable skills. They push students to use both practice examples and theory together in the same exercise, so that they learn how the two relate to each other. They require students to be actively involved in their learning so that they prepare the materials used in discussions with other students in class or with their tutors and practice teachers. This fits wells within the enquiry and action learning approach to social work education developed at the University of Edinburgh (Cree and Davidson 1999). Our experience is that students enjoy these exercises and that, when used in the classroom, often lively and heated discussions have had to be drawn to a close due to time limitations. It has also been gratifying to see how students subsequently use pieces of the analysis from these exercises in theory-to-practice assignments, to good effect.

CHAPTER THREE

Planning the Integrated Theory-and-Practice Assignment

This chapter discusses the process by which students choose their topics and start planning their integrated assignments. Unlike most other essay-type assignments that students complete, the integrated assignment is usually not based on one pre-set topic which all students must complete. Instead students must choose a topic about which to write. Some people find the idea of choosing their own topics a bit nerve-wracking or intimidating. They are afraid of getting it wrong. Nonetheless, it is a crucial part of completing an integrated assignment and something which has to predate all the rest of assignment preparation since it forms the basis for everything else. In this chapter we have discussed the process of preliminary planning which is followed in the Norfolk Diploma in Social Work. We are explaining how it works *here*. Other programmes may have slightly different arrangements. However, we would argue that the arrangements in place on this programme provide high levels of very good quality support to students starting an integrated assignment. This is why we would recommend them to students and other programme providers, even though we recognise that they would need tweaking to accommodate the differences of individual programmes. We have included some common questions (with some answers) that students ask about this process. We have chosen this format because students have told us they found it particularly accessible.

A golden opportunity

Choosing their own topic provides students with a tremendous opportunity. This will be the one chance students have to write about something which really interests them, instead of writing about a topic someone else has chosen. Additionally, the process of devising their own topic or question to answer demonstrates valuable analytical thinking skills – skills which are transferable to practice when they are qualified.

Despite the seemingly free choice, there are still some restrictions about the focus of the topic and content of the final paper which will affect students' choice of subject matter for the integrated assignment. This chapter explains the broad parameters of content which every paper – like all other students' papers in courses throughout the United Kingdom – must eventually satisfy. The initial task for the students will be to choose a specific topic or question for their paper to address which can fulfil these broad parameters.

Content and focus of the integrated assignment

This assignment is meant to *integrate* both practice and academic knowledge. Therefore the topic that students choose must have both a practice component, based on the work they are doing on their placements, and an academic component, based on academic modules already completed, any college-based academic work they may take while on placement and further library research (specific to the integrated assignment). Very early in placement, students should develop a plan for an assignment which can fulfil these criteria.

Students need to plan a topic and assignment which take as a starting point the following content:

- their work in the areas of assessment and planning services or intervention
- their understanding of issues regarding the care versus control debate and professional accountability.

These are the key competencies that CCETSW requires courses to assess in students through the final stages of course completion (CCETSW 1996a).

However, the assignment is not limited merely to this. It should also address and clearly include the following:

- evidence of the integration of what students have learned at college or university about theory, research, policy and law with their *own* practice with individuals, groups or a community

- evidence of students' ability to reflect on and critically evaluate their *own* practice, and transfer knowledge, skills and values between practice situations.

In addition, it should include:

- material from a variety of modules throughout the programme

- analysis about how theory and research inform policy and practice

- evidence of anti-discriminatory and antiracist practice

- evidence of students' individual professional development, and how they expect these skills and knowledge could be implemented in future practice situations

- evidence of implementation of core social work values into practice.

Students will need to negotiate with their tutors and practice teachers assignment topics which will cover all these points. Different courses have differing arrangements for this, although all start with the same basic approach: to require the *students* to take the initiative in considering the topic first, with advice or guidance following from practice teacher and/or tutor only after the students have made some choices about what interests them. On some courses students discuss their plans with practice teachers and tutors in tutorials but are not required to submit a written plan. However, at the Norfolk DipSW, students are required to submit written plans; this is a model we would endorse as good practice which better supports students to succeed.

The written preliminary plan

The Norfolk DipSW expects students to submit a brief plan or outline of what they expect to write about in the final assignment. The written preliminary plan describes the student's proposal for the assignment. A plan is actually a fairly short piece of written work (approximately 1500 words including bibliography); it involves far more thinking than writing. It serves to outline the pieces of practice the student intends to analyse, the theoretical framework for the work, the question or theme the student has chosen to address and the way the student intends to do this. The written plan is not marked but it must be submitted both to the practice teacher and to the college or university tutor for review. The student subsequently (within one to two weeks) receives feedback about what has been written with guidance about how to change it in plenty of time to revise plans for the actual assessed assignment. It is the one time a student can get a piece of written work utterly wrong and not have it affect a mark, since the preliminary plans do not form part of the formal assessment process for students.

Timing for the preliminary plan

At the Norfolk DipSW the preliminary plan is written by students within three weeks of the start of placement. By this time they will have actually started the social work practice that provides case material and practice examples to incorporate into the assignment. They will also have had a couple of supervision sessions with their practice teacher and so will have had a chance to discuss the assignment focus with the teacher. Students are often quite anxious about writing the preliminary plan because it is the first time they have had to choose their own topics and write essay proposals. They may feel uncertain because so much rests on the assignment which is eventually written. In addition, students often complain about the pressure they feel having to complete the preliminary plan so early after they start their placement. They want to settle into placement. They want to get to know the people they are working with (colleagues and clients) better before choosing a topic. They don't understand the urgency behind completing a plan early in the placement when the assignment is not due until the end of placement. Nonetheless, as a programme we continue to pressure students to plan early since it ensures they do not delay thinking about the assignment until the last minute.

Below is our suggested format for writing a preliminary plan. This is followed by the answers to many of the questions commonly asked by students about the plan. We have kept the language used in this section of the chapter deliberately direct and informal so that it is easy and readable. Examples of some topics chosen in the past by previous students have been given. Examples are provided of common reasons why draft plans are returned by tutors with suggestions for changes. Two examples of good plans submitted by former students – plans which eventually facilitated good written assignments – have been included as Appendices 1 and 2 at the end of the book.

Format for the preliminary plan

The Norfolk DipSW requires students to use the format shown in Box 3.1 when submitting their plans. We recommend this format because:

- it ensures tutors have a certain standard amount of information to use in considering the viability of the student's plan

- it gives a message to students that the plan needs to be taken seriously and requires some reading, thinking and written work

- it helps students to formulate their ideas and ensure that they have not missed anything obvious.

Box 3.1 Preliminary plan for the integrated assignment

ASSIGNMENT TITLE

STUDENT'S NAME

TUTOR

PRACTICE TEACHER

PROPOSAL

Introduction

This should be between one and three paragraphs which identify the type of placement and work undertaken in the team, discuss the general topic for the assignment, underlying theoretical framework and theme or question around which the assignment will be focused. A thumbnail sketch should be provided of the items of (suitably anonymised) practice (derived from the placement) which will form the basis for analysis.

Practice issues

This should identify the issues that the assignment intends to cover and how they will inform the student's learning. This should take the form of six objectives. Students should develop objectives by use of words such as 'evaluate', 'analyse', 'investigate', 'examine', 'compare', *not* 'understand', 'discuss' or 'describe'. The issues should be written in such a way that they incorporate both the theoretical framework for the assignment and the practice evidence. In addition, the practice issues must relate to the overall theme or question chosen so that once the practice issues have all been fully analysed in the assignment, they will provide sufficient evidence and argument to provide an answer to the question or theme chosen. Practice issues also need to focus on analysing the student's own practice.

Specific areas of college-based study

This should identify what parts of which college modules the student intends to integrate into the practice issues, as those most relevant to this assignment. This must include modules which covered theoretical material related to social work assessment, planning social work intervention, the care versus control debate, and professional accountability, as well as reference to social work ethics and values and anti-discriminatory and antiracist practice.

Methods of inquiry

How are you going to do this? Where do you intend to look for material?

People involved and their roles

Who will you need to talk to and involve (e.g. college tutor, line manager, practice teacher)? What type of guidance or support can they offer for the assignment?

Preliminary literature search

A formal bibliography using Harvard (author and date) referencing must be provided of sources which you expect to use.

SUBMITTED BY: **Date:**

(student's name and signature)

AGREED BY: **Date:**

(practice teacher's name and signature)

Clearly this format would need to be amended by individual programme providers to ensure it meets the needs of that particular course.

Common questions asked by students about submission of the preliminary plan

What is the purpose of the preliminary plan?

The plan serves several purposes:

1. to assist you in planning the integrated assignment

2. to assist you in reflective practice

3. to provide a focus for your tutor and practice teacher to assess the validity of the planned work and to support you in preparation and completion of the assignment.

The preliminary plan is also a method for starting the dialogue between you and your tutor (albeit often at a distance) and between you and your practice teacher about the integrated assignment.

How long will it take me to write the preliminary plan?

A good preliminary plan cannot be written in 30 minutes. You need to start thinking about your preliminary plan from the very first day of placement. There is a formal academic content to the preliminary plan (particularly the methods of inquiry and the literature search) and you will need to use an academic library to complete it properly. Therefore a good draft preliminary plan probably includes the equivalent of *at least* one full day's solid work (i.e. eight to ten hours). Depending on the topic chosen (and the care with which it is written) it may include two or three days' work.

Why bother if the preliminary plan isn't marked?

Past experience has shown that students who are unable to formulate a good preliminary plan in the early stages of their placements often struggle to complete good integrated assignments and may fail this work. In contrast, students who complete good analytical preliminary plans have a head start in completing their assignments and often get better marks. We cannot guarantee that you will pass the assignment with flying colours if you do a good preliminary plan within two or three weeks of starting your placement, but we believe you have a better chance to pass and do well in the final assignment.

How do I choose a good topic?

Most students find it easier to choose a topic if they first identify specific pieces of practice or allocated cases which particularly interest them, or which are likely to absorb a great deal of their time and energy while they are on placement. Try working back from the specific practice examples to identify the theory, policy, legislation and research which inform that area of practice. If you choose a theory first and then try to find a piece of practice which fits the theory, you will probably find it harder to choose a good topic for the assignment. The general topic you pick is clearly determined to some extent by the type of practice you are doing on placement. However, your topic is also related to the theme you choose for analysis or the argument you hope to develop (see below).

How many pieces of practice should I pick?

This depends on the complexity of the pieces of practice or cases which you are involved with, which varies from placement to placement. Sometimes people use information drawn from more than one case when that information all relates to one theme (e.g. comparing how the same theory can be implemented in contrasting ways in different situations with two or three clients). Sometimes people analyse one very complex case in depth. Sometimes students don't hold cases as such but are involved with work with a number of people, where case responsibility is held by someone else (e.g. therapeutic group work). In such situations students may choose to use information drawn from the project they are working with and the people it serves, rather than any one specific case. The question of how many pieces of practice to choose is interrelated with the question of choosing your argument or theme for analysis (see below).

How do I choose a theme or question for analysis?

In addition to identifying the pieces of practice and the theory (or theories) which underpins this area of work, it is important to refine your topic by choosing a theme or analytical argument. This is something which students often can feel confused about. However, it is very important to try to pick a theme. This will help you to develop the kind of sophisticated and academic critical analysis and evaluation which is so important in a final year assignment (where higher marks tend to be awarded for critical analysis while lower marks are awarded for simple description). In addition, choosing a theme or analytical argument will help you to focus your background reading and research so that you use your time wisely reading in depth those academic books and articles which are most relevant to the topic, rather than going off on a tangent.

Most people find it easier to choose a theme if they set themselves a question to answer. This should be a question which keeps coming up, over and over, in the practice you are doing. The more central the question is to your everyday practice, the more relevant it will feel to you and the more interest you will (in all probability) be able to maintain in completing the background reading. Another strategy is to choose a theme (related to the practice you are doing) about which you hold strong opinions and about which you would like to do some more reading and research.

For example, students who are completing a placement in the area of youth offending and criminal justice might complete several pre-sentence reports and supervise several teenage clients on supervision orders. Clearly they would choose a topic related to issues of youth justice and the work they are doing – perhaps choosing to compare and contrast the work involved with two or three pre-sentence reports, or possibly analysing in depth their work supervising one client on a youth justice supervision order.

Choosing the pieces of work helps to choose the topic, but more is needed than this alone. The next step would be to consider the different aspects of theory, policy, etc. which inform the practice. In this example the students could include social psychology and adolescent development and behaviour, theory and research about issues specific to the problems faced by these clients (e.g. literature about addictions if dealing with a drug user, or literature about domestic violence if the young person lives in a family where this is a known problem), criminological theory, sociology of deviance and social control, different theories of social work intervention, criminal justice legislation, national and local policy, and so on.

Following this, it is important for students to choose a theme, or devise a question to answer, which encompasses both the practice element *and* one or more chosen theory. In this example, students might choose a variety of questions, depending on the practice they are involved with and the cases they have been allocated. Here are four sample questions and themes:

1. Is it possible to be simultaneously caring and controlling in supervising young offenders?

2. Using task-centred practice to address underlying causes of adolescent car crime

3. Does the assessment of risk in pre-sentence reports corrupt the welfare principle of social work with children and young people?

4. Therapeutic intervention in youth justice with teenage drug users.

Any one of these questions or themes might help students develop an analytical argument in relation to their practice in youth justice. However, although some of the background reading of theory would need to be the same regardless of which question or theme the student chose, some would be different and the same theory might be used differently when analysing practice in relation to the different questions or themes. Thus, the final paper would read quite differently depending on which question or theme was picked. The background reading which the student uses, and the work on placement which the student does, will eventually be written up in an integrated assignment which analyses both elements in relation to the question or theme the student chose at the beginning of the placement. The question or theme the student chooses usually becomes the essay's title.

How do I develop my practice issues?

Once the main question, topic or theme has been chosen, the student should then break down the question into the various smaller components or issues which need to be addressed in order to provide a full answer to the main theme or question which has been chosen (see Box 3.2). These issues need to incorporate the various aspects of day-to-day social work the student will be completing with the chosen pieces of practice.

Box 3.2 Example of analytical practice issues

Suppose the student were a middle-class, 45-year-old, white female involved with a weekly therapy group for teenage drug users and wanted to complete an integrated assignment about this work. The student might choose the topic of 'Therapeutic intervention in youth justice with teenage drug users'. In the introduction section of the preliminary plan, she explains that what interests her is the tension which exists between therapeutic social work objectives of caring, empowering, helping and individual personal growth, and a criminal/youth justice system which is more concerned to prevent, control or punish antisocial behaviour. She wonders whether it is really truly possible to do good therapy within the constraints of youth justice. Practice issues which might be developed from this could include:

1. I will evaluate whether the help I was providing helped these young people to stay straight.

2. Therapy is often seen as a soft option, rather than as punishment; I will analyse the ways my practice was caring or controlling and why, and the impact this had on the young people.

3. I will investigate the impact my statutory responsibilities had on my ability to develop a trusting relationship with the group members, communicate with and engage them constructively in group activities.

4. I will assess the impact my gender, age, class and ethnicity may have had on my practice with a group of predominantly working-class male youths and I will assess the impact that gender, class and ethnicity differences between group members may have had on my ability to help.

5. I will analyse the impact my record-keeping had on the therapeutic relationships within the group.

6. I will examine the ways policy and procedures within a framework of national standards supported or limited my social work practice to be therapeutic.

The example in Box 3.2 shows how interconnecting practice issues could be developed which would sum up to give a comprehensive answer to the topic chosen. We recommend that students develop six interrelated practice issues for a 6000-word assignment, although sometimes students find fewer are sufficient. As we have previously mentioned, it is usually helpful to develop these practice issues using words such as 'evaluate', 'analyse', 'investigate', 'examine', 'assess', 'compare', *not* 'understand', 'discuss' or 'describe', since it is important right from the beginning to think in analytical terms rather than simple descriptive terms about the study you are undertaking.

Consider how differently you would need to be thinking and writing about a practice issue which was merely descriptive from how you would need to be thinking and writing about a practice issue that was analytical. For example, consider the differences between practice issues in Box 3.2 with those in Box 3.3. The former involves the student analysing and evaluating her own practice in relation to a specific question or issue she wants to answer; the latter merely requires her to describe what was done.

Box 3.3 Example of descriptive practice issues

1. I will discuss whether or not these young people stayed straight.

2. I want to understand how the young people viewed the therapy group – as caring or controlling.

3. I will describe the way I fulfilled my statutory responsibilities.

4. I will discuss gender, age, class and ethnicity issues.

5. I will discuss the record-keeping I did for the group.

6. I will describe how the group worked within policy guidelines of national standards.

Practice issues should always be written from the perspective of analysing the student's *own* practice. Doing this helps to build in, right from the start, self-reflection and self-evaluation. Note that the practice issues in the example have all been written from the perspective of looking at the student's own practice. It is critical to remember that your task is not to analyse theory, but to analyse how you *used* theory in your practice, or how policy or research *informed* your planning and decisions. All too often students write practice issues from too wide a perspective, so that they analyse theory and policy, not their own work (see Box 3.4). This is a common mistake but it is potentially quite serious since it can lead a student off track to such a wide degree that the final assignment does not fulfil the requirements for self-reflection.

Box 3.4 Example of broad theoretical practice issues

1. I will analyse the values emphasis over staying straight and whether this focus is right for therapeutic work in youth justice.

2. I will examine the care versus control debate in youth justice and assess how young offenders in Britain view the roles of youth justice professionals.

3. I will assess statutory changes in Britain over the last ten years to consider the fundamental values position incorporated in the recent legislation.

4. I will compare the racial, gender, age, class biases of youth offending teams in Britain with these issues in youth justice in other countries.

5. The youth offending team's policies and procedures about record keeping will be analysed to determine if they are ethical.

6. I will assess the theoretical basis for standardised practice.

Remember also when you are developing your practice issues to ensure that they include:

- all the major issues or sub-questions needed to provide a comprehensive answer to your chosen theme or question

- appropriate mention of the theories you plan to use in most, if not all, of your practice issues

- ethical issues related to your area of work (*with reference to anti-discriminatory and antiracist practice*).

Could I complete a research project for my integrated assignment and use my preliminary plan to set this up?

Sometimes students want to complete research projects as part of their integrated assignments. While the possibility for this is not ruled out, it is also not recommended, because of the difficulty of designing and implementing a good research project in the short period on placement using academically sound research methodology. In addition it can be difficult to design and implement a research project which will also fulfil the required content and marking criteria for this assignment – which are strongly focused on self-reflection, personal evaluation of one's own practice and professional growth and future learning. Please do not be confused by this book's use of the term 'research'; it does not imply that you are going to complete primary field research. In general it refers to library research and background reading.

While it is true that increasingly researchers and theoreticians are aware that theory is tested in practice, and it is equally true that social work as a profession is now recognising the need to develop practitioner research, that is not the point of this assignment. Students who want to incorporate some kind of research into their integrated assignments (e.g. customer satisfaction survey as a part of evaluating their own practice) should discuss this in detail with their practice teachers and college or university tutors to ensure this kind of project does not result in a change of focus away from the parameters which will fulfil the marking criteria.

What is my practice teacher's role in the preliminary plan?

Through supervision, practice teachers usually help students to identify an interesting practice-focused topic which can form the basis for a good assignment. They can also help students pick the specific pieces of practice or cases which they will use as sources of information for the final assignment. Practice teachers may sometimes help students identify a relevant theoretical framework for their assignment. Often practice teachers can help students to identify key policy documents or legislation as well as give guidance or suggestions about other people it may be helpful to talk to (e.g. 'Why not have a chat with …, she knows a lot about that area'). Discussion with practice teachers often helps students to formulate their practice issues. Further detail about the practice teacher's role in relation to the preliminary plan and integrated assignment in general is included in Chapter 4.

What is my tutor's role in the preliminary plan?

Your tutor's role is an advisory one. Once you have submitted the draft preliminary plan your personal tutor will read it. Preliminary plans may also be shown to a subject specialist tutor. In the Norfolk DipSW we have a system which requires tutors to contact the student after they have reviewed the draft plan. Usually this is done by letter. A few people's preliminary plans are accepted as they are. However, more often advice is given (e.g. 'Have you thought about...?').

Why don't they just ring me?

Advice about the draft plan can sometimes be quite detailed. It can be difficult to remember every detail about advice given over the phone. Therefore, it can be more appropriate to give this kind of advice in writing so that students have a record they can refer to at a later stage if they wish. An alternative to a written letter might be a person-to-person tutorial. However, this can cause delay, particularly since students have limited contact with tutors while on placement (or during holiday periods). If students were on placements some distance from college this might also lead to delay. It is more important students get the feedback quickly, rather than in person – hence a letter.

What does my tutor do when he/she gets my preliminary plan?

Tutors look at your preliminary plan to check that:

- you have chosen a sufficiently complex subject which involves sufficient theory and practice issues to provide enough material to complete an integrated assignment which will meet the marking criteria

- you have not chosen too theoretical, too broad or too large a topic to complete within the 6000 word limit

- you have developed a question or theme around which to focus your analysis

- you have started to identify the parts of *your own* practice or allocated cases from which you will draw material to use in the assignment

- you have started to identify what you learned in certain college or university modules which inform this area of practice (the corollary of which is that you have also started to identify other things learned in other modules which have less relevance in this situation)

- you have correctly identified the most relevant theories

- you have picked a topic which relates to *your own* practice, not practice in general

- you have developed practice issues which analyse your own practice (not your placement, policies, theories, other people's work, etc.)

- you have started to identify academic books or articles which you will use as a basis for integrating theory, policy and research evidence with practice

- you have identified a reasonable plan for library or other research to obtain further relevant reading (or other) material to include in your assignment.

If I have to resubmit my preliminary plan, does this mean I am failing?
Every year at the Norfolk DipSW *most* students are asked to substantially revise and resubmit their preliminary plans because the tutor has identified a problem with the planning which, if not corrected, would probably mean the student's final work would not fulfil the marking criteria and could not pass. Your tutor's comments and criticisms about the original preliminary plan you submitted are intended to help you to devise a topic and plan of work which will stand a good chance of eventually fulfilling the marking

criteria. Needing to rethink and revise substantially your preliminary plan should *not* be viewed by students as a sign of failure; it is quite common. Even students who have never had to resubmit anything frequently have to resubmit their preliminary plans.

If it is so important and so hard to write, should I have a tutorial before I complete my preliminary plan?

Students should expect to submit their preliminary plans without formal tutorials before they are written. Both academia and professional programmes have long and effective traditions of students learning through doing and through changing mistakes. The system of receiving tutorial advice about the preliminary plan *after* submission follows this tradition. We appreciate that subjectively students might feel better about submitting a preliminary plan after they have a tutorial. However, our experience has shown that this makes little or no difference to the actual draft preliminary plan submitted.

What does make a difference in students' planning for this assignment, and in the quality of the assignment which eventually is submitted, is for students to submit a preliminary plan in writing (as soon as possible after the start of the placement) in which they make a few mistakes or misinterpretations, which are picked up by the tutor, who provides feedback, and for the student then to submit a revised preliminary plan.

We appreciate that until they have gone through this process students will be quite sceptical when we say this. Nonetheless, years of helping people with their preliminary plans and integrated assignments have demonstrated to tutors that preparatory tutorials before attempting to write a preliminary plan really are not very effective.

But there is such a lot riding on this final assignment that I have to get it absolutely right and I need a tutorial!

Students can sometimes become very anxious about preliminary plans and planning for their integrated assignments. However, it is also important to keep this in perspective. The preliminary plan is a *working document* used as an outline for the work for the assignment. The point of this exercise is not to get it absolutely right – there is no such thing as a perfect preliminary plan. The plan will inevitably change slightly over time as students' work progresses. The preliminary plan is not an end result in itself, but will form the basis for assignment planning.

Part of professional practice involves managing anxieties. Students who find it difficult to manage their anxieties about the preliminary plan and/or integrated assignment are encouraged to seek support through student counselling services and/or their GPs.

Why do I have to complete it so soon?

One purpose behind the preliminary plan is to assist you with planning the long assignment. If you wait for two or three months to think about the plan, then you have lost a lot of time to do the work. We know from experience that the process of developing the preliminary plan from first draft through tutor's comments to final version usually takes approximately five to six weeks. The longer you wait to start this, the less time you leave yourself to complete the assignment. At the beginning of placement the due date for the assignment may seem a very long way off; however, you will be surprised how quickly it comes round!

The assignment is intended to show how you implemented theory, ethics, policy and research evidence into your own practice. Insisting that you complete the preliminary plan at the beginning of the practice placement ensures that right from the start you begin to think about which theories, policies and research evidence will be helpful to you in completing the work allocated to you on placement, and the ethical dimensions of using theory, policy, research, etc. This, in turn, emphasises the significance of the academic–practice link for the assignment.

Why do I have to do this type of assignment while on placement? It makes it difficult to concentrate on what I ought to be doing – my placement, not college

Requiring students to submit a preliminary plan soon after the start of placement is not ideal, but then few things in practice are absolutely ideal. Students who have completed their course have told us that requiring them to do academic work whilst on placement has been a powerful way of preparing them for the demands and realities of social work practice, that of juggling many balls in the air all at once.

Moreover, the preliminary plan and integrated assignment should not be considered as something separate from your placement – something specific only to college work which drags you away from the real work of a social work placement. The preliminary plan and the assignment itself both involve *integrating* theory/research/policy/law learned in college *with* the practice done on placement, and with the development of self-reflective practice. Comparison between the required content of the integrated assignment and the practice learning objectives for an 80-day placement (the core competencies required by CCETSW) will show there is considerable congruence between the two. Thus the work for the preliminary plan and the assignment should *enhance* practice learning and *support* you to achieve the core competencies.

How can I possibly complete it so soon? I'm on an induction programme for the first two weeks of placement

Even when you are on an induction programme, you will be learning about the types of work done on your placement and the various policies, procedures, theories and research-based knowledge which inform this area of work. Moreover, your practice teacher and/or on-site supervisor or line manager will usually be identifying cases or pieces of practice to be allocated to you once the induction programme has been completed. As a part of supervision, it is important to discuss these pieces of work so that one or more can be selected for the integrated assignment, even while you are completing induction.

Occasionally you may complete an induction programme for the first two weeks of placement and not be allocated any work during this period. If this is the norm for your placement, this should be identified in the placement learning agreement and you, your tutor and the practice teacher can all then discuss special arrangements for the submission of the preliminary plan. It might be suggested that you should take another week before submitting the preliminary plan. Alternatively, depending on the type of placement, you might decide to submit a preliminary plan within the usual time-frame based on a theme or question common to the work setting, with theory and practice issues that commonly arise in all social work in that placement. You will, however, not be able to include information about the pieces of practice you have chosen, since no work will yet have been allocated. This makes it harder to complete the preliminary plan, since it is more difficult to identify a good theme and then relate that to practice and easier to identify or choose practice first, and then work back from it to the theory that informs it. In this situation, you should *expect* that when the preliminary plan is returned by the tutor one of the recommendations will be for you to identify and discuss the pieces of practice you plan to use.

But I cannot complete it this soon – I haven't been allocated a really good case

It may be tempting to wait until something better comes along, but students who do so often find they wait indefinitely in the hope of a good case. There is an assumption among many students that an integrated assignment must be based on one large complex, difficult and meaty case. However, the reality of your placement, and the type of social work practice typical for students on your placement, may be that complex cases are few and far between and none may arise (or if they arise, none may be allocated to you) until midway or even later in the placement. If you wait and wait like this, then you are preventing yourself from using your time most effectively to complete the relevant background reading, thinking and analysis. It will not be possible to do it all in a rush at the end. *All* social work practice is based on theory, research, policy and law, not just those complex cases. Thus it is better to choose from the cases readily available at the beginning of your placement, rather than wait before choosing pieces of practice and delay the preliminary plan. Just make sure that if you are being allocated lots of small, short open-and-shut cases that you choose more than one piece of practice, and that a central theory, theme or issue (common to all cases) can be identified and used as the basis for analysis.

What is the penalty for submitting the preliminary plan late?

There is no penalty as such: the preliminary plan is not assessed and marked in the way that formal assignments are. The only penalty is to *you*.

The longer you take to complete the plan, the longer it will take before you receive comments and advice back from your practice teacher and tutor – advice you may really need in order to do a good assignment. In addition, tutors cannot guarantee a quick turnaround if you delay in submitting the preliminary plan. Tutors arrange time in their schedules to review the plans based on when they expect to receive them from students. If you send it in after that window of opportunity, there may be a delay in your tutor being able to review it and send it back with suggestions.

What if I change my mind about my topic mid-placement?

Often students find when they write the final assignment that they did slightly different analysis and practice from what was originally proposed in the preliminary plan. Considering how and why these minor changes developed can assist you to evaluate your own work as a part of reflective practice. For example:

> I thought I would be implementing information from Jones's research study in my practice. However, in the end, although I used some of what I read about in Jones, because agency policy required that I do X and the client chose A rather than B, as I had anticipated, this meant that Jones's research findings were of limited relevance. Instead I found I was using what I'd read in Smith.

However, if, midway through your placement, you find that there are *substantial* differences between what you now plan to do and what was approved in the preliminary plan, then it is *vitally important* you seek a tutor's advice. Experience has shown that students who change horses midstream often do badly in the final assignment and may well fail.

Why do I have to list all the college modules I've taken? – you already know that

The point of the 'Specific areas of college-based study' section (see Box 3.1) is not to list the titles of all the modules you have taken throughout the course. The intention behind this section is to have you go through the exercise of considering which parts of various modules are most relevant to the topic you have chosen. Pull the reading lists, core textbooks, class handouts and other reading material you collected for each module out of that dark dingy cupboard where you threw them once the modules were finished! Look over your notes and handouts. Which ideas, theories, research evidence, etc. from each module appear most relevant to *this* topic? This exercise will help you to remember the different topics and ideas you learned about throughout the course so that you do not miss anything obviously relevant when planning the work for this assignment. If students are struggling with this we would suggest they complete the following two exercises.

First, draw a mind map or spidergram. This is a quick-think exercise. In the centre of a blank sheet of paper put the topic you have chosen. Then around the sides of the page put all the key words or concepts or ideas that you can think of that are related to this question. Try to group these concepts together in ways that make sense or draw arrows between ideas to show that they are related (see Figure 3.1). This is a useful preliminary tool to help you identify which issues form a part of your chosen assignment topic. It is a technique that is useful for all academic essays, not merely the integrated assignment.

Second, devise a chart for yourself to help you to consider what parts of what academic modules might be relevant to the concepts or ideas covered in the chosen topic or question. This involves taking a piece of paper and dividing it into three columns. In the left column list the modules you have taken during the course (first and second year). In the middle column list the ideas, concepts and theories each module covered. In the right column list the issues or ideas which are a part of the topic you have chosen. Once you have done this, draw arrows between the different ideas in the middle column and the issues they relate to in the right column (see Figure 3.2). Once you have done this, you are ready to transfer the information to the 'Specific areas of college-based study' section of your preliminary plan. The ideas or aspects of each module that did *not* match with the issues included in the assignment topic do not need to go into the written plan.

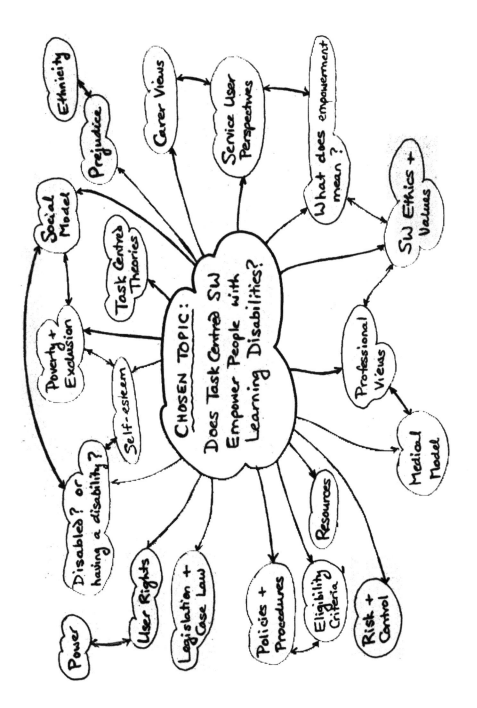

Figure 3.1 Example of a spidergram

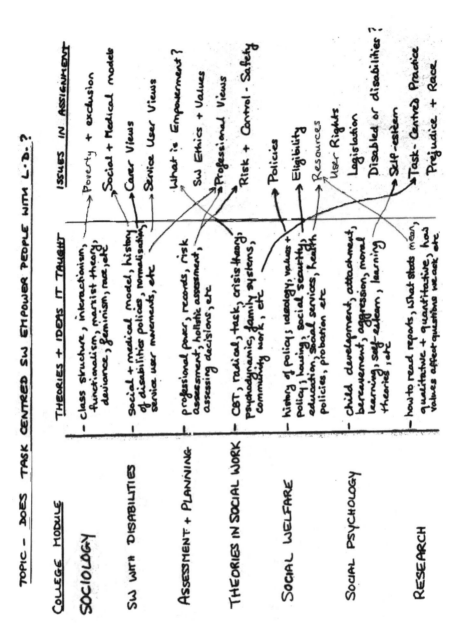

Figure 3.2 Example of a chart linking academic modules to assignment issues

Why must I include a literature search in the preliminary plan? I cannot possibly know in July all the sources I'm going to use in November

The list of books and articles is *not* intended to be a definitive list of all the sources you will eventually use. It is intended to show your tutor and practice teacher that you have started to identify the key sources which are relevant to the topic you have chosen and area of practice. It is important to include as sources:

- books and articles relating to your specific area of practice (e.g. students working with a 3-year-old who has suffered gross neglect should include sources relevant to this area, not sources relevant to a sexually abused adolescent)

- key policy documents which guide practice in this area

- key legislation.

At this stage, your list of sources should not include general social work texts even though you may eventually use them for the assignment and may include them in your bibliography when it is submitted in November. A good list of books and articles at the preliminary plan stage should include approximately 12–15 sources. More sources will be needed for the final assignment. Some of the sources included at the preliminary plan stage may eventually not be used in the integrated assignment (i.e. when you started you thought they might be helpful, but in the end you did not use them).

What if my college tutor and I cannot agree about my preliminary plan?

Some programmes may require preliminary plans to be approved. However, we do not go that far in the Norfolk DipSW. Instead we have said that the decision about your assignment topic is made – ultimately – by you, not your tutor. College tutors act as advisers at the preliminary plan stage and, technically speaking, their agreement is not mandatory. However, experience has shown that students who reject good advice from tutors at the preliminary plan stage are more likely subsequently to fail the assignment. This is because tutors are considerably more experienced than students. They have written equivalent kinds of assignments in the past (for their own professional courses) and have also had the experience of reading and marking previous integrated assignments (both those which passed and those which failed). Thus they have a very good idea of what kinds of preliminary plans assist students eventually to write good assignments which pass, and what kinds of preliminary plans lead students off track so that they later have serious difficulty writing assignments which fulfil the marking criteria sufficiently to pass.

Your tutor's advice is simply intended to help you to devise a topic which can fulfil the required content guidelines, expected standard of work and marking criteria, *not* to prevent you from studying any particular area you find interesting. If you disagree with their advice, you may choose to reject it. However, please note that the final assignment will be assessed in accordance with the required content, expected standard of work and marking criteria established for all integrated assignments. Should these substantially differ from the content and standard of work contained in your final written assignment, even if what you wrote is consistent with the plan you set out in your preliminary plan, you must expect the assignment to fail.

Another way to consider it is to take a consumer approach to the situation: you are paying good money (through your course fees) in order to get good advice from your tutor and practice teacher. When you receive the advice you may not like it, but liking it is not really the issue. The main point is to get the advice you need. Having obtained the advice, you might as well use it!

What if my practice teacher and I cannot agree about my preliminary plan?

Your preliminary plan must be agreed by your practice teacher. If you have an off-site practice teacher and an on-site supervisor or line manager, *both* must agree your plan. Serious disagreement between the practice teacher and on-site supervisor or line manager about a preliminary plan is very rare. However, should this unusual circumstance develop, *you must change your plan*. This is because the practice teacher and on-site supervisor or line manager have professional responsibilities to clients, carers and social work agencies to ensure that practice examples and case material drawn from the placement experience are used ethically, sensitively and appropriately in accordance with legal requirements and policy directives. The judgements of practice teacher, on-site supervisor or line manager about the appropriateness (or otherwise) of a student's preliminary plan take priority over the student's individual wishes in relation to these issues.

Examples of topics

The following are some examples of integrated assignment topics which have been completed in the past:

- How far can a theory of advocacy and empowerment inform my social work practice with older people living in the community?

- Sibling attachments and their importance in social work practice

- How does 'blame' affect a social worker's assessment about child care difficulties in a family where domestic violence is an issue?

- Segregation or inclusion? The policies affecting disabled children

- How does the multidisciplinary hospital setting affect social work practice with older people?

- An analysis of the relevance of the person-centred approach to after-care support for people leaving psychiatric hospitals

- Kinship fostering – dilemmas for grandparents in meeting the assessment criteria for foster carers: implications for a social work assessment

- The direct payments scheme – 'willing and able' and the implications for social work practice.

Common difficulties with preliminary plans

The following are some of the most frequent reasons why preliminary plans are returned to students with requests for revision:

- The preliminary plan does not follow the required format and several sections have been omitted.

- The student has not identified which cases or pieces of practice will be used for the assignment.

- The student has identified the cases to be used but has failed to provide sufficient information about these cases to allow the tutor (a) to form a judgement about whether they provide sufficient material for an assignment of this length and complexity, and (b) to form a judgement about whether or not the preliminary reading list the student has included is on track.

- Too many pieces of practice are chosen involving very complex cases, meaning that the completion of a good analytical assignment on this topic would span far too wide reading over a variety of specialist areas of practice (e.g. bibliography of 150+ sources) and far too many words (e.g. 15,000 words, rather than the required 6000).

- The student has not identified the theory or theories which form the basis for analysis.

- The student has not developed a question to answer or theme around which to focus the analysis.

- The question which has been developed is too general and not linked to the student's *own* practice.

- The practice issues are written from too general or too broad a perspective of analysing theory, policy or statistical trends, or the procedures and work of the placement/office in general, rather than one of the student analysing his or her own practice and how theory, etc. was incorporated into practice and the implications of this.

- The practice issues bear little or no relation to the main question or theme chosen for the assignment, and do not flow from this main theme as sub-questions which need answering in order to address the topic as a whole.

- Various module titles are listed as 'Specific areas of college-based study' but there is no mention of which parts of these modules are relevant to the chosen topic and why. For example, psychological theories of ageing would probably have more relevance in a placement with an older persons' team, while theories about children's cognitive development would have limited relevance. However, the student merely listed the module title 'Social and developmental psychology' and did not specify which parts of this module he/she thought would be relevant.

- Confusion is shown between the 'Methods of inquiry' section and the 'People involved and their roles' section (see Box 3.1), with people who have agreed to assist the student in the assignment being listed as 'Methods', when in fact they are 'People'. Conversely, library literature searches, use of case records and use of the Internet are listed as 'People'.

- Everybody the student encounters on placement is included in the 'People involved' section. Only those people who have specifically agreed to provide a student with guidance or support about the integrated assignment should be included.

- The preliminary literature search has been omitted.

- An idiosyncratic method of referencing has been used for the preliminary literature search.

- The preliminary literature search includes general social work texts and does not include sources specifically relevant to the subject area.

- The preliminary plan has not been discussed with or signed by the practice teacher and on-site supervisor or line manager.

Once students have received their tutor's comments about their preliminary plans, we suggest they revise and send in a final version within a week or two. In practice, some students delay doing this for several weeks. However, even if there is a delay before the revised plan is received by tutor and practice teacher, by this time the true purposes of the preliminary plan have been fulfilled:

- the student has started to develop a plan

- the plan has been checked to ensure the content can fulfil the assignment requirements so the essay will not be wildly off topic

- the plan has been checked to ensure it is appropriately focused and manageable

- a constructive, helpful dialogue has been started about the assignment between student and practice teacher, between student and tutor and between practice teacher and tutor

- the student has been helped to start the assignment promptly rather than delay until the last minute.

Summary and conclusion

A start needs to be made on all integrated assignments soon after the placement begins. The first step for any student is always to choose a good topic for the essay. This can provide an exciting opportunity for students to write about topics dear to their hearts. However, no matter how encouraging tutors and practice teachers may be, students are often worried about whether or not they will get it right as they choose what to do. This chapter has provided some guidance to students about the process of choosing a relevant, focused and manageable topic for their integrated assignments. Students *are* right – it *is* important to take enough time to consider carefully what the assignment should be about. In the Norfolk DipSW, we require students to submit written plans for their assignments soon after the start of their placements. These plans require some academic work to complete and cannot be done properly without careful thought.

The process which students need to follow in developing these preliminary plans has been discussed. We have explained how a written plan can help students to start off on the right foot, so that they understand the focus needed to develop a good integrated assignment. The roles which college or university tutor and practice teacher play in helping students to develop their plans have also been discussed. Common difficulties that students experience in choosing their topics and planning for the assignment have been mentioned as the process is not always completely smooth and easy. Even if sometimes frustrating to students, the time spent planning is critically important. We hope that this guidance will help students to understand the process better so it becomes more effective for them.

CHAPTER FOUR

Tutorial and Practice Teacher Support

This chapter discusses the tutor's and practice teacher's roles in relation to the integrated assignment. As a fairly long academic essay which incorporates practice, it is appropriate for both practice teacher and tutor to be involved in supporting the student through the preparation process. Students need to know what support they can and cannot expect from both tutor and practice teacher. Some social workers who have been practice teaching for several years may be very experienced in supporting students in the throes of academic writing. However, some practice teachers come to this fresh. Just as students may feel deskilled by the new challenges facing them through a theory-to-practice assignment, so too may practice teachers. They feel confident in commenting on the student's practice but less confident giving advice about academic standards. Just as students need to know what to expect, so do practice teachers. The purpose of this chapter is to provide both students and practice teachers with an idea of the purposes of tutorial and practice teacher support and the strengths and limitations of this.

The personal tutor's role

In Britain most students taking higher education courses are allocated a personal tutor. Usually this individual has specific responsibilities related to monitoring and supporting the personal and academic development of the tutee. The tutor acts as a link between the student and the university or college administration, and gives advice about course regulations as they may impact on the student's progress. There is also a welfare role attached to being a personal tutor. The personal tutor is one point for the student to access support or pastoral care for personal issues (e.g. family crisis) which may have an impact on academic progress (Wheeler and Birtle 1993). Pastoral care does not always rest easily with the personal tutor due to the academic requirements of the tutorial role, so that most colleges and universities also have specialist support services for students (e.g. counselling, chaplaincy, etc.).

Nonetheless, many students discuss very personal issues with their personal tutors, valuing the link between pastoral care and academic guidance that the tutor is in a unique position to offer. Higher education involves change and the process of change can sometimes be painful:

> The prospect of change often engenders anxiety. There is comfort in familiar, predictable routines and anything which threatens to disrupt them disturbs the individual. Change brings in its wake the uncertainty which in turn induces stress. (Wheeler and Birtle 1993, p.142)

This is particularly pertinent for professional courses which are designed quite deliberately to change students – to inculcate in them a professional identity and to challenge them both intellectually and personally in terms of their values base (Dingwall 1979). Student anxiety associated with academic learning and fear of failure is well known in universities and colleges. The personal tutor often helps students to manage anxieties and keep them in perspective (Wheeler and Birtle 1993).

Within professional social work education, the personal tutor has additional responsibilities as a part of the professional requirements for the course. Monitoring and review of practice learning are key parts of the tutor's role. Tutors play a part in assisting students to identify their own practice strengths and weaknesses on entry and to assist them to grow and develop as practitioners throughout the programme until they achieve professional competence. The personal tutor is not *solely* responsible for this. Every component of the course is designed to help students to develop as professionals as well and the tutorial role is only one small part of this. In addition, students have to take responsibility themselves for their own development. Nonetheless, personal tutors will be involved in helping students to develop problem-solving methods and study skills, either by providing advice themselves or through referrals to other services that can help. At the end of the 50-day placement, the personal tutor will be a part of the process by which future practice learning needs are identified and carried through to the second placement. In addition, the tutor provides a link to practice teachers about college or university based learning and the progress of students, both academically and professionally (Bines and Watson 1992).

The partnership between the tutor and the practice teacher helps to ensure that the student gets the maximum benefit from the period of assessed practice. Direct teaching on placement is provided by the practice teacher, who also assesses the level and quality of the student's achievement. However, the personal tutor monitors the student's achievement through practice and needs to be aware of how this is progressing as a part of the student's overall professional development. Modularisation has affected the academic social work curriculum significantly since the early 1990s (Lyons 1999) and this has had an impact on the tutorial role. Nonetheless, the umbrella oversight of the student's development from an holistic perspective remains part of a personal tutor's responsibilities. Through periodic tutorials, from beginning to end of programme, the personal tutor can sometimes facilitate the radical self-development, critical understanding and self-knowledge or catalytic awareness that spark breakthroughs in learning (Woods 1996) which accompany the development of professional role.

Last, but by no means least, the personal tutor holds a high level of responsibility within a programme in ensuring anti-discriminatory and antiracist educational practice. Students who join social work courses may have suffered from discrimination and oppression. It is extremely important these experiences are not compounded through oppressive experiences in education. Personal tutors need to be able to identify and counter bias and discrimination by examining their own attitudes and considering how sexism, racism or age bias may affect their performance (Walklin 1990). In the past, social work courses have been criticised for their inability to build positively on the experiences students bring with them to the course, particularly in relation to developing anti-discriminatory and antiracist practice (Northern Curriculum Development Project 1991). Personal tutors who develop a sensitive awareness about their students' backgrounds and experiences are in a good position to use their understanding in anti-oppressive educational practice to facilitate positive professional development.

The tutor for the integrated assignment

Support for students completing an integrated assignment often falls on the personal tutor, who visits the student on placement and liaises with the practice teacher, acting as a link between college or university and practice. Occasionally, tutorial support for the assignment may be provided more effectively by a different academic tutor. Nobody can be an expert at everything, and this is as true of the social work personal tutor as it is for everybody else. Social work is completed within a wide range of practice settings. Students may choose topics for their integrated assignments which cross specialist areas of practice or about which their own personal tutors have little experience or knowledge. In this instance the personal tutor may suggest that students talk with the course tutor or lecturer who has most knowledge of that specialist area.

The tutorial

Tutorial support and the tutor's role in helping the student to develop a good essay topic were discussed in Chapter 3. The main method for supporting students in completing assignments, particularly as they approach the writing stage of the assignment, is the individual tutorial. In essence, a tutorial can be defined as

> a meeting between a teacher and a student, or a very small group of students, characterised by discussion and/or personal face-to-face teaching, generally based on the content of an essay or other material written by the student(s) or on questions raised by the tutor or the student(s). (Curzon 1985, p.213)

Tutorial support is not without limits. Students and tutors have limited amounts of time to spend in tutorials. Thus, it is crucially important for students to use the tutorial as effectively as possible. Below are suggestions to help ensure students gain the maximum benefit from tutorials for their assignments. They may seem very basic and too obvious for words.

However, in our experience, it is those students who forget these issues who are most likely to complain that they did not get enough help to complete the assignment.

Scheduling tutorials

Students should find out before the placement starts if there is a limit to the number of tutorials allowed as part of assignment preparation. Sometimes courses set specific limits (e.g. only one or two); some courses may not set a specific limit but a de facto limit may be in place due to the tutor's availability within a specific time period. This needs to be taken into consideration in planning when to have a tutorial and how best to use it. Often the course handbook will indicate how much tutorial time each student is allocated.

In most programmes it is students' responsibility to contact their tutors to arrange a mutually convenient date and time for a tutorial. We *strongly* recommend that students do not leave it to the last minute. If students find at the last minute that they are not able to keep a tutorial (e.g. because of illness), then it is their responsibility to contact the tutor to arrange an alternative date and time. Few tutors will remind students about tutorials and the initiative for rescheduling tutorials missed or cancelled by the student needs to be taken by the student.

Tutors also cannot be expected to provide tutorials at a moment's notice. Other students who have booked a tutorial will normally be given priority. If a genuine emergency developed, most tutors would make every effort to discuss the situation with the student as soon as possible. It is important to remember, however, that a crisis which has developed due to the student's own lack of forethought or planning may not normally be dealt with on an emergency basis.

Occasionally students may feel the need for more tutorials than a programme would normally allow. This raises the issue of equity: courses need to ensure that one student is not given a greater advantage or opportunity to pass a programme through unfair access to tutorial advice, access which another student did not receive. Courses will, however, usually try to apply regulations about limits on tutorial time in flexible ways, sensitive to individual differences and the varying levels of need among students.

This is particularly relevant with regard to anti-discriminatory practice, or when dealing with students who have been identified as struggling academically due to non-traditional academic backgrounds, who may, therefore, need additional support.

Sometimes students supplement in-person tutorial advice by phoning their tutors. Teaching schedules permitting, most tutors will try to be available for telephone consultations. However, students should remember when contacting tutors that they are not chained to their desks eagerly awaiting telephone calls. If you ring when a tutor is in a meeting or teaching a class, you may be asked to ring back later. If you leave a message, normally the tutor will undertake to return your call. However, few tutors guarantee to return phone calls within the next hour.

Focusing tutorials to get the most from them

Tutorial time is a precious resource and needs to be used in focused ways which help students to get the advice or support they most need. The best way to ensure the most helpful focus is for students to prepare for the tutorial and decide what they want to achieve. Is it:

- suggestions for additional reading because the student is having difficulty locating reading material about a particular subject area

- analytical debate about the strengths and limitations of a particular theoretical perspective in order to clarify the issues related to a specific point and the argument the student wants to develop

- advice about how to incorporate examples of professional experience into paragraphs which discuss theory

- advice about how to incorporate theory into paragraphs which discuss practice

- discussion about how the student learned from experience and how to incorporate this into the developing argument

- guidance about a change in focus or topic

- help in revising the essay plan
- advice about how to reference properly?

All these topics are appropriate to bring to a tutor for advice. The more that students help to set the agenda for a tutorial, the more they are likely to feel they got the help they needed. Students should bring notes to the tutorial or a list of questions to ask, so that nothing is forgotten. The more that students can show about what studying has been done, the better able the tutor is to focus advice on the areas where help is most needed.

However, there are limits to this. Tutors cannot allow a tutorial to be turned into a mini-class which teaches students everything there is to know about a particular theory or issue. Tutors will give some guidance and a few suggestions about what to read, but they will then expect students to pursue the topic through independent reading and research. Equally they cannot offer students so much advice about how to revise draft assignments that it has the effect of rewriting substantial parts of the assignment. One paragraph might be pulled apart and revised as a teaching example to show students how to do this, but then students would be expected to do the rest on their own.

The more that tutors are told by their students about how the work is progressing and what areas are causing confusion, the more likely it is that the tutorial will be productive and helpful. In order to get the most from a tutorial, students need to be able to discuss openly and fully their background research, how they are planning to write the assignment and what parts they are finding difficult. That way, tutors know how to target advice.

Getting advice that was not expected

Every tutor has the experience of giving a student unwelcome advice. This does not happen often, but once in a while a student comes to a tutorial expecting to get a pat on the back for a job well done. Instead the tutor poses seemingly unanswerable questions, or offers criticism which from the student's perspective seems harsh. The tutor may be asking the student to consider issues from a radically different approach from the one the student chose. Why? Usually this is because the tutor has identified a gap in the student's background research or difficulties in the way an argument has been focused or constructed which could lead to failure unless corrected. The tutor is not being critical because of a personal dislike of the student or a desire to see the student fail. Quite the opposite – the tutor is pointing out the criticisms in time for the student to address them well in advance of submitting the assignment. This is done in order to help the student to pass. Listening to the criticism may well be painful, but ignoring it may be more perilous!

Reading and critiquing first drafts

It is worth checking the course regulations to discover if tutors are allowed to read and critique first drafts of assignments. This is not permitted under many regulations, but if it is permitted, it can provide invaluable assistance to a student. This would involve a student submitting a draft to the tutor a week or two in advance of the scheduled tutorial. The draft paper would then form the basis for subsequent tutorial discussion. If course regulations do not permit this, the student can bring notes to the tutorial and use them as a focus for discussion. Or, why not take a draft assignment to a writing workshop or learner support service for advice? Sometimes students think there is shame attached to using a writing workshop, yet there may be more hurt feelings to deal with if an essay earns a low mark or fails. The practical help offered through a writing workshop or learner support service may make the difference between students passing or failing or being awarded a high or average mark.

Tutorial records

Tutors often keep some brief notes about the focus of tutorial discussion. However, it is normally *students'* responsibility to take detailed notes during the tutorial if they believe notes of this kind might be helpful. We would suggest that unless a student has an eidetic memory, it would be wise to keep detailed notes. Some students like to audio-tape tutorials.

The practice teacher's role

Supervised practice placements are an important part of the training for many professions and may be called by many names: accountants complete a year of articling, doctors complete an internship, barristers become pupils, while social work students complete placements. The principle remains the same: professionals cannot qualify without completing a period of experiential learning, where they receive on-the-job training under close supervision from a practice teacher.

Practice teachers are not primarily teachers – they are practitioners first. That is why they offer such an important service to social work courses and students. Research has shown that academic tutors on social work courses are not always in touch with the reality of agencies and practice. 'Some tutors have clear frameworks for placement links and are very helpful. Others seem to have very little idea about the nature of social work practice' (Player 1990, p.53). This is part of the reason why professional social work training is not solely based in an academic setting nor taught solely by career academics but involves people currently in practice.

In our view, practice teachers fulfil a vital role within social work education by:

- helping to provide students with a safe environment in which to learn
- arranging work and other training opportunities for students
- monitoring students' practice
- teaching students about procedures, law, theory and agency policy
- helping students to understand the links between theory and practice
- helping students to understand the links between college or university-based studies and the work they are doing on placement
- helping students to reflect on their work and learn from their experiences
- helping students to develop more skills
- assessing the quality of students' practice

- taking accountability for students' practice (to a point)

- acting as professional mentors and role models to students.

This is a demanding role for anyone to fulfil. To this list must be added two interrelated tasks. Practice teachers may not only support students with academic assignment preparation but also mark theory-to-practice assignments. Not surprisingly, supporting students with assignment preparation will often take a back seat to other aspects of practice teaching. Understandably practice teachers often feel the main supportive role for an academic assignment is vested in the academic tutor, but they still have a part to play.

Practice teaching supervision

The main vehicle that practice teachers use to support students in completing assignments is practice teaching supervision. A lot is already packed into supervision. The National Organisation for Practice Teaching (NOPT 2000) recommends that students receive a minimum of one and a half hours' formal supervision per week; into this practice teachers and students need to fit an already crowded agenda if they hope to fulfil the requirements of the above list. How then can supervision *also* serve as support for an assignment?

Throughout the placement, practice teachers provide supervision and support for students' practice. Students will be discussing their plans for pieces of work, the theory, research, policy and legislation and ethics which inform their work, and reflecting back on practice they have done, evaluating its effectiveness and looking at ways to improve. This supervisory process, *in itself*, supports the student to complete the integrated assignment, given that the major foci of the academic essay are:

- the ways the student integrated theory (research, policy, law, etc.) and ethics with practice

- the student's ability to reflect on and evaluate his or her own practice.

These are also focal points for practice teaching.

Stages of practice teacher support for the integrated assignment

Identifying a good topic and developing a preliminary plan

The first stage in assignment preparation is identifying a topic and developing a plan. Students are often quite anxious about this and may look to their practice teacher for emotional support and guidance about how to choose what to write about. The student's allocated work will be discussed as a part of supervision. In supervision, practice teachers will pull apart pieces of work with students. Together they identify the tasks which form parts of the whole and the theory, law, research and policy which underpin this. This process can help students to identify pieces of practice they will analyse in their assignments and to develop their practice issues (see Box 4.1).

Box 4.1 Case study

Katie was allocated to co-work a children and families' case with Doris, an experienced practitioner. Care proceedings were being taken by the social services department for two of Tessa's children, Liam and Maria, due to longstanding concerns of neglect. Doris was responsible for completing a court-ordered assessment about Liam and Maria and Tessa's ability to care for them. Katie was allocated the role of supporting Malcolm, who was the natural father of Glenda (Liam and Maria's younger half-sister). Malcolm had permanently separated from Tessa and was caring for Glenda full time; he had applied for a residence order. The SSD was supporting him in this plan for Glenda's care. Doris and Katie would co-write a report to the court about this.

In supervision Katie and her practice teacher Max discussed the various aspects of her work with Malcolm and Glenda. They identified the following components and issues to consider in day-to-day work:

- Direct work with Malcolm about parenting skills
- Direct work with Glenda to determine how settled she is with her father and how she is developing
- Is Glenda safe and happy and what are her wishes?
- Is Malcolm empowered to be a good father?

- Liaison with relevant professionals working with Malcolm and/or Glenda (e.g. health visitor, paediatrician)
- Record-keeping about Glenda and Malcolm's progress
- Liaison with Doris about how the care proceedings are progressing for Liam and Maria
- What are the boundaries of co-working between Doris and Katie in relation to the report about Glenda and Malcolm?
- Meetings with extended family and friends of Glenda and Malcolm to help them to develop appropriate support and check on their progress as a family
- What are the boundaries of confidentiality – what can or should be shared with other professionals, with Glenda's family and friends, with Doris, with the court?
- Legal framework under the Children Act 1989
- Policy and procedural guidance under Area Child Protection Committee (ACPC) guidelines, the Department of Health (DoH), Department for Education and Employment (DfEE) and Home Office (2000) *Framework for the Assessment of Children in Need and their Families*, and local SSD policy and procedures
- Attachment theory and child development theory
- Sociology of the family and single parent families and the role of fathers.

Katie told Max that when she took the 'Child protection' module at college she was concerned about the difficulty of working 'in partnership with parents' while also working within an adversarial court process using a risk-assessment framework that substituted professional judgement for parents' opinions. She wanted to find a way to explore this more fully in her integrated assignment. Max pointed out that they had identified too many issues and components for Katie to include everything in one assignment. She would have to choose what to include and what to leave out.

Katie thought about it overnight before coming to a decision. Her own interest in the question of partnership, coupled with her identifying the different components of her social work, led her to develop the following assignment topic and practice issues:

Title

What meaning does 'partnership' have for social work practice within court proceedings?

Practice issues

- I will evaluate how the sharing of information and the negotiation of boundaries of confidentiality affected my development of partnership with Glenda's father, mother and extended family.
- I will examine the impact of my co-worker's practice and decisions in the assessment on my own practice and decisions and whether this facilitated my attempts to empower Malcolm to become a full partner in the court process.
- I will investigate how the framework of risk assessment within the court process affected my ability to develop a partnership with Malcolm.
- I will evaluate my use of the *Framework for the Assessment of Children in Need and their Families* (DoH, DfEE and Home Office 2000) and the impact this had on the development of partnership with Malcolm.
- I will investigate the extent to which a partnership is achievable with a pre-school child within the court process and what steps in my practice I took to attempt this.
- I will analyse to what extent in developing a series of different partnerships with various professionals within the assessment process I was safeguarding and promoting Glenda's welfare as the paramount concern.

Katie and her practice teacher felt satisfied that the topic and practice issues incorporated several aspects of Katie's own day-to-day work with the father and daughter with legal and policy guidance, theory about empowerment and Katie's own interest in the concept of 'partnership'.

Gathering evidence and completing background research

As a part of regular supervision sessions, practice teachers discuss with students the work they are undertaking. Good supervision about social work practice is an excellent form of support for students as they gather evidence and complete background reading. Practice teachers can discuss with students the relevance of what they are reading to the work they are doing, and help students to reflect about the efficacy of their work and the ethical dilemmas they face. This fulfils the 'educational', 'supportive' and 'evaluation' models of supervision (Kadushin 1976) while also helping students to prepare their assignments.

Writing the assignment

It is rare for any practice teachers to have the time to give detailed guidance about technical aspects of essay writing (e.g. how to reference correctly, how to structure an essay, academic style, etc.). It is also unlikely that practice teachers will have the time to read and correct draft assignments before final submission. By the time a student starts to write the assignment, the practice teacher's supportive role is mostly complete. Occasionally a student may want to discuss aspects of assignment writing with the practice teacher, or may need to negotiate a few days away from placement to put the final touches to the assignment. However, by this time, the supportive role of the practice teacher is essentially being replaced by an assessing role.

Marking the assignment

Practice teachers are experts at assessing students' practice on placement but in our experience few practice teachers would describe themselves as expert markers, confident about academic marking criteria, because they mark assignments only occasionally. However, practice teachers are not being asked to mark the integrated assignment because they are expert at assessing its academic quality. That is the role of the academic tutors. Practice teachers are being asked to read and assess the assignment because they bring different skills and qualities which are no less important than the ones that academic tutors bring.

Practice teachers are being asked to assess the following:

- Does the assignment accurately portray the practice the student completed on placement?

- Does the assignment reflect the unique style the student brought to his or her work?

- Does the assignment provide evidence that the student was a safe, effective, ethical, anti-discriminatory and reflective practitioner?

- Does the assignment indicate that the student is ready to practice?

Many courses ask practice teachers to mark the integrated assignment simply on a pass/fail basis. If a course asks a practice teacher to provide a numerical mark (e.g. 40%, 50%, 60%) or grade (e.g. C, B, A) or class mark (e.g. 3rd, 2:2, 2:1), then we would recommend the practice teacher ask the course for written guidelines about what qualities are needed for an assignment in each category or mark.

Summary and conclusion

In this chapter we have outlined the partnership role between the college or university tutor and the practice teacher in providing support to the DipSW student in writing the integrative assignment. The importance of the interface between the practitioner's perspective and that of more formal academic teaching is highlighted. We hope that in providing a framework for understanding these differing roles, relationships and responsibilities that each partner in this process will find the experience positive and rewarding.

Suggested further reading

Evans, D. (1999) *Practice Learning in the Caring Professions*. Aldershot: Ashgate.
Hinchliff, S. (ed) (1992) *The Practitioner as Teacher*. London: Scutari.

CHAPTER FIVE

Gathering Evidence

Most of the time and energy devoted to the integrated assignment take place during the research, preparation and practice stage, which runs from the beginning of the placement to approximately one month before the assignment is due to be submitted. This is a stage when students complete the bulk of their background reading and also complete the majority of the practice from which they will draw examples to use in the final assignment. This chapter provides some guidance about how students should approach background reading and research for the assignment and how to access support for their studies.

Maintaining focus

During the placement period students have relatively little contact with the college or university. Often they are enthusiastic to be away from college and back in practice. They are spending most of their time at their practice placements; they may be starting to feel a little more comfortable in their placements (perhaps feeling they are starting to become part of the team). Traditionally, during this time students focus on their practice or work on placement and, to some extent, forget about the academic side of their course. Particularly at the beginning, they can sometimes feel enormous lethargy about their integrated assignments – that the due date is in the far distant future and they do not need to bother right now. The demands of working full time in practice may make it difficult to find the time to get into the college or university library and, apart from doing practice and meeting with their practice teachers, students may do little towards their integrated assignments.

Nonetheless, it is crucial that during this period students do not lose focus on the integrated assignment but continue to work on their plans for their essays – including the formal academic side of those plans (see Box 5.1). The bulk of the library research and background reading which is needed will have to be completed during these months. Only a very small amount of supplementary reading should be completed once they move into the writing and revision stage of the assignment. This means that, however hard it is to fit it all in, students must be very self-disciplined during this stage, to ensure they complete the academic library research and background reading – in evenings, at weekends, using time-off-in-lieu, whenever there is a spare moment – in addition to the hands-on practice they are doing on placement.

Box 5.1 Tips for maintaining focus

Set yourself a series of small goals or targets of what you want to achieve (and when), so that you do not drift. For example:

- 'I will spend a day at the university library by …'
- 'I will put in all my inter-library loan requests for journal articles by …'
- 'I will skim read these three articles by the end of the week.'
- 'I will highlight the examples of practice in my log this weekend.'

You may find that making notes on a wall calendar helps you to stay on track.

Finding information and background reading

By the end of a two-year full-time professional course most students are familiar with the academic library at their college or university. When a tutor suggests they do some background reading, one of their first ports of call will be the university or college library where they have, by now, learned which shelves tend to hold the books relevant to their field of work. Another is likely to be handouts and various photocopied material they have collected from tutors and other students, and in the course of completing other assignments. However, students do not always look beyond these obvious sources. When completing a complex piece of work like an integrated assignment, it is helpful to use a variety of sources to obtain the necessary information. For example:

- policy and procedure documents available through the placement

- policy or practice guidance published by government departments (e.g. Department of Health, Department of Social Security, Home Office)

- policy statements, guidance documents and other publications from key voluntary organisations that also work in the specific area of practice (e.g. MIND, National Society for the Prevention of Cruelty to Children, National Foster Care Association, National Association for the Care and Resettlement of Offenders)

- policy statements, guidance documents and other publications from key statutory organisations that also work in the specific area of practice (e.g. police, probation service, National Health Service (NHS) trust)

- policy statements, guidance documents and other publications from key voluntary organisations that publish generally about the social work role and practice standards (e.g. National Institute for Social Work, National Association for Probation Officers, British Association of Social Workers)

- recent research and statistical reports available through statutory and voluntary organisations and from academic journals and books (see also Box 5.2).

Box 5.2 Tips for finding information

Reading lists you receive throughout the course are a starting point for reading but do not limit yourself to these. Typically you need to read far more widely when completing your background research. The following suggestions should help you to find relevant information:

- Use the library computer systems in a subject literature search (you may need a librarian's help with this if you have not done one before).

- Search the Internet for websites of key voluntary and statutory organisations (e.g. Department for Education and Employment, Barnardo's).

- Use major social science abstracts (e.g. Social Science Citation Index, Applied Social Science Index of Abstracts) to find relevant academic journal articles.

- If a book is not available at your college library it can probably be ordered through inter-library loan (leave yourself enough time as it may take two to three weeks).

- Contact key voluntary and statutory service providers in your local area to ask for advice and help with finding relevant sources.

- Locate new sources through bibliographies and references in recent books you know are useful for your topic.

- Ask your tutor and practice teacher for suggested reading.

Making sure you do enough background reading

When your assignment is eventually assessed, the practice teacher and tutors who mark it will be looking for evidence of both breadth and depth of reading. In order to achieve this, you will need to collect and read academic and professional literature from a wide variety of subject areas relevant to your chosen topic. Consider the following example: the chosen topic involves a community care assessment about providing supportive services in the home for an older person who is suffering from dementia. Reading material potentially could be drawn from a wide range of sources and subject areas.

Example

Local and national policy, legislation and case law relating to community care assessments would be needed. In addition, you would need to read sources about dementia and about working with older people. Psychological theory about ageing processes might also provide useful background reading. Sociological theory about the position of older people within our culture might be relevant. Possibly you would need to read theory about communication with older people or people who are suffering from dementia. Background reading about age-bias, sex-bias and cultural discrimination would be relevant. Professional literature about empowering individual clients and promoting client choice in services would undoubtedly be helpful, and social work ethics and academic texts about professional accountability and the use of power and authority are related to this.

Theory about the model of intervention you use with this client (e.g. task-centred, crisis intervention, etc.) would need to be read and it is possible you might need to access evaluative research literature about what types of programmes are effective in helping older people with dementia. Theory about models of assessment (and possibly risk assessment) would be relevant and possibly also literature about financial assessment and fiscal policy. Sociology and psychology relating to family structures and family dynamics and professional literature relevant to working with carers and carer's needs assessments might be relevant depending on the circumstances of the older person. If sheltered housing were being considered, literature about housing policy, etc. would be needed.

These are some examples of subject areas which could be read. Depending on the case circumstances, undoubtedly more areas of theory, policy and so on would need to be added to the list.

Sources of information

It is essential to maintain a detailed list of all sources of information:

- legal statutes
- case law precedents
- local and national policy and procedures
- practice guidance and national standards

- academic texts

- professional leaflets

- academic journal articles

- professional magazine articles

- broadsheet newspaper articles (of limited use, but occasionally of some benefit)

- Internet publications (some care is needed in assessing the academic level and standard of such material).

This list will later be used to develop your bibliography. Remember to record page numbers of any key articles you wish to quote from or use as sources for statistics. During this stage you will inevitably gather more material than you eventually use. This is normal and is actually a sign of good, wide reading. When you eventually sit down to write, some of the background reading will be discarded as less relevant to the final assignment (or reduced to one brief mention). However, at this stage, you want to be sure you have collected widely enough to allow yourself a choice later when you start writing. If you severely limit your reading at this stage to only those few sources you know are absolutely necessary, you won't be able to do this kind of wide reading later (due to having even less time). Subsequently you may well find there are huge and glaringly obvious gaps in your reading that are difficult to fill in with last-minute reading.

Clearly if you collect background reading material on all the fields related to your chosen topic, you are ensuring breadth of reading, but there is also a potential danger in that you could lose focus on your specific topic and go off on a tangent. Equally, there is a time-management issue: no one is able to read everything of any possible relevance to the topic; there simply are not enough hours in the day.

Skim reading

One of the keys to this kind of wide coverage of a variety of background reading is to skim read (see Boxes 5.3 and 5.4). Certainly you will read in depth (word for word) some sources which you are actively using in your work every day or which are specially relevant to those particular cases or pieces of practice you are doing. In addition, you will read in depth several sources from those fields of literature most directly related to your chosen question and practice issues so that you thoroughly understand the *most* relevant theory, policy, law, ethical debates and research evidence that you are actively using day to day. However, in general you will find yourself simply skimming over the surface of most of the material you collect at this point, making a few brief notes or highlighting passages for reference in case you subsequently need to go back and read them more thoroughly. You are simply making sure you know where the information you may need is located. If you are not sure how to do this, you may find it helpful to seek advice about study skills through a student support or study skills service operating at your academic institution.

Box 5.3 Preparing to skim read effectively

- Set aside enough time for this – you cannot skim read ten books in half an hour.
- Do not expect to do too much all at once – you cannot do it all in a marathon 18-hour session.
- Make sure you are in comfortable surroundings (good chair, lighting, etc.).
- Take frequent short breaks (stretch your legs, make a cup of tea) – this *will* improve your concentration.
- Make sure you will not be continually interrupted by friends or family members.
- Make sure you are well rested – if you fall asleep over the book you will not remember it.
- Make sure you have writing paper and a selection of pens with different coloured ink and/or highlighter pens.
- Post-it Notes are very helpful for marking passages or relevant chapters.

There is a fine balance to be maintained between trying to read everything of any possible relevance and reading too narrowly. Judicious use of skim reading versus in-depth reading can help you to achieve a good balance which should later allow you to demonstrate both breadth and depth of reading in your written assignment. Unfortunately, a study guide of this kind cannot give you a definitive answer to how to get this just right. However, take heart: you will have developed considerable skills at this delicate balancing act when completing background reading for class and writing earlier assignments for the Diploma in Social Work. Thus the research skills you will need to complete the background reading for the integrated assignment are merely an extension of those skills you have previously learned (building on what you already know well) rather than something brand new.

Box 5.4 Tips for effective skim reading

- Read the introduction to the book quite thoroughly.
- Read the conclusion to the book quite thoroughly.
- Choose which chapters appear most relevant; within them read just enough of the sections that appear most relevant to understand the main ideas they are conveying.
- In the margins note the key points or use highlighter pen to pick them out or use Post-it Notes (reminder: please do not mark library books – it is preferable to make notes separately or mark a photocopy of the section).
- Use different colours for different ideas or themes – this will help you to keep things organised for later.

Choosing relevant reading

A common concern of many students is the difficulty of finding the right things to read. Their difficulties do not stem from a lack of reading, but from not always accessing the best books or articles. They read sources that are lateral to their topic, rather than clearly and specifically central to the issues they want to write about. For example: students might spend a lot of precious time reading a psychology text about self-esteem, which has some relevance, when what they really want is to read something about the relationship between disability, oppression and low self-esteem.

The following steps should help you to locate relevant reading:

- check the title, subtitle and table of contents

- look in the index for key words for your topic

- turn to the relevant chapters or sections that look as if they might be relevant

- check the headings and subheadings within the chapters and sections

- read a *brief* section you think is most relevant to see if it really is helpful to you

- check the introduction to learn what issues the book discusses

- check the conclusion

- compare the issues covered in the book with the topic or question you chose.

Collecting practice or case material

It is never too early to start collecting the practice or case material that you hope eventually to incorporate into your written assignment. You may want to collect copies of examples of client records (properly anonymised). If you are thinking of doing this, you *must* first seek permission from your practice teacher and line manager to ensure this is done in accordance with agency policies and legal requirements. In addition, you should consider seeking the permission of clients whose stories you are using to illustrate your practice.

Using a practice log

Does your programme require you to complete a practice log while on placement? If not, you may find it helpful to start a log or journal for the purposes of assignment preparation. Practice logs are a useful source of case material. If you have to complete them anyway for your placement, using examples drawn from your practice log does not duplicate effort (always important when time is limited and work is pressured).

Practice logs are a useful tool for integrated assignments because:

- they record experience
- they facilitate learning from the experience
- they support understanding
- they help students to develop critical thinking and a questioning attitude
- they encourage synthesis
- they increase active involvement and student ownership of their own learning
- they enhance students' abilities to do reflective thinking
- they improve problem-solving skills
- they can act as a rough draft for writing
- they are a step in planning the assignment.

There are various formats you can use for practice logs. We do not have any particular format to recommend. People are all individuals and what seems effective and helpful to one person may not be as useful to another. However, we suggest you consider using different coloured pens, high-lighting bits in contrasting colours, or using various styles of print (if typed or word processed) or columns as a part of organising the log *at the time of writing*. This should save you time in locating material when you move on to the organising and writing stage of the assignment.

Independent study

All students need to be very self-directed in this stage of the integrated assignment. They cannot expect frequent lengthy consultations with either the college/university tutors, or with their practice teachers whose *sole* focus is the integrated assignment. It is expected that by the end of the final year of the course, social work students will have developed consider-able skills and competence at independent library research and self-directed study. They should no longer need the hands-on type of teaching that they received in the early stages of the course. Having said this, we recognise that people have different styles of learning and some students struggle with self-directed learning and need to have an outside agency to help direct their time and keep them on track. If you know you are like this, is there someone you can turn to who will help provide this (e.g. partner, colleague, fellow student)?

Despite working largely on your own, you are not expected to work *entirely* alone, without any help whatsoever. During this stage you can expect some tutorial support from the college or university, some help from the student support/study skills/writing workshop services at your institution, and some support from your practice teacher as a part of the regular supervision received on practice placement. This was discussed more fully in Chapter 4.

Managing anxiety

Research and background preparation of the integrated assignment usually bring some anxiety. It is only as you get involved with the background research that you start to fully appreciate the complexity of the task facing you. At this point confidence may waver. You may even start to panic. In understanding your own response to stressors it is helpful to ask yourself the following questions:

- How much is the stress and anxiety created externally by the demands of the assignment competing for time and attention alongside the demands of your placement and your personal life?

- How much is it a product of the internalised beliefs you have about yourself?

Psychology about stress and emotion does not provide definitive answers (Lazarus 1999) to these questions. Each person manages stress differently. One way to help you to manage your own stress, however, is to be self-aware about how these issues may be affecting you (see Box 5.5).

Box 5.5 Common anxieties and fears that students talk about

- 'It's getting too big – I'll never get it down to just 6000 words.'
- 'I keep coming across all kinds of things that are really interesting and it's really hard to stay on topic.'
- 'It all just seems too overwhelming.'
- 'I am afraid I won't get it finished.'
- 'What if I cannot find enough material?'
- 'I know I cannot do this – I'm not academic.'
- 'They expect too much – I'm just a practitioner.'
- 'I don't have the time.'
- 'I just know I'm going to fail.'
- 'If I don't pass this I'll be a total failure.'

Sometimes people find it supportive to discuss with other students the stage they have reached in their background reading and evidence gathering and what they plan to do next. However, sometimes this only heightens anxieties as inevitably somebody in the group of students will seem to have done a bit more than you. We have no ideal cure-all for anxiety and stress (although we have provided some tips in Box 5.6). All we can suggest is that you should monitor your stress and anxiety levels carefully. If they rise too high, you ought to seek appropriate help (e.g. talk with your GP, go to the student counselling service, etc.).

Box 5.6 Tips for managing anxiety

- Keep reminding yourself that everybody works on assignments in different ways – speed of evidence gathering is not the point of the exercise.
- Do relaxation exercises.
- Take a break and listen to soothing music.
- Dance and work off some energy.

- Eat properly – sleep properly – get exercise – do not use alcohol excessively.
- Change the script: instead of 'I cannot do this', say 'I am learning how to do this'.
- Change the script: instead of 'I'm going to fail', say 'I am working hard to pass'.
- Set goals (see SMART goals in Chapter 11) and be methodical in working to achieve them.

Summary and conclusion

This chapter has discussed the process of locating good background reading. Information gathering, both academic and about practice and case examples, needs to be started as soon as possible. Students need to be self-disciplined and methodical in their approach to the assignment, even when they may be tempted to procrastinate. At this stage it is important to gather a wide range of material from a variety of sources. This will mean students are later able to demonstrate both breadth and depth of reading and it will also allow choice at the later stage of actually writing the assignment. It is also never too soon for students to collect examples of evidence from their own practice. Practice logs can help tremendously with this, and also can help later when students are reflecting and analysing their practice in the written assignment. Finally, we have included some suggestions for students about how to manage anxiety, which can start to develop, even at this stage of assignment writing.

Suggested further reading

Fairbairn, G. and Fairbairn, S. (2001) *Reading at University: A Guide for Students.* Buckingham: Open University Press.

Moon, J. (1999) *Learning Journals: A Handbook for Academics, Students and Professional Development.* London: Kogan Page.

CHAPTER SIX

Demonstrating Ethics and Values in Practice

The context of social work practice is complex and this creates tensions for many social work students in providing evidence of an ethical and values-based framework in their integrated assignment. In this chapter we consider ways in which students can illustrate the process of describing their practice in an ethical context in their written assignments. In so doing, they will provide evidence of achieving the values base and competence that CCETSW requires: 'It is clear, consistent and thoughtful integration of values in practice that students must demonstrate and programme providers seek evidence of in all assessable work' (CCETSW 1996a, p.18).

As with concepts such as reflection and reflective practice discussed in Chapter 9, the notion of values is a complex one. It is hardly surprising, therefore, that students struggle to understand what is meant by the term 'demonstrating ethics and values in practice'. Giddens (1993) defines values as 'abstract ideals'. Similarly, Banks (1995) acknowledges the problematic nature of the term 'values':

> 'Social work values', 'the value-base of social work', 'social work as a value-laden activity' are all common phrases in the social work literature... Values is one of those words that tends to be used rather vaguely and has a variety of different meanings. (Banks 1995, p.4)

The vagueness and variety of meaning associated with the notion of values is compounded by the *context* in which [social work] is practised, as part of a welfare bureau-cracy with a social control and resource rationing function, [which] also places ethical duties upon the social worker which may conflict with her [*sic*] duties to the user as an individual. (Banks 2000, p.119)

In addition, Clark notes that social values 'are not things that can be directly and unambiguously observed' (Clark 2000, p.27). Values are, however

an important influence on our actions and attitudes… In this way, values are not simply concepts – they are concrete in the sense that they have a very strong influence over what happens… It would, therefore, be very foolish to underestimate the significance of values to social work. (Thompson 2000a, p.105)

The centrality of values to social work practice is recognised by the requirement that all social work students are required to demonstrate adherence to core professional values requirements in all their work:

- Identify and question their own values and prejudices and their implications for practice.

- Respect and value uniqueness and diversity and recognise and build on strengths.

- Promote people's rights to choice, privacy, confidentiality and protection whilst recognising and addressing the complexities of competing rights and demands.

- Assist people to increase control of and improve the quality of their lives while recognising that control of behaviour will be required in order to protect children and adults from harm.

- Identify, analyse and take action to counter discrimination, racism, disadvantage, inequality and injustice using strategies appropriate to role and context.

- Practise in a manner that does not stigmatise or disadvantage either individuals, groups or communities. (CCETSW 1996a, p.18).

We would suggest, therefore, that in the context of the integrated assignment, demonstrating ethics and values in social work practice requires that students should be able to:

- indicate explicitly where core social work values were incorporated in their work

- identify a range of practice issues which identifies decisions they made about ethical dilemmas and show how they resolved them

- demonstrate an ability to reflect on the relationship between personal and professional values

- provide a framework for resolving problems where values may conflict with each other

- illustrate how they worked within an anti-discriminatory and anti-oppressive framework whilst integrating values into their work.

The integrated assignment gives students a wonderful opportunity to develop and demonstrate these abilities. Sometimes, however, students view ethical issues as something distinct and separate from theory, self-reflection, research-based knowledge and use of policy in practice. Viewing ethics as separate from these elements of practice is, in our experience, not helpful. Indeed, this attitude can actively hinder students from identifying how they evidence ethics in their work. It also acts as a barrier to the analysis about ethical practice in their assignments. It is essential, therefore, that students should approach the integrated assignment fully aware of the need to incorporate and integrate ethical perspectives throughout and to recognise values as an integral element of practice. As Thompson states: '...the relationship between theory and practice...needs to be seen in the context of values' (Thompson 2000b, p.16).

This bond between values and practice is supported further by the consensus of professional and academic opinion that ethics are an integral part of our use of theory, policy and research. In completing an integrated assignment, therefore, students will need to recognise and demonstrate this link between these three elements.

The link between values and use of theory to guide practice is illustrated in this example from a student's paper:

> ...task centred approaches involve aspects of partnership and include an emphasis on the impact of environmental pressures on individuals and/or families and therefore can be invaluable in anti-discriminatory work with service users in 'offering empowerment and dealing with structural oppression' (Ahmad 1990, p.51). This is particularly relevant to Pat's situation. (Example from student paper)

Here the student has identified the explicit link between theories of task-centred practice, how it can support anti-discriminatory practice and its particular relevance to the work she is undertaking with Pat.

It is also possible to demonstrate the intrinsic link between policy and values:

> Because concepts of the state's role in relation to children hinge partly on underlying values – values to do with children, with adults as parents, with the family as a unit, with welfare and suffering, and with the state itself – the four [policy] positions are referred to as value positions. (Harding 1997, p.9)

And:

> These 'awkward questions', and many others, give rise to the situation where there can be no certainty as to what the state should do, when it should do it, or how... Disagreements are not merely intellectual therefore, but are bound up with personal feelings and experiences. (Harding 1997, p.3)

As can be seen, Harding (1997) clearly demonstrates the link between underpinning values and policy developments. While it is true that students do not write policy, they often have some latitude in how they implement policy (Lipsky 1980) which in turn reflects their own personal and professional values. There is also a 'general expectation that social workers take an active part in policy formation and development' (Pugh 2000, p.82), as was recognised in one student's integrated assignment:

> I believe it is possible and essential for practitioners like me to work creatively with other professionals and service users to provide

services and interventions that meet identified need; also to pursue policy and practice changes that seek to ensure that the impact of children witnessing domestic violence is of central concern for social work.

...having established that the family needed support and the children appeared to meet the criteria of being 'children in need' I needed to look at what support could best help this family. The definition of a 'child in need' is contained in Section 17 (10) of the Children Act 1989. I realise, however, that 'eligibility criteria' for a 'child in need'...varies between local authorities, depending on interpretation. Authorities can and do redefine 'need'. This leads me to question whether assessments and/or service provisions are actually 'needs led' as in the spirit of the Children Act 1989, or 'resource led' due to increasing need and diminishing funding. I therefore need to be aware of my own department's policies and procedures before offering...services...In addition, it was important that I had a thorough assessment of and familiarity with all other local resources. This could facilitate directing Pat and her sons (or advocating on her behalf) for further or additional help/services (e.g. Family Friends, Home Start, counselling women's and/or parents' groups, children's support groups etc.). (Example from student paper)

This extract illustrates how the student acknowledged the ways in which policy can shape the delivery of services and her potential role in shaping policy and practice. It also demonstrates a commitment to anti-discriminatory practice and evidence of meeting the CCETSW values requirements.

Finally, the relationship between research and values is demonstrated by Fortune and Reid where they state that 'social work's professional values and ethics also influence the shape of a research study' (Fortune and Reid 1999, p.53).

We would extend this statement in relation to the integrated study. We argue that, as social work students, your personal ethics and values will influence your choice of which research evidence you incorporate into your assignment. Evidencing the implementation of research into your own practice is itself a reflection of good ethical practice and a way of demonstrating you are an ethical practitioner. As Thompson states: 'Research has a valuable role to play in helping to promote an *informed* approach to health and social welfare practice' (Thompson 2000a, p.17).

In the following example from a student paper, the writer was able to illustrate the way in which her reading of research had an impact on her understanding about the experiences of the person she was working with:

> Worryingly, on the evidence available to me it appears that attitudes towards domestic violence amongst professionals tend to mirror society's, in that denial of the extent of domestic violence and minimisation of its effects in women and children is all too common (Farmer and Owen 1995). I reflected that for Pat and her sons fleeing the violence had not meant the end of unequal power relations. (Example from student paper)

Incorporating consideration of ethical issues in an assignment requires an ability to reflect on practice as well as being able to demonstrate an understanding of theoretical perspectives which inform social work. Issues of reflecting on and evaluating practice are discussed more fully in Chapter 9. For the integrated assignment, however, it is important when evaluating the ethical context and values base which informs social work to be able to integrate this element *throughout* written assignments. The integration will reflect (or *should* reflect) the underpinning values base and ethical framework upon which social work is founded. In practice, then, this element cannot be seen as an add on to social work but should be incorporated in everything we do. This is not as easy as it may initially appear, however, as core values and the general ethical principles that flow from them may sometimes be in conflict with one another (Eby 2000b), as two students noted:

> In my work I could advocate so far, on an individual level, but I was always aware of the conflict of duties to my service users, the profession, to the agency and to society (Banks 1995). (Example from student paper)

> The issue of confidentiality arose between [the father] and myself... This posed a dilemma between my primary duty to safeguard [the child's] welfare and [the father's] right to confidentiality. The

> outcome…did not immediately alter [the child's] circumstances or her welfare; however [the father's] intent may have done so. But was it clear 'evidence of serious danger' to [the child] (BASW 1996)? …I was unable to endorse the 'negotiated consent' to confidentiality [the father] was seeking (Thomas 1995, p.60). (Example from student paper)

Here one student has identified that conflict was inherent in her work when wanting to act as advocate for the service user, but that she was limited in this undertaking by wider factors which determined her role. The other student has identified two separate duties which were in conflict with one another, one of which had to be given priority over the other.

Students may also find that the task of integration of values into the final assignment is confusing. This is because of the complexity of issues surrounding values and their continually changing nature:

> MacIntyre (1985) argues that we should indeed abandon the notion that we can rely on ethical statements of universal validity in order to make sense of particular situations…

And:

> …if our principles are derived from a robust, relevant and living tradition we must expect them to be constantly disputed and constantly evolving. (Donnison 1994, p.28, cited in Hugman and Smith 1995b, pp.10–11)

Moreover, values may be interpreted differently depending on the circumstances, particularly where there is no one clear straight and easily discernible path. 'Timms [1983]…argues that ethical principles are not fixed directions in the manner of an instruction manual but are the basis for making choices in situations where a range of actions is possible' (Hugman and Smith 1995b, p.2).

The following extract from a student's work demonstrates this kind of debate where principles of working in partnership may be put into practice using opposing frameworks:

> Our different approaches to partnership caused much debate and reflection between [the social worker] and myself. Would pursuing the deontological principle of self-determination for [the father] lead to a good outcome for [the child] (O'Sullivan 1999)? …our different practice

approaches were reflected in our views on decision making, for instance, by our differing responses to [the father's] marriage proposal. It was [the social worker's] view that [the father's] intent and secrecy signalled that he was placing his own...needs before [the child's] and [the social worker] questioned whether he was committed to safeguarding [the child's] welfare as his primary concern. [The social worker] felt that we should therefore suggest to [the child's] grandparents that they apply to become party to proceedings for a residence order... I felt that this was premature. [The father] was a non abusing parent, his basic care of [the child] appeared good... As such I felt that [the social worker's] view was excessively interventionist, which, in itself, could be harmful to [the child] in her future family life. (Example from student paper)

Social work involves a wide range of practice issues and involves *us* as individual workers in the evaluation and resolution of ethical dilemmas on a daily basis (Watson 1998). Thus, 'ethical issues cannot be divorced from the standpoint of the actors involved' (Hugman and Smith 1995b, p.3). Therefore, as a watchdog for the social work profession, CCETSW requires that social workers (the 'actors' Hugman and Smith refer to) demonstrate adherence to core values in their qualifying studies. Individual interpretation of ethical practice requires consideration of personal and moral values as well as those dominant social values that inform what social work should aspire to (Payne 1996). Values and ideology can be seen to be inextricably intertwined: 'Basic values embrace the grand aspirations or big ideas of morality and politics, such as freedom, justice, autonomy and community' (Clark 2000, p.28).

The political realisation of these values becomes enshrined in the policy and theory that we choose to use in our practice: 'Rescher [1969] suggests that, because values and their realisation are bound up with a *vision* of a *good life* (for self or others), values are fundamentally ideological in character' (Huxley 1994, p.176). Thus the ways in which we use our personal and professional values in our social work practice is bound up with both our understanding of what is the good life to which the people we work with want and aspire and also with what *we* want and aspire to.

A hundred and fifty years ago, charity workers accepted a values base that linked with and was consistent with the dominant welfare ideology of Victorian society – one of the 'deserving poor' and that 'God helps those who help themselves' (Fraser 1984). Our values have fundamentally shifted, however, and in modern social work we hold instead to respect for persons (Butrym 1976) as of human right (Human Rights Act 1998), rather than categorising people as 'deserving' or otherwise.

Thompson (1998) suggests that contemporary western society is characterised by inequality. Social work clients can be seen as amongst 'the most marginalised and excluded groups in society' (Stepney 2000, p.13). This requires workers in human services to recognise the challenge we face in either making decisions which may move us towards a greater degree of equality or reinforcing existing inequalities. Thompson argues that a crucial role of the worker is to promote equality 'rather than reinforcing or exacerbating the inequalities that already exist in society and in people's lives' (Thompson 1998, p.1). This requires us, therefore, to recognise these social divisions, the experience of disadvantage, discrimination and oppression that result as a basis for understanding these inequalities and that 'good practice must be anti-discriminatory practice' (Thompson 1998, p.3).

Again, the term 'anti-discriminatory practice' is one fraught with confusion and a range of interpretations of its meaning exists in social work literature. Definitions of the term anti-discriminatory practice tend to provide a clearer insight into what it is, but offer a more limited insight in terms of how to do it or what it looks like. For example: 'The term anti-discriminatory practice [can be used] in a broad sense to refer to forms of practice that challenge discrimination and oppression' (Thompson 1998, p.77).

Langan and Day (1992) see anti-discriminatory social work as

> recognising the specificities of oppression, according to gender, race, class, age, disability and sexual orientation. It seeks to develop an understanding of both the totality of oppression and its specific manifestations as the precondition for developing an anti-discriminatory practice relevant to all spheres of social work. (Langan and Day 1992, p.3)

Trevithick provides an example of anti-discriminatory/anti-oppressive perspectives in social work as being 'where the emphasis is on ensuring that people's rights are not violated' (Trevithick 2000, p.165).

The academic debate regarding the relationship and distinction between anti-discriminatory practice and anti-oppressive practice may also provide a further source of confusion for the student in evidencing this in the integrated assignment. Some writers stress the importance of the distinction and difference between anti-discriminatory practice and anti-oppressive practice (Dalrymple and Burke 1995; Phillipson 1992) but there are those who see this distinction as unhelpful (Thompson 1998) and as not having wide currency (Thomas and Pierson 1995). As a result of this ambiguity and confusion, it may be difficult for the student to provide clear evidence of anti-discriminatory practice. It may be that one person's anti-discriminatory practice is another's experience of oppression.

The following extracts from two students' work illustrate a range of ways in which they have incorporated evidence of anti-discriminatory practice:

> I have seen similar booklets…in the past, referring to the child's new 'mummy and daddy'. However, I felt that this may be misleading as Lorna's new family may be a same sex couple or a single person for instance. Despite the fact that recent research by BAAF [British Agencies for Adoption and Fostering] (2000) found that 95 per cent of adopters are married couples (McCurry 2000, p.10), family structures vary enormously (Thompson 1990, p.20). (Example from student paper)

> I also took offence when she was referred to as 'a piece of work' by members of the team as I felt this was like referring to catwalk models as 'pieces of meat'. I felt this terminology went against the values of social work and decided to challenge the use of such language in a team meeting. (Example from student paper)

It is possible for students to demonstrate integration of values and ethical decision-making at a range of levels. Kohlberg (1969) understands moral reasoning to develop through six stages. This may start at a simple level of 'I do it because I will be punished if I do not' and progress to a level of reasoning that demonstrates internalised norms and values, owned personally but linked to overriding principles. The level of moral reasoning required of students in the integrated assignment should reflect the most sophisticated of Kohlberg's stages where

> what is right or wrong is based upon self-chosen, ethical principles which we arrive at through individual reflection... The principles are abstract and universal such as Justice, Equality...and respect for the dignity of human beings as individuals, and only by acting on them do we ultimately attain full responsibility for our actions. (Gross 1996, p.548)

Sometimes, students demonstrate integration of values through a more simple approach of 'I do it because policy says so' or 'because the BASW code of ethics say so'. We would not recommend this. While it is true that students must adhere to policy and codes of ethics, we would suggest that the student's level of critical reasoning about ethical decisions needs to reflect the sixth stage of Kohlberg's model. Analysis about ethical decisions in the integrated assignment should demonstrate that the student linked abstract principles with the complexity of the ethical dilemmas which he/she faced in specific case situations.

Case-related ethical dilemmas can cause a crisis of conscience in practitioners. This is to be welcomed as a good opportunity for students to learn and grow as individuals as well as professionals. Stressful situations can challenge our belief systems; they challenge the principles we hold dear. The essence of good ethical practice is work that adheres to core social work values, regardless of environmental pressures (i.e. anything affecting the practitioner in their work). We recognise that intellectual and emotional synthesis of behavioural standards (what we think, what we feel and the value we place on something) may shift slightly as a result of inconsistencies we perceive between principles and reality and the ways our consciences mediate this dissonance (Aronfreed 1968). Nonetheless, we would suggest that at the core, the values remain the same.

In other words, we often work in organisations that are under pressure. We may struggle to administer policies which have at their core values we disagree with. We may be tired, the building we work in may be overcrowded, perhaps we lack the practical resources our clients need. All these factors create dissonance. We have in our minds a standard of practice that incorporates both our social work ethical and values perspective and skills and knowledge. Our conscience tells us what ought to happen and prods us not to accept less. Yet we live in the real world. Nonetheless: 'The subtleties and flexibility of professional discourse provide workers with sufficient tools to resolve working problems' (de Montigny 1995, p.47). Thus, practitioners may 'argue that the need to provide good professional social work outweighed the limits imposed by "a few bad policies"' (de Montigny 1995, p.46).

An example of how a student mediated between 'good professional social work' and 'environmental pressures' is illustrated in this extract:

> For my own peace of mind I wanted to explore the possibility of Mr N returning to live in the community even though this would necessitate twenty-four hour waking care. In so doing I began to realise further tensions between social work ethics, the centrality of the service user (Coulshed and Orme 1998) and the multiple accountability that Adams (1998) acknowledges is inherent in social work practice. The cost of providing such assistance would have far exceeded the budgetary limits placed on home care and in turn could have jeopardised what was available to others (the principle of the greatest good for the greatest number). Cost was compounded by lack of human resources necessitating live-in carers to be recruited from London. It is a poignant comment on the nature of racial discrimination and poor status and pay of such work that the vast majority were black women. Mr N would not have tolerated this and we were accountable to both him and the carers. (Example from student paper)

Students must demonstrate they were able to hold fast to social work values and anti-discriminatory practice, even in the face of pressure to abandon them. Questions can be raised about social work values in multidisciplinary work, where a worker is faced with having to explain or defend decisions to a member of another profession, who may share some of the same values, but who may place different emphasis on them. For example:

> In agreement with Mrs S I set up a package of care, to provide assistance with personal care in the mornings for a minimum of two

weeks and left a message with the OT [occupational therapist] to advise the outcome of my assessment. The OT was dismissive of the care provision, stating that most of the large support network were very elderly and I was putting Mrs S at risk by not providing the care package [she] had mentioned in the original referral. She also revisited Mrs S on the ward and undermined her confidence by emphasising the level of risk to which the OT felt Mrs S was exposing herself and the burden she was placing on her elderly friends. The infantalisation of older people as being in need of care and protection is an ageist attitude and should be challenged (Thompson 1997). I feel sure that the high levels of accountability to which medical staff feel subjected influenced the OT's behaviour in this case and the notion of being seen to have failed if Mrs S should be admitted to hospital again after a fall was the major contributing factor. The increasingly litigious atmosphere in society generally has impacted on the health service, as on other services, to raise the management of risk as one of the highest priorities in work with vulnerable people (Finlay 2000). However, challenging ageist attitudes is an essential component of anti-discriminatory and anti-oppressive practice (Thompson 1998). In the case of Mrs S I organised for a voluntary agency (Red Cross Home from Hospital) to visit each afternoon because Mrs S's confidence had been undermined. I felt that once she was at home, in her own environment, she would cope well. This proved to be the case and Mrs S cancelled the afternoon visit within two days of returning home. (Example from student paper)

The example demonstrates how clearly the student fulfilled core social work values of assisting the service user to control her own life, building on her strengths and respecting her right to choose while taking action to counter age discrimination. Yet the student also demonstrates a nice appreciation for the dilemma faced by another practitioner, and respect for that professional's values and the pressures she was facing – a lovely example of sensitive, caring and anti-discriminatory practice.

Social workers so commonly work with people who have experienced varying forms of discrimination that most students manage to provide evidence of anti-discriminatory practice in their assignments. However, students sometimes are confused about how to provide evidence of antiracist practice. One of the most frequently asked questions of tutors is how a student can provide evidence of adherence to antiracist values and the development of antiracist practice when the pieces of social work chosen for the assignment involved white service users.

It is true that examples of antiracist practice are relatively easier to develop in assignments which are based on work involving people from Black or Asian ethnic minority backgrounds. For example:

> I felt that foremost if I were to uphold Jenny's right to participation I also had to provide her with an anti-discriminatory service. Jenny and her adult family members were white British. However, Jenny's brother and sister had a dual heritage. Therefore I had a duty to Jenny to elicit Mr Jones's views about how he would promote this racial diversity positively to Jenny in the future. Mr Jones recognised the importance of this to Jenny, but felt unsure as to how to promote positive images of her brother and sister. Alderson suggests that 'all children can benefit from having black dolls and respectful books about black people' (Alderson 2000, p.34). I informed Mr Jones of this, so that Jenny could begin to internalise positive images of, not just her brother and sister, but of other members of society who have diverse ethnic and racial backgrounds. (Example from student paper)

However, the mere fact a social work student has chosen to analyse a piece of practice involving a white client, or is working in a geographical area with predominantly white demographic characteristics, is no excuse for ignoring the requirement for antiracist practice. To suggest that antiracist practice is needed only with a Black or Asian client is itself racist since it ignores the institutional dimension of racism. Moreover, it suggests that 'race' and the need to address discrimination is being viewed in simplistic terms as a Black/white/Asian issue – an approach which leads to culturally insensitive practice (O'Hagan 2001) and inappropriate social work intervention.

In the past students have reported a range of issues arising in practice with white people which involve antiracist awareness and anti-oppressive practice. For example, one student discussed how they addressed a white foster carer's colour blind attitude that 'race didn't matter because she was a white carer working with a white child who only had white friends'. The foster carer was ignoring both the cultural diversity among white people and also ignoring the experiences the child was having at school and in after-school activities where they both encountered people from Black and Asian backgrounds. In another example, a Black student commented about how she encountered racism when arranging for a white Jewish woman to move into residential care. The home was sensitive to the possibility that an Asian or Black person might have particular dietary requirements but expected all white people to eat bacon at breakfast! Yet another person discussed how difficult it was to access interpreters when working with asylum seekers. The local service was well equipped to provide interpretation in European languages such as French, Spanish and German but had no one able to interpret languages from other areas of the world. Thus the needs of someone who spoke an Eastern European, Middle Eastern, African or Asian language could not be provided for. This was having a major impact on social work service delivery to refugees arriving from Ethiopia, Afghanistan, Bosnia and Croatia. White students discussed how they initially looked to the sole Black worker within the team as the expert who could answer all their questions. Through self-reflection, they learned it was inappropriate to invest expertise about all cultural or racial backgrounds in one person and instead learned to take responsibility for seeking out culturally appropriate information for themselves.

Ethical practice involves students questioning how their values or assumptions may affect their practice. This not only is intertwined with self-reflection but also needs to be seen as a part of the core values requirements and adherence to high ethical standards. Examples of how four different students integrated this standard into their assignments are illustrated below:

> ...when faced with a son caring full-time for his mother it did invoke some preconceptions in me that I had to counter. I had questioned the propriety of a son attending to all his mother's personal care but had to challenge this when considering whether I would have reacted as strongly were a woman fulfilling her role as a

'natural' carer (Graham 1997) to meet her father's personal care needs. (Example from student paper)

I spoke to Mrs F before the home visit and it was clear that she had felt she needed her husband's permission before becoming involved with social services. When we discussed financial matters she made it clear that she had felt financial affairs were her husband's responsibility… Feminist perspectives would argue that this is disempowering and infantalises Mrs F (Pascall 1986) but I would argue that social workers should be aware of the values and attitudes of older women particularly in relation to their attitudes towards married life and their roles therein. (Example from student paper)

I was very aware that my assumptions, attitudes and beliefs about family life could fundamentally affect my working method, as I carried my individual baggage to assessments, planning meetings, etc. Assessment could [thus] become as much a product of my own views and experiences as it was the information I gathered. I soon recognised and understood the possible influence of perceptions and subsequent decision-making (MacDonald 1989). (Example from student paper)

I did not feel confident that Sonia would be able to communicate sensitively with Lorna about this issue. However, I was aware that for Sonia, this was also a very difficult time and that if I was to ensure she was not discriminated against, I needed to do my utmost to enable her to participate in this work… Sonia, in fact, surpassed my expectations and effectively apologised to Lorna for what she had been put through when she was younger and gave her blessing for Lorna to have new parents. (Example from student paper)

We have demonstrated ways in which students are able to draw upon their professional ethics and values and how this can be used to inform and illustrate anti-discriminatory practice. The following checklists can be used to help students achieve the required standard in demonstrating integration of ethics and values in practice. In completing the integrated assignment, students will need to illustrate evidence of the following:

- adherence to core social work values and ethical standards and their implementation in practice

- appreciation of the complexity of ethical issues and ability to resolve practice dilemmas related to ethics and values

- anti-discriminatory and antiracist values incorporated into practice undertaken on placement

- awareness of the potential for practice which could become discriminatory or oppressive or awareness of the potential for practice which might not reflect core social work ethics and values and how they managed to avoid these pitfalls.

This requires from students analysis of:

- how various aspects of the student's practice fulfilled ethical requirements, with appropriate links made to academic and professional literature about ethics and values

- ethical dilemmas that the student encountered and how they were resolved

- how the student's awareness and academic knowledge about prejudice, bias, discrimination and individual and structural oppression was used in practice in anti-discriminatory ways

- the continuum of care and control used in the student's practice and discussion about his/her professional accountability intertwined with core social work ethics and values and practice dilemmas the student dealt with on placement.

Box 6.1 Common pitfalls to avoid in discussing ethical issues

As we have stated earlier, students sometimes view ethical issues as something distinct and separate from theory, self-reflection, etc. In this situation they may pay more attention (i.e. devote more words in the assignment) to discussing using theory in practice at the expense of discussing ethical issues and anti-discriminatory practice. Any discussion about ethics or anti-discriminatory practice then becomes a minimal addition which is never fully analysed. For example:

- One paragraph is devoted to anti-discriminatory awareness, one paragraph is devoted to ethical issues and they are not discussed in the rest of the assignment.

- Discussion of ethical and anti-discriminatory issues consist of simplistic slogans (e.g. 'I made sure my practice fulfilled social work ethics because they are important' and 'Social workers should strive to be anti-discriminatory') but there is little detail about how practice implemented these values while also fulfilling legal and policy requirements and using theory, research, etc.

- No awareness is demonstrated about ethical dilemmas common to the practice setting, where conflicts may arise between two or more core ethics and values when trying to implement them both in practice, or where legal and policy requirements (or the practice setting) mean the implementation of social work ethics is not simple or straightforward, or where the interests of one party are sacrificed to another client's need.

- No awareness is demonstrated about issues of discrimination common to the practice setting, where difficulties may arise in fulfilling legal and policy requirements while still maintaining anti-discriminatory practice due to structural inequalities (e.g. in an assignment about working with a client who has Down's Syndrome, the student does not analyse how the client has experienced disabling and discriminatory attitudes about their ability to make choices for themselves and the student does not discuss the measures taken to combat this discrimination, nor link this discussion to the literature which supports this approach).

- Issues of antiracist practice are either ignored or dismissed through a simple statement like: 'Antiracist practice was not an issue as this client was White.'

- The way the student resolved practice dilemmas is not fully discussed or is explained in ways which raise concerns about unethical or discriminatory practice. (Students sometimes make mistakes as a part of learning. This issue is considered more fully in Chapter 9 as part of reflective practice.)

Summary and conclusion

We have stressed throughout this chapter the complexity of issues surrounding social work values and their relationship to the constantly changing context of social work practice. These complexities are bound up with notions such as the range of work social workers undertake with people, definitions of the role of social work in society and 'newly emerging professional values' (Shardlow 1998, p.25).

The centrality of values to social work practice is also stressed. This centrality is reflected by our role and position in society: 'As social workers we do not merely help our clients. Instead, clients' lives become the terrain for exercising our professional powers' (de Montigny 1995, p.222). We practise within a role which consists of elements of both care and control – with the potential for 'both…empowerment and…oppression' (Thompson 1997, pp.10–11). This 'exercising of power' requires us to practise in ways which acknowledge this, support 'emancipatory practice' and 'promote equality'.

We hope that the examples cited from students' assignments have illustrated a range of ways in which it is possible to incorporate consideration of ethical and values issues into social work practice. They should show how students can demonstrate that their practice reflects core professional values (CCETSW 1996a) and that they practised in an anti-discriminatory way. In this way, these professional values can be seen to be a common thread which runs through practice and which draws it together with the wider elements which inform social work practice.

As authors, we are committed to supporting students to go out as practitioners, with increasing clarity about the issues and dilemmas that ethical practice presents us with. As de Montigny states:

> ...liberating social work is not without values... We must create values that are catalysts for practical action. We need values that demand decent housing, ending exploitation of working people, fighting racism, sharing wealth and building communities. (de Montigny 1995, p.226)

The process of writing an integrated assignment, reflecting on practice, and bringing together the range of elements which inform social work will support the creation and further development of such emancipatory values.

CHAPTER SEVEN

Incorporating Theory and Research

This chapter focuses on the uses of theory and research in practice and how students can develop this aspect of their assignments. Academic literature acknowledges that, even though linking theory and practice together is a requirement for professional qualification, the relationship between theory, research and social work practice is not an easy one (Cosis Brown 1995). Social work students are often told that theory and research are integral parts of good practice. They are exhorted by their tutors to read books and learn theory (rather in the way a revivalist preacher exhorts sinners to repent). Nonetheless, asking students to identify the ways they incorporated theory and research into their work can create anxiety. A long theory-to-practice assignment consolidates this anxiety.

After taking a quick look around the office at the practice placement, where often fully qualified social workers rely more on personal experience or co-workers' advice to make decisions, rather than theory or research (Carew 1979), students may be left still more mystified by the academic tutor's insistence that good practice includes theory. Their sense of unease grows. The anti-theory stance of some practitioners has been eroded of recent years through the movement towards evidence-based practice, where research is used to demonstrate the value of various theoretical approaches to practice (e.g. Corcoran 2000). In our experience, however, students rarely approach the topics of theory and research with anything but trepidation. The prime purpose of this chapter is to ease those fears – to explain how students' use of theory and research can be evidenced in their day-to-day practice, and to demonstrate (through the use of examples from previous assignments) how it is possible to do this well.

Let us examine the fear and anxiety of the knowledge bases of social work. Research is often seen by students as something that brainy people with lots of degrees do; it involves statistics and leads to incomprehensible reports (to the lay audience). Research 'conjures up images of white-coated boffins, dry-as-dust statisticians, deep thinkers, closely-typed and table-packed reports, the mystique of the expert' (Fuller and Petch 1995, p.3). The corresponding stereotype about 'theory' might hold that 'theories are sets of abstract ideas and hypotheses developed…by academics' (Carter, Jeffs and Smith 1995, p.3) – and perhaps the image of Einstein pops into one's mind! When the three of us discussed our own underlying stereotypes about theory and research that we held years ago when we first started as practitioners, they bore a striking resemblance to the images we have presented here. We would like to suggest an alternative, more user-friendly approach to theory and research in social work. For theory substitute the word 'idea'; for research substitute the word 'information'. Those are probably less frightening words.

Theory and research 'give a framework for analysing the situation and generating a number of possible options' (Thompson 2000a, p.35) for intervention. Cosis Brown points out:

> Social workers, approaching any piece of work, have to ask themselves, and be able to answer, three simple questions: what am I going to do?, why am I going to do it? and how will it be accomplished? (Cosis Brown 1995, p.9)

Explicitly pointing to (referencing) theory and research in an integrated assignment helps students to answer these questions.

In addition, each person's choice of exactly which theories to incorporate into practice is unique. It reflects the individuality of that specific piece of social work, and that practitioner's own values, ideology and beliefs. The theories and research information reflect the paradigm of beliefs and assumptions which underpin all work (Kuhn 1970). Thus, incorporating theory and research throughout an assignment also provides a vehicle for students to integrate analysis about values and ethics into their practice (otherwise known as killing two birds with one stone).

It all sounds good but how is this actually achieved? We would argue that using both research-based knowledge and theory together within an argument helps a student to make the link to practice: '...research needs to be recognised as a significant part of the process of integrating theory and practice' (Thompson 2000a, p.55). This is because '[research] poses a challenge to established theory...by producing data which theory finds hard to explain' (Thompson 2000a, p.55). Students, like 'most social workers...value research that is applied and useful to advance social work practice' (Fortune and Reid 1999, p.52).

In addition, we would suggest that incorporating both in relation to a given situation strengthens the evidence that the student was carefully analytical, aware and professionally accountable in their practice. This is not as difficult as it sounds. See how these two students achieved it in their assignments:

> I would argue that it is how we as social workers use our legal power in practice that is the crux of developing partnership. That we have legal power does not absolve us of our professional duty to our clients. Jenny and her family members had a right to be treated with respect, openness and honesty (Banks 1995) in my interventions with them. To me, this included acknowledging to them the impact on their lives that my legal power to intervene to safeguard and promote Jenny's welfare was having. Research indicates that family members stressed the importance of being cared about as people (Thoburn, Lewis and Shemmings 1995). This extended to identifying and acknowledging areas of Mr Jones's care where he was safeguarding and promoting Jenny's welfare. As Morrison suggests: 'Partnership is about working with parents and their networks to enable them to carry out the responsibility shared by both the state and parents to promote the welfare of children' (Morrison 1996, p.136). (Example from student paper)

> I met A in the ward office of the hospital. My aim was to discover what she wanted when she came out of hospital, the first part of the assessment for an aftercare plan under the Care Programme Approach (Department of Health 1990a). As a person-centred worker I expected to listen to her, accept her unconditionally and

try to empathise with her. Her first words were: 'I've just had a baby!' I knew she only had one child who was six. However, I accepted what she said while being aware of the 'thought disorder' I was told was part of her illness. She then said: 'I've just come back from Greece. Did you know I was a mermaid?' I realised that a person-centred approach was going to present problems. Rogers found working with 'frankly psychotic' clients difficult but stressed the importance of congruence (Rogers *et al.* 1967, p.86). The essence of the person-centred approach is communication and 'if the lines are crossed' empathy is blurred. Laing's psychoanalytic approach to schizophrenic patients involved engaging with them, listening to them and attempting to 'enter their world' by empathy (Laing 1965). He found it very demanding and was only partially successful (Clay 1996). I had to be very directive to bring A back to a reality we could share. (Example from student paper)

These are very different examples. The students were working in different areas of practice – one with children and families services, the other in mental health services – and were in very different geographical locations. Both students also brought to the placement (and to the specific piece of work being analysed) their own unique approach to the situation – different from something anybody else in the world could possibly do. Yet what these examples have in common is the way both students demonstrate the interweaving of awareness and use of theoretical ideas and principles, and research-based information, into their day-to-day practice.

The integrated assignment should demonstrate students' ability to implement theories and research evidence about practice into their own work in a social work agency. This may involve an appreciation for how book learning related to the environment in which students are operating. The following example shows how issues that a student read about came to life as a result of her practice experience:

Care provision is not a matter of fitting clients into whatever space is available which was the perspective of one of the doctors within the team who felt that a bed booking bureau run by the health service would be a better method of finding residential and nursing home placements. 'A multidisciplinary team without conflict is a contradiction in terms' (Ovretveit 1993, p.139). (Example from student paper)

It is important to incorporate the discussion of theory with practice throughout the assignment. An excellent paper will integrate some aspect of theory and practice together in almost every paragraph of the entire assignment. It is not easy. However, done well the intertwined theory and research with practice is like a good ballet: the dance looks smooth and effortless, as if the people are floating on stage. All the sweat and nerves, hard work and blisters are known only to dancers on stage – or to you, the student, as the writer. The finished product reads as if it came naturally.

Students' understanding of their clients' situation is frequently based on research-based knowledge. This is often a starting point for students to use in integrating theory and research into assignments. The next example shows how one student demonstrated the use of research in helping her to understand clients' circumstances:

> Wilma was 16 and leaving care, had low self-esteem and was lacking in confidence. She had been in and out of short-term foster care due to her mother's ongoing mental health problems. 'When a parent's mind is filled with delusions, pre-occupations or fears and their interpretation of events is dominated by abnormal beliefs, the capacity for necessary perceptions of the child may be eliminated' (J. Hill 1996, p.22). Waldo was 17 and deaf/dumb (Waldo's preferred terminology) and had self-referred as homeless due to domestic violence between his parents. He had just left residential school, was very capable, but felt vulnerable at home due to his disability (which he was proud of). Research by Cleaver, Unell and Aldgate (1999) has shown there is a link between parental mental illness and domestic violence and the parents' capacity to respond to the needs of their children. (Example from student paper)

The next step is to consider how research-based knowledge could help you to make decisions or predict outcomes of intervention. See how skilfully this student related relevant research about the predictive factors for success of a foster placement to her own practice situation, showing the limitations of research-based knowledge in guiding decisions:

In presenting predictive indicators, Triseliotis, Sellick and Short (1995a) identify both positive and negative factors, adding that 'it is the accumulation of factors rather than the presence of a single one that matters' (Triseliotis *et al.* 1995a, p.28). The following can be attributed to the five grandchildren: of the seven negative child-related factors, only two applied, which were lack of preparation (the children were placed as an emergency measure), and rivalry between fostered child and the family's own children – found in most studies (in individual interviews, all the children told me that they argued and fought frequently). Predictors that were not present were: child very disturbed, long periods in residential care, placed in adolescence, ignorance about origins and separation from siblings. According to these studies, there were few negative predictors, implying that the placement should have a good chance of success. Of the foster-home-related positive factors, the following applied: no children younger than the foster child; foster carers are inclusive of the natural family; willingness to work with social workers – the grandparents valued the financial and day care support; are getting enough satisfaction from carrying out their caring tasks – they wanted the children there; foster mother is over 40. Crucially, however, a positive predictor that wasn't present was: have been trained, prepared and are supported to work with children who have been abused (Berridge and Cleaver 1987; Strathclyde Social Work Department 1988; Rowe, Hundleby and Garnett 1989). On balance, the predictors would suggest the placement should have succeeded. Nonetheless, this placement broke down. (Example from student paper)

In contrast, the following student found her expectations of how a client would act, based on her knowledge of research, were confirmed by practice experience:

Wilma was horrified by most options... I also reminded her that the time limit she had set on achieving her goals was fast approaching, and that it was she who wanted to be housed and settled before commencing college a week later. A study by Reid and Shyne (1969) showed that short-term work becomes more effective as the deadline gets closer, as proved to be the case with Wilma, when having explored all her options she decided the housing association was preferable to hostels, re-applied and had moved within a fortnight. (Example from student paper)

The next example shows how a student used her awareness of the findings of research to promote better understanding in her work with a client:

Her description of her mother's physical abuse linked in with the findings of Williams and Watson (1996) that 50 per cent of women using mental health services have a history of physical or sexual abuse… Shirley's history of violence and attempt to burn down her house reminded me of a description of women in Ashworth Hospital, where 'there is a common existential experience shared by the women of not being heard and rarely believed, of feeling chronically frightened and overwhelmingly powerless, except in outbursts of impotent rage against property, self or others' (Potier 1993, p.340). (Example from student paper)

Another way of demonstrating the use of theory and research in practice is to analyse how the ideas in books and articles affected one's attitudes to practice and vice versa. For example, this student found that experiences on placement reinforced her commitment to work in innovative client-focused ways she had been introduced to at college:

Admission to hospital followed often by invasive surgical treatments, transfer to another ward for further treatment, detachment from the normal home environment and natural anxiety about future prospects is stressful for any human being. 'Their difficulties in understanding what is going on seem compounded by the sense of crisis in their lives' (Richards 2000, p.38). I found that in many ways the medical environment strengthened my resolve to practice in a holistic, client centred manner (Rogers 1951). Many clients were glad to tell their life story during the assessment process which often showed how resourceful people were at coping with problems, finding solutions (Slater 1995) and using their own support networks. This was the case with Mrs S, and Mr and Mrs F. (Example from student paper)

Of course implementing theory in practice is not always without drawbacks, as one student found when using task-centred approaches with two teenagers:

> I tried to advise Wilma not to rush into making a decision about her housing as I felt it was important we looked at a choice of accommodation. This would be needs, not resource, led and give due consideration to the planning and funding of her individual support package (Broad 1998). However, I was also aware that the sooner we acted the more motivated she would be (Marsh 1991). Wilma was set on her own tenancy with a local housing association and despite my advice she applied and was successful, but when told where the property was, immediately refused it as it was not in a 'trendy' enough area. This was when I first realised all may not be plain sailing as she said it was up to me to find her something else. I tried to explain that the tasks identified in her written agreement were of joint responsibility (Coulshed and Orme 1998), but as much as I tried to encourage and empower her, it was becoming obvious she expected me to do everything. I found it frustrating that Wilma would not try to help herself and I had to be careful not to use her failure to achieve tasks as evidence of general incompetence or lack of motivation (Doel 1996). (Example from student paper)

> My initial intervention with Waldo was totally different, as he was an emergency referral... He was homeless and in a state of crisis... Task centred intervention at this point was not appropriate as when in crisis our habitual strengths and coping mechanisms do not work. We fail to adjust if the situation is too alien, has not been accepted or when a series of events become too overwhelming (Coulshed and Orme 1998). Waldo was in crisis, could not think straight and had trouble conceptualising his problems and possible solutions. He was, at this point, certainly not ready to solve problems through joint planning (Doel and Marsh 1992). All he was concerned about was finding a bed for the night. I suggested bed and breakfast, he agreed and I duly arranged it. I then asked him to return the following morning when he was less stressed. (Example from student paper)

Critical analysis about the relevance of theory in a wider context may sound very grand, but can look deceptively simple when done well in an assignment. For example:

> That the partnership did not have equal power was a dilemma. Braye and Preston-Shoot (1997, p.238) expound that 'involving service users in problem definition and analysis of need' is an imperative of partnership. I was unable to involve Jan and Jack in defining problems as they denied abuse had taken place. They did not accept that the children previously witnessing domestic violence was abusive, or that physical abuse of their own children had occurred. Thoburn, Lewis and Shemmings (1993) argue that partnership is hardest to establish when the latter factors are present. Thoburn *et al.* (1993) also note that partnership is not an absolute concept, rather a 'continuum ranging from non-involvement in the decision making processes to carers being treated as equal parties' (p.97). (Example from student paper)

Through the incorporation of theoretical academic discussion about the meaning of partnership and power into a discussion of the minutiae of their work with two people, this student skilfully related wider structural issues to the specific situation she was dealing with. This kind of analysis is not easy to achieve, and so when it is done well, it tends to earn high marks.

We have demonstrated ways in which students are able to draw upon relevant research and to show how this, together with theory, can be used to inform practice.

The following checklist may provide a useful framework to help you achieve this integration at the required standard in your assignments:

1. Evidence that you correctly understand the most relevant theories and research evidence which inform this area of practice.

2. Evidence that you have correctly applied theory and research evidence in this situation.

3. Evidence that you are aware of other theory and research evidence which could inform this area of work but which may

not be fully discussed in this assignment (due to assignment word limits).

4. Evidence that you have implemented theory and research-based knowledge throughout your practice.

5. Evidence that theory and research has been implemented in social work assessment and/or intervention planning.

6. Inclusion of detailed analysis about using theory in your individual practice which examines how this kind of 'micro' analysis informs (or fits within) analysis about wider societal (structural or 'macro') issues. Analysis about the interrelationship of theory, ethics, research, policy, self-evaluation and practice would allow a complex argument which synthesises detail about individual casework within a broader argument. (Many students who achieve quite good marks nonetheless do not do this kind of intricate and complex analysis which includes several levels of critical examination. This kind of complex discussion is rarely achieved and is *not* a requirement to pass. However, if included and done well, an assignment which synthesises different levels of analysis generally earns a high mark.)

This requires from you detailed analysis of the following:

- how you used particular aspects of different theories and research evidence in different aspects of the work you did

- why specific theories were relevant to your practice

- how your knowledge of certain theories and research evidence helped you to make decisions in your work

- how your understanding of specific case details was enhanced by your underpinning theoretical/research knowledge so that your analysis about the implications of certain 'facts' about a case/situation was affected by this

- the strengths and/or weaknesses (limitations) of implementing this theory and research evidence in this situation

- analysis about how theory and research evidence was integrated into your *own* social work assessments and the way intervention was planned (and implemented) with this discussion linked to various areas of academic/professional literature informing this

- critical analysis about the relevance of theory in a wider context with analysis about power structures, cultural factors, ethics and values, etc. which affect this, the implications for practitioners' own use of theory in their day-to-day work and the role this plays at different levels (the 'micro'/'macro' analysis mentioned in point 6 of the checklist above).

Box 7.1 Common pitfalls to avoid when incorporating theory and research

Often students include both theory and research evidence and practice in their assignment but these elements are not integrated throughout their essays. Sometimes students' own weaknesses at understanding theory become glaringly apparent as the theory is misapplied. For example:

- Students describe what they did in their practice but only barely mention the theory which informs this and never expand on this through critical analysis.

- Students describe in detail what different authors have said about theory or this kind of social work, and may compare and contrast what each author has said, but never relate this to what they did themselves in their own practice placements and in fact barely mention their own practice.

- One half of the essay describes (in great detail) a case situation, the client's circumstances and what the student did, and the other half of the essay describes what several different authors said about theory and research evidence, but these two elements (case description and theory) are never related one to the other.

- Students discuss a particular theory and research evidence which has dubious relevance to that area of practice and misses theory which is clearly much more relevant.

- The theory which is discussed is relevant to the area of practice but it becomes apparent the student seriously misunderstood the theory and/or has misapplied it.
- Students discuss the agency/office/work environment in general or discuss and analyse other people's practice and fail to analyse their *own* work.

Summary and conclusion

This chapter has provided some guidance about how to incorporate theory and practice in integrated assignments. Theory and research-based knowledge should be an integral part of good social work practice. Knowledge of theory and research by themselves is not enough. Social work students need to demonstrate that they understand the relevance of theory and research to the day-to-day tasks they perform in practice. They must demonstrate how their understanding of theory and research-based knowledge guided their actions. This is different for every student and the diverse and wide-ranging ways theory and research can be implemented into practice need to be respected by the academics and practice teachers who mark integrated assignments. Some examples of how students have evidenced their use of theory and research in practice have been provided. The examples demonstrate how differently this can be done. All the examples came from good assignments that passed. No matter how different they are, however, they all have one quality in common: they incorporated both theory and practice and demonstrated an awareness of theory and research-based knowledge on the part of the students in their every action.

The ways in which we can incorporate theory to fit our style of working can be illustrated by the sweater analogy used in Chapter 2. If I were to make a pullover, I would probably choose different colours from you, the pattern I knitted would be different, and it would be a different size – the right size to fit me. However, you, the student, are knitting this sweater. Perhaps it will be a cardigan, not a pullover. Perhaps you have chosen various different shades of pink wool, while I chose peacock blue. Perhaps I chose a cable knit, while you chose Fair Isle. Of course, it will be a different size – the right size for you. And a sweater you feel comfortable wearing. It suits you and your style. Within reason, both approaches are valid. What is common to both approaches, however, is that the pattern chosen – the theory – would underpin the final piece of work. Without the pattern there would be no sweater just as without theory there would be no professional social work. Theory, research and social work are thus inextricably knitted together.

CHAPTER EIGHT

Using Law and Policy

It is usually not difficult to convince students that policy and law have direct relevance to their work. This is something they realise very quickly as they start the programme (if they did not already know it before). From the very first week of most placements, students also become aware of how agency procedures guide their work because this is something practice teachers actively teach their students. The wider policies (developed by central government) and legislation which lie behind agency procedures are factors which students also become aware of, although to a greater or lesser degree depending on the type of placement. For example, students placed within a busy children and families fieldwork team or area office which does a lot of child protection work would probably quickly become aware of Department of Health policy and guidance documents and be very conscious about the legislation governing the work. In contrast, students placed in a day centre for older people suffering from dementia might be less immediately aware of how legislation framed their decisions.

Why then do students sometimes struggle with this area within assignments? Why is evidencing how students used policy and law within their practice not a simple matter? Surely all a student needs to do is say: 'I did X and I did it because policy Y told me to'?

There are two main reasons why this is not as simple as it seems. First, policies are based on assumptions about how people behave; they have at their heart certain value judgements about how our society ought to be and how to influence people's behaviour (through policies) to achieve that (LeGrand 2000). This means that policy contains ideology within it; as policies change this may be a result of ideological shifts which have taken place within the governing bodies that initiate new policy and law. For example, one such shift was evident in the late 1980s and 1990s as community care legislation and policy changed:

> The community care legislation of recent decades considerably affects social relationships and caring; it also starkly reflects the overall ideological shift in Britain's political climate at the turn of the 1980s when New Right inspired perspectives and policy prescriptions came to replace a general consensus on social democratic approaches to the welfare state. (Cowen 1999, p.13)

Ideologies may have shifted over time but social workers may still be using old legislation that is based on values we now consider old fashioned (e.g. National Assistance Act – Ministry of Health 1948). Even when dealing with modern legislation and policy, there are times when the underpinning values and ideology do not rest easily with social work values. For example, policies and legislation surrounding child support payments when parents separate have at their heart a belief that estranged parents ought to support their children financially and that punitive measures should be taken when they do not. The introduction of the Child Support Agency was designed to reduce the cost of providing social security to parents with children, since it was believed that these families became dependent on the welfare system because non-resident parents were avoiding their financial responsibilities (Garnham and Knights 1994). The values and ideology of reducing the state role in providing support to families and reducing costs to the taxpayer reflect a very different perspective from the core social work values which CCETSW requires students to demonstrate and the code of ethics adopted by BASW (1996).

There are also times when policies and law are based on assumptions about social circumstances, assumptions which may not reflect the modern reality or the situations that social workers face. For example, embedded within much policy is the assumption that women are predominantly carers, that they

> should assume caring roles with regard to children [and] there will often be assumptions about similar responsibilities towards adults with disabilities and health problems...an expectation that unpaid caring for elderly

parents (in particular), but also for other relatives, will be undertaken by females without financial rewards and perhaps at the cost of abandoning opportunities to participate in the paid labour force. Inasmuch as the government regard community care as family care and, thus, reducing demands upon public funds, this means female care. The availability of female relatives may be used as a specific criterion for the denial of social care services. (M. Hill 1996, p.273)

What do these assumptions mean when a social worker is working with a family where the husband is carer for his sick wife? What does this mean when the adult learning disabled son is caring for his elderly father? How does a social worker reconcile the dissonance between these assumptions and the reality she faces when it is a 12-year-old daughter taking care of her mother? Or when an adult daughter says bluntly that she will provide her disabled parent with a home to live but her career is also important to her, and she has no time to provide personal care?

Moreover, policies and law, as they have been traditionally implemented, may reinforce discrimination, or act as forms of institutional discrimination. For example, Alcock (1996) notes how

the development of voluntary and informal support to replace the inadequacies within, and exclusions from, formal welfare services has in some ways compounded the discrimination experienced by black people. For the existence of self-protection can act as a confirmation that formal services [through the statutory sector] are not needed by black communities, because they can be relied on to 'provide for themselves'. Exclusion from welfare services thus becomes translated into apparent disinterest in them. This is a view that can encourage both direct and indirect discrimination by white service providers. (Alcock 1996, p.236)

What implications may this have for a social worker trying to support an Asian mother with severe postnatal depression? What is the impact on practice with a Black Catholic family who lives in an area where most of the local services that Black families are referred to are provided by the local Baptist church? What does this mean when a Black community is very poor and lacks voluntary or community-led services in the local area?

The second main reason why students sometimes struggle with integrating policy into assignments is because policies and procedures usually do not cover in infinite detail every aspect of a person's job with each and every individual they might encounter. This was recognised by Lipsky (1980) when he discussed how policies are interpreted differently by different people as they are implemented at street level by line workers. This can mean the same policy has a different impact on different people. Davies (2000, p.221) asks: 'Is there always a gap between policy and practice or at least a tension between what is on paper and what happens in the real world?' She goes on to suggest

> By seeing policy not as something that is given to people to implement but as something to be owned and developed by them, outcomes can be more positive. It may be that we have expected either too much or too little from policy pronouncements from the top. (Davies 2000, p.221)

Similarly law, also, is not something which merely comes down from above, in detail, to be implemented slavishly verbatim by practitioners. Cull and Roche (2001) point out that

> individuals working in social work are still faced on a daily basis with dilemmas over what they can and should be doing. Despite the new role accorded to law within social work, the law does not and cannot provide an answer to the complex human questions that lie at the centre of the social work task. In many senses, however, the law is an indispensable partner for social work. The law regulates social work practice, holding it to account and providing social workers with the powers and duties they need to do their job properly; it provides social workers with the authority they need as professionals. The law also structures their discretion through providing them with specific legal powers and duties in a range of situations and with 'advice' in the form of guidance. In addition, the law, like social work, is a dynamic and human process constantly changing and impacting on the lives of service-user and professional in different ways. (Cull and Roche 2001, p.xiii)

Thus, just like policy, law also is open to interpretation by practitioners at street level (subject always, potentially at least, through the courts).

The task for students to fulfil, in the integrated assignment, is to analyse how they used policy, procedures and law (including both statute and, if appropriate, case law) in their work on placement. They need to demonstrate their awareness of the complexity of what policy and law mean to practice. They need to show they used policy and law with imagination and sensitivity and showed a fine sense of appropriately discriminating judgement. This is closely linked to the core competencies (which they also must demonstrate) to assess and plan, intervene and provide services, work in organisations and develop professional competence (CCETSW 1996a).

Once again, this is not an easy task and the ways that students do this are as different as both the students, and their various placements. Sometimes students may fundamentally agree with or accept the values or expectations of the professional role which underpin policy. For example:

> Social work is not solely a 'therapeutic relationship'. There are also issues of care and control. It has been defined as 'the paid professional activity that aims to assist people in overcoming serious difficulties in their lives by offering care, protection or counselling' (Thomas and Pierson 1995, p.357). I am happy with this definition but many would not be. Since the 1980s most professions have changed under the pressure of the managerial revolution. In social work, a more managerial set of tasks has taken the place of intensive face-to-face work with users (Hanvey and Philpot 1994). Social workers and service users are both 'socially constructed' (Payne 1997). In mental health social work, the way of working is defined by the dominance of the medical model and the legislation and policies derived from it, by society's wishes expressed through its political representatives, and by the managerial revolution that has occurred in all the 'caring professions' (Smail 1993). Today's social context is for professional social work to be 'seen by government and public alike as an essentially "containing" or "monitoring" activity' (Thorne 1997, p.177). Individual care in social work is increasingly mediated by care management, especially in mental health. The Department of Health (DoH 1991a) defines care management as a method of systematically linking the process of identifying and assessing need with the arrangement of monitoring and review of service provision. 'The care manager is not herself a provider of services; the social worker acts as manager rather than therapist' (Sheppard 1997, p.319). This care management takes place within the Care Programme Approach (DoH 1990a). (Example from student paper)

The student, clearly locating her work within a policy framework, not only indicated that she was aware of professional controversy about the shift from a more therapeutic casework approach to one of care management, but also indicated clearly her position that she accepted fully the twin duties of care and protection. The next two examples show in different ways how another student agreed with the principles contained in policy and law, although she experienced difficulties implementing them:

> Advocating on behalf of S, I recognised my professional limitations in this role. As Atkinson (1999) comments: 'social workers are not advocates (although they may have an advocacy role)' (Atkinson 1999, p.34). Advocacy, if it is to work effectively, needs a coherent policy framework, which was meant to have been provided via the Disabled Persons Act 1986. However, this part of the legislation has never been implemented (Banks 1995; Lesnik 1998) and according to Walker (1997) 'in the absence of clear guidelines for such involvement, it is not surprising that professional opinions have continued to dominate' (Walker 1997, p.211). Nevertheless I did advocate for extra services on behalf of S. (Example from student paper)

In another section of her assignment she explores this further. Section 22 of the guidance states:

> Local authorities have the discretion to refuse direct payments to anyone who they judge would not be able to manage them, but should avoid making blanket assumptions that whole groups of people will necessarily be unable to do so. (Community Care (Direct Payments) Act S.22; DoH 1997, p.9)

In relation to women as a group, it is important to understand the 'inter-relationship between social policy, social work and sexism/patriarchy' (Thompson 1997, p.41). According to Williams (1989) the personal sphere is dominated by issues of power. At a macro level, S's husband was probably socialised into being the traditional head of the family. At the micro level this had manifested itself into their personal relationship and S's identity. Accordingly with S, I drew attention to how sexism may be acting as a barrier. However, S made the decision not to participate in Direct Payments and the guidance does state that the local authority 'will arrange services in the normal way if someone decides not to accept direct payments…[and] should not pressure him or her to accept' (Community Care (Direct Payments) Act S.30; DoH 1997, p.13). (Example from student paper)

Clearly this student fundamentally approved of the values or ideology behind advocacy and direct payments. However, the student's opinions about the value of this initiative meant little when faced with client resistance to the idea (because of the client's values) and because the student realised legislation had been only partially implemented. Appropriately she responded to the circumstances she was facing and arranged as many services as possible in the traditional way.

In contrast, another student was concerned that the underlying ideology or values behind policy were not helpful to the situation she faced:

If Fahlberg is correct in stating 'when social workers separate siblings, at some level they are accentuating the impression that family relationships are not really important' (Fahlberg 1994, p.262), then the question is: does policy, based on opinions and values that are defined socially and culturally, or the principle of the Children Act to keep siblings together (Sec. 23(7)(b)), support this? Was it not possible due to lack of appropriate resources, those being family or suitable foster carers (Beckett 1999)? It is apparent that lack of resources was responsible for separating these siblings, and one underlying ideology of policy (that of minimising costs of foster care: Triseliotis, Sellick and Short 1995a) that permits this situation, could be the widely held assumption that this is acceptable, even if not necessarily preferable. This implies, therefore, social construction and cultural definition imposed by the dominant ideology in an era of reducing family sizes. (Example from student paper)

Although this student had serious misgivings about the values base of some of the policy and procedures being used, it is interesting to note that this student also subsequently provided a ringing endorsement of the helpfulness of certain procedures and law in decision-making:

> The F2 [form and guidance for the assessment of a family as prospective carers] proved an invaluable tool. It enabled me to evidence, both through conversation with them, and in the revelations of their older children, that they had little insight into the harm inflicted upon children witnessing or receiving violence. It was nevertheless a daunting conclusion for me to reach as a student. The impact of my assessment/interviews meant that the sibling group of five were removed into foster care, and split up against their wishes. For my future practice, I have learned the rationale for paramount consideration of the child's welfare (Sec.1(1) Children Act 1989). (Example from student paper)

The potential dissonance between the legal framework for practice and a student's own approach is something which another student noted in her assignment:

> Applying this model, it becomes clear that the Court process's negative framing of risk [through the threshold criterion of significant harm and welfare checklist] induces risk-seeking decision-making in this environment, and thus by proxy, of the worker also. For example, this model illustrates that [the social worker's] decision-making, described earlier, mirrored the process of the Court's risk assessment framework. My decision-making was more cautious. I wanted 'certain' evidence that [the father] could not protect [his daughter] before opting for the less certain but greater gains to [the child] of [the social worker's] approach. In this sense, my decision-making was risk averse, and therefore contrary to the style encouraged by the socio-legal framework. (Example from student paper)

This example also shows how reflection allowed the student to identify the differences between her approach and that mandated through the court system, so that she could respond dynamically to the situation (reflection is an element discussed more fully in Chapter 9). In contrast the next example shows how a student agreed with the intent behind legislation and policy, but was concerned about how it was implemented in practice:

> The next stage of Andrea's assessment for discharge was the Section 117 Mental Health (Patients in the Community) Act 1995 Aftercare Co-ordination meeting which took place a few days later. Present at this were the professionals involved with Andrea's care and Andrea's mother. It was decided... Andrea was then called into the meeting and told about these arrangements. She was not happy with them... I accepted that there had to be a measure of control because of the risk of danger to herself and [her daughter]. However, I challenged the psychiatrist's rationalisation of Andrea's disagreement with the after-care plan. It was clear to me that Andrea knew what she wanted, whether or not she had a short attention span. Because her wishes were considered impractical did not mean they were not genuine. I was unhappy that the meeting had taken place, and decisions were made, in her absence, which disempowered her. Most of the other professionals felt that Andrea in the room during the discussions would have caused chaos. Perhaps some chaos should have been allowed so that she could have more readily accepted her need for containment. 'It is important that the individual concerned and his or her carer(s) are involved as much as possible in the care planning process. If this has been done, there is a better chance that the patient will keep to the care plan' (Department of Health 1995, p.49). (Example from student paper)

Similar concern about how policy and legislation were implemented were discussed in the next example:

> My primary legal duty under the Children Act 1989 was to act in the best interests of Waldo and Wilma, which includes their rights to express an opinion and to have that taken into account (Triseliotis *et al.* 1995b). The support for greater user involvement is complemented and reinforced by the children's rights movement and the Convention on the Rights of the Child (United Nations 1989) ratified in the United Kingdom in 1991 (Alderson 2000)... Wilma was a young person leaving the care of the local authority at

16 as is the current trend (Stein 1997) and as such I attended her statutory review in accordance with local procedures, where:

> Young people should be fully involved in discussion and plans for their future. Well before a young person leaves care a continuing care plan should be formulated. This should specify the type of help the young person will be receiving and from whom. (Stein 1997, p.127)

Throughout the review I was concerned at the jargon being used and wondered if we were manufacturing a situation that prevented Wilma from feeling excluded as opposed to truly represented. I also had reservations as to the effectiveness, if any, that [Leaving Care] schemes had in combating isolation and providing social support (Inglehart 1995). I was aware at the time of leaving care her ability to cope would be affected by her housing situation (Coles 1995). However, Wilma was more positive about the whole process and in her evaluation of the Leaving Care scheme said that she had been truly involved. She felt that life, practical and interpersonal skills had been tackled in a participative manner (Lynes and Goddard 1995). (Example from student paper)

Once again, the example shows how a student's analysis about how policy was implemented in practice was linked to reflection through seeking feedback from the client, reflection which satisfied the student's concerns. Linking detail about how the student used policy and law in practice with reflection about the effectiveness of the student's work is one method of incorporating analytical discussion of policy and law in an assignment. For example:

> Nevertheless, in my opinion, S's short-term memory difficulties should not automatically exclude her from participating. Specific ways of overcoming this particular barrier should be sought and according to Hull and Griffin (1989) techniques should be explored in order to help individuals to communicate and record by other means. On reflection, I could have given more time to this issue, which in the context of guidance practitioners are asked

...if they are considering offering Direct Payments, they build time into the assessment process...to give him or her as much time as possible to think about this (Community Care (Direct Payments) Act 1996, s.21; DoH 1997, p.9). (Example from student paper)

Once again, it can be seen that these examples are all very different. The differences in placements and students mean that while all demonstrated use of policy and law in their work, there was considerable diversity in the ways this was done. The important point to remember is that an excellent paper will integrate some aspect of policy, procedures, law and practice together in a substantial proportion of paragraphs throughout the assignment. The following checklist may prove a useful framework to help you achieve the required standard of incorporating policy and law into your essays.

In completing the assignment you will need to provide the following:

1. Evidence that you correctly understand the most relevant policy, procedures, legislation and case law which inform this area of practice.

2. Evidence that you have correctly applied or implemented policy, procedures, legislation and case law in this situation.

3. Evidence that you understand the implications that policy, procedures, legislation and case law hold for social work as a profession and social work practice with vulnerable people.

This requires:

- detailed analysis about how you used particular aspects of different policy, procedures, legislation and case law in different aspects of the work you did and how they helped you to make decisions

- analysis about why policy, procedures, legislation and case law were relevant to your practice

- analysis about the strengths and/or weaknesses (limitations) of implementing these policies, procedures, legislation and case law in this situation

- critical analysis about the relevance of policy, procedures and law in a wider context with analysis about power structures, cultural factors, ethics and values, etc. which affect this, the implications for practitioners' own use of policies, procedures and law in their day-to-day work and the role this plays at different levels.

Box 8.1 Common pitfalls to avoid when including policy and legislation analysis

Often students include policy, legislation, case law and practice in their assignments but these elements are not integrated together throughout their essays. Sometimes students' own weaknesses at understanding policy analysis become glaringly apparent. For example:

- Students describe what they did in their practice but only barely mention the policy and procedures or law which inform this and never expand on this through critical analysis.

- Students describe statutory legislation in detail (citing what powers each section of the Act bestow) but never relate this to what they did themselves in their own practice placements and in fact barely mention their own practice.

- One half of the essay describes (in great detail) a case situation, the client's circumstances and what the student did, and the other half of the essay describes what several different authors said about policy, legislation, case law, but these elements (case description and policy and law) are never related one to the other.

- Key authors who have written about relevant policy in the area of practice are discussed but it becomes apparent the student seriously misunderstood what these authors have said.

- Students discuss the agency/office/work environment in general or discuss and analyse other people's practice and fail to analyse their *own* work.

Summary and conclusion

This chapter has provided some guidance about how to evidence use of policy and law within practice. Students usually have no difficulty understanding the importance of policy, procedures and law for their work. However, they can struggle with discussing in assignments how they used policy and law in practice. Their struggles may partly be due to the dissonance they experienced between underpinning ideology of some policies and core social work values. It may also be due, in part, to their awareness that national and local policies may be differently interpreted, depending on circumstances, by various people. We have suggested that students use this dissonance as a way of focusing analysis about policy and law in their assignments. Examples given from previous assignments show that this approach has served students well in the past to achieve good analysis and argument that lifts the discussion above the simplistic level of merely saying: 'I didn't like X and I did it because policy/law Y told me to.'

CHAPTER NINE

Reflecting, Analysing and Evaluating Practice

Reflection and self-evaluation are integral parts of professional competence. Just as with other key qualities discussed elsewhere in this book, the importance of reflection to professional work is not unique to social work. It is, however, central to CCETSW's expectations of the skills and abilities that qualifying practitioners will demonstrate while undergoing training. Social work students must 'demonstrate that they have...reflected upon and critically analysed their practice' (CCETSW 1996a, p.17). In this chapter we examine concepts of reflective practice and the process of evaluating practice and how this can be evidenced in the integrated assignment.

Reflecting on practice includes the process of evaluation. In this context we do not mean evaluation through research (although research might support us in evaluating the effectiveness of our practice) but recognising that 'questions of evaluation lie at the heart of what social work means' (Shaw 1996, p.1). Shaw suggests that the question 'how do I know if I am doing [social work] well, or even well enough?' is central to the development of critical, disciplined practice. In this context then, evaluation can be seen as a process which promotes and supports addressing developmental needs (Feltham and Dryden 1994).

So what does reflection, reflective practice and being a reflective practitioner mean? It should not surprise anyone that students struggle to understand these concepts given the confusing messages they receive from the academic literature about reflection. 'Reflection' has been defined in many ways by various authors over the years. For example, reflection has been described in the following ways:

> ...the kind of thinking that consists in turning a subject over in the mind and giving it serious thought. (Dewey 1933, cited in Moon 1999a, p.12)

> ...those intellectual and affective activities in which individuals engage to explore their experiences in order to lead to new understandings and appreciation. (Boud, Keogh and Walker 1985, p.3)

> ...looking backwards...and projecting forward to the future. (Jarvis 1992, cited in Nash 2000, p.74)

> ...reflection enables individuals to make sense of their lived experiences through examining such experiences in context. (Eby 2000a, p.52)

> Reflection is the way practitioners weigh up the possibilities in any given situation and evaluate the extent to which existing theory is adequate. (Stepney 2000a, p.22)

We would argue that reflection, within the context of an integrated assignment, means:

- being open and honest about our practice
- explicitly reviewing how we used values to guide our decisions
- explicitly reviewing how we applied theory to our practice
- understanding our use of self in our work (past experiences, feelings, skills and knowledge)
- demonstrating an awareness of our professional role and boundaries
- recognising how we might approach things differently – or the same – in future.

However, understanding what the concept 'reflection' means *still* is not enough. One must move from an appreciation of what reflection means to a more active position of 'doing'. Once again, the professional literature about this concept provides competing interpretations, which students may find confusing. For example:

> Reflective practice is more than just thoughtful practice. It is the process of turning thoughtful practice into a potential learning situation...reflec-

tive practice entails the synthesis of self-awareness, reflection and critical thinking. (Eby 2000a, p.52)

[Reflective practice is] a set of ideas to be drawn upon critically and reflectively as part of the continuing challenge of integrating theory and practice, as opposed to a set of ready-made technical solutions. (Thompson 2000b, p.116)

...the reflective process also includes becoming aware of feelings. (Evans 1999, p.69)

Reflective practice provides an opportunity to review our decisions and decision-making processes, and to learn from the lessons of the past. (Trevithick 2000, p.170)

Thus reflective practice for an integrated assignment requires students to:

- synthesise different elements of their work (for example, values, legal framework, policies, theories, accountability, etc.)
- analyse (not describe) *how* they did what they did
- identify how skills and knowledge they have learned in other settings have been used in this piece of work
- identify how skills and knowledge learned from this piece of work could be used in the future
- analyse *why* they made choices and decisions
- accurately identify the influences on their decisions
- demonstrate awareness of the implications of decisions for all parties (clients, carers, advocates, agencies, the profession, etc.)
- evaluate whether or not practice was effective, ethical and anti-discriminatory
- consider ways in which their practice can be improved upon
- identify what they need to learn for future professional development.

Of course, discussion of each element outlined above may not be included in every example of reflective practice in an assignment. These assignments show individuality because all students are different and because the practice experiences on placements vary. However, all reflective practice should include some of these elements.

How do people learn to do reflective practice? This may seem to be a tautology but the simple answer is: by doing it! Experiential learning is an essential part of learning to reflect on and analyse one's practice. This is why reflective practice is so much a part of the practice placement, and why the teaching exercises we developed (see Chapter 2) depend so much on students using examples from their own social work/social care experience. 'Reflection is presumed to have a key role either in experiential learning or in enabling experiential learning' (Moon 1999a, p.21).

Theories of experiential learning (Eraut 1994; Kolb 1988a) suggest that learning is a continuous process. People develop skills and experience through an interaction with their environment. They try; they do – and then they consider their actions and their effect. They relate 'what happened' to the theories they have learned (or been taught through social work education) about 'what ought to happen' or about 'what it means'. They consider what they might have done (Gibbs 1988).

They may experience dissonance. Jarvis (1995) says that learning occurs when there is conflict between prior expectations and current experience. However, in order to benefit – or learn – from experience we need to go beyond a recognition that it is uncomfortable, and engage with it and *reflect* on it.

> Without reflecting on the experience it may be lost or misunderstood…reflection needs to lead to conceptualisation and analysis, so that meaning can be attached to the experience and generalisations can be generated…it is from generalisations that we become better able to tackle new situations, or to try innovative solutions to current situations. This is how theory is translated into practice. (Horwath and Morrison 1999, p.51)

The theories about experiential learning therefore support what we stated earlier: we learn how to do reflective practice by doing it. In this way, the integrated assignment becomes a vehicle for students to learn how to do reflection and reflective practice by writing about their work within an analytical format. Thus, as Schon (1983) would put it, the assignment becomes a

> reflective conversation with a situation… Through his transaction with a situation, he shapes it and makes himself part of it. Hence the sense he makes of the situation must include his own contribution to it. (Schon 1983, p.163)

Reflective practice can be taught and as a skill can be refined and developed. There is a difference between reflection and intuition. The former can be taught by tutors and practice teachers and learned by students, which is why it is included in the formal social work education curriculum. The latter involves an innate quality or skill which does not easily respond to formal teaching (Nash 2000) and which cannot, therefore, be made part of a formal curriculum to be assessed or examined – hence the emphasis on reflection rather than intuition.

Some students may be innately intuitive from the earliest stages of their work. They appear to be naturally gifted practitioners who intuitively and sensitively adjust their approaches to situations to achieve best practice. These students often struggle with the difference between intuition and reflection and have trouble consciously identifying the components of their decisions or elements of reasoning they used to inform their practice. This is because intuition is 'understanding without rationale' (Nash 2000, pp.76–77). Intuition involves quick response to events without careful thought. This is sometimes appropriate, as can be seen in the following example:

> There is an oral account of a social work experience in which a female practitioner interviewing a male client intuitively felt very unsafe and left the building at once, only to discover subsequently that he had just murdered his wife. (Evans 1999, p.60)

We recognise that criticisms can be levelled at the emphasis within professional education about reflection and reflective practice. There are times when professionals need to act quickly, without endless reflection which might stymie swift action (James and Clarke 1994). Moreover, reflection may in some circumstances be considered a 'masculine' paradigm which does not give sufficient weight to feminist notions of 'intuition' as a respected way of knowing (Wetzel 1986). Non-objective and qualitative ways of understanding and intuition are part of everyday practice (Moffatt 1996; Schon 1983).

Even though we recognise the inherent limitations of reflective practice, it is an important component of practitioner competence and involves a commitment towards continuing education and professional development. This is why so much emphasis is placed upon evidencing reflection in the final academic work done for the Diploma in Social Work (CCETSW 1996a) so that students become reflective practitioners. They need to be able to absorb into themselves, their self-perceptions and professional identities the qualities of being reflective practitioners:

> The self image here is one of a facilitator whose role is to help find an optimal course of action or solution to problems in an uncertain world. (Jones and Joss 1995, p.26)

> …reflective practitioners require an awareness of their own humanity, of how their own experiences can enable them to empathize with people who seek help and use services. (Walmsley *et al.* 1993a pp.1–2)

> Unthinking, uncritical practice can be dangerous, especially where uncertainty and change are to the fore. It is therefore necessary for practice to be reflective – carefully thought through and reflected on, open to change and development where necessary. (Thompson 2000a, p.22)

Excellent integrated assignments should demonstrate that from the point of completing their qualifying training, students are reflective practitioners. Students are able to reflect on their own practice and the implications of their intervention, and are evaluating their own work with a view to improving future practice. It should also demonstrate that this self-reflective process is an integral part of all of the work that students do. Individuals are all different and unique in how they examine themselves and their practice, and so there is considerable originality and variety in the way this is done in assignments. Nonetheless, despite differences, some common themes generally emerge in the ways students reflect on their work.

Good reflective practice usually includes some discussion by students about possible areas of personal bias. They acknowledge how their own personal values, assumptions or experiences may differ from a client's and analyse how they used this awareness in their practice. The following examples show the different ways three students confronted this issue:

> I am myself influenced by the cultural conditioning within my own social group and it is important that when observing and assessing the behaviour of adults and children I reflect about the 'conceptual differences which underlie ostensibly common experiences' (Dwivedi 1996, p.153). (Example from student paper)

> But this was not the case with Wilma as she was very specific that she did not wish her mother to know how or where she was. As a parent, I initially found this request difficult to adhere to as I could not imagine being in a similar situation with my own daughter and was aware it was my own values and experiences of family life that led to these feelings. Wilma continually asked me to respect her decision so I explained that she was my client and that my social work ethics and values (BASW 1996) ensured I would respect her wishes and confidentiality at all times. Her mother phoned me constantly and I found myself quoting the Data Protection Act 1998 at her, as this required me to be very clear about seeking the approval of people in advance of sharing information with them, and Wilma had been very explicit about not sharing anything. (Example from student paper)

> Having said all this I have to acknowledge my own prejudices about mental illness and its treatment. Not only am I biased in favour of the 'talking therapies' because of my own experiences of person-centred counselling but I am also biased against mainstream psychiatry through having a sister on long-term medication. I knew that I would have to face my prejudices when I came on placement and it has taught me a lot. (Example from student paper)

Closely linked to demonstrating awareness of possible sources of personal bias, and questioning how one's own values affect practice, is the 'use of self' which develops in sensitive, responsive practice. How do student social workers maintain appropriate personal and professional boundaries in practice? Where such issues arose on placement, some students demonstrated reflective practice in their assignments through their discussion of how they dealt with boundaries of practice:

> It aroused some anxiety in me initially, partially because death seems a taboo subject and one I find particularly difficult to confront. (Example from student paper)

> Working with Mr M I felt I had some insight into his situation following a similar experience within my own family, although I was careful not to self-disclose inappropriately (Rogers 1980). (Example from student paper)

> Personally, the experience left me feeling powerless which in some small way may serve to give me some indication of the feelings that service users are likely to experience. (Example from student paper)

Good reflective practice also includes frequent review of one's actions and decisions. Were they effective? How could they be improved? A good integrated assignment will include discussion about the ways students incorporated self-evaluation into their work. The following four examples show how this was done by students:

> The extent of D's feelings was brought to the fore during what was seemingly one of many straightforward telephone conversations. D became very abusive toward me personally and although immediately hampered by lack of non-verbal communication I was able to utilise Berne's (1961) Transactional Analysis... D affirmed through subsequent conversations that he had felt listened to and had his feelings validated. (Example from student paper)

> When I went to visit she had a flat full of friends. However on this occasion I didn't consider it appropriate or conducive to confidential discussions regarding personal and financial matters. Wilma was also angry when I said she could not have money from her 'leaving care' grant for [another] pair of shoes as they did not constitute an essential living item and started to make derogatory comments about social workers in general. I am aware that adolescents can be highly egocentric and find it difficult to see others' views, which makes them touchy and hypersensitive to

rejection as their social skills are, as yet, underdeveloped (Hendry *et al.* 1993). However, it was unusual for Wilma to be rude and dismissive and on my return to the office I was surprised to find she had requested a new social worker. Initially I was disappointed and questioned my own practice – whether I had been unreasonable and not responded appropriately. But on the other hand I felt she had made progress in that this was quite an empowering thing to have done for someone previously resistant to self-help. (Example from student paper)

...although when first on placement my natural anxieties about a new work place probably inhibited my ability to challenge other professionals... Due to my inexperience I felt I did not challenge this attitude appropriately at the time but worked to develop a relationship with my fellow professional which enabled us to work together in partnership with another client. (Example from student paper)

I acknowledged the need to plan for our first meeting but learned valuable lessons from some visits undertaken earlier in this placement. I had been anxious to ensure these encounters were as effective as possible within an empowerment framework and planned rigorously. Contrary to guidance (Social Services Inspectorate/Social Work Services Group 1991) these interviews were protracted, generating a vast surplus of information. When reflecting on this I realised I had unintentionally planned to the extent that the interviews were very formal and structured even though I had tried to employ an exchange model that would allow for mutual understanding (Smale, Tuson and Statham 2000), resulting in 'vertical imposition' rather than 'horizontal exchange' (Fook 1993). With supervision and increased confidence through practice I was able to rectify these early errors endeavouring to nurture a climate more conducive to exchange. I was able to become less focussed on outcomes and more attuned to offering the potential for a partnership process that could aim to address what service users have voiced as important to the social work interaction such as clarity, honesty, approachability and interest (Howe 1987; Seden 1999). (Example from student paper)

Part of reflection and self-evaluation involves being aware that you always have more to learn and know what helps you to learn. Should any changes of heart occur (any breakthroughs in learning as mentioned in Chapter 4) discussing these experiences in the integrated assignment can provide evidence of reflective practice. For example:

> It is easy to talk about the importance of individual liberty in theory but more difficult to be so dogmatic in practice. When someone is threatening you with a knife, you tend to favour a policy of restraint and containment. Issues of care and control have to be faced. Correct risk assessment can mean the difference between life and death. This is where I found supervision so helpful. It is important to be able to step back and reflect, and not be blinkered. Supervision enabled me to view situations from a different perspective, and to realise that my original perspective could sometimes be naive and often plainly wrong. I now feel that the medical model is often the *best* way of treating severe mental illness, as long as adequate resources are provided of social care in the community. I continue to believe that it is an inappropriate way of treating 'minor mental illness'. (Example from student paper)

All these examples are as different as the students and the placements, yet all are indicative of self-reflection about the boundaries of personal and professional, self and others and what was effective in practice. They show that these students were learning through experience and demonstrate their commitment to developing practice knowledge and evaluating the impact of their interventions to become more effective social workers. They demonstrate sensitive and ethical use of self.

We have demonstrated ways in which you may be able to illustrate reflection and self-evaluation in your practice. The following checklists may provide a useful framework to help you achieve the required standard in demonstrating reflective practice in your essays. In completing the integrated assignment, you will need to provide the following:

1. Evidence of self-reflection about different influences on your practice.

2. Evidence of your critical awareness about the strengths and weaknesses of your own practice.

3. Evidence of the development and use of transferable skills.

4. Evidence of your awareness of your professional role and the implications of your own decisions for clients, carers, organisations, society, your profession and yourself.

5. Evidence of developing awareness about professional boundaries and limitations and the identification of future learning needed for professional growth.

This requires analysis and evaluation of the following:

- How your own past (personal and professional) experiences, skills, education and training, etc. helped to inform current practice.

- How decisions were made.

- The effectiveness of social work practice and how and why this might be changed (improved upon) in future.

- The implications of your own practice decisions, for clients, carers, etc. in terms of accountability and professional competence: this should incorporate, where possible, the views of various stakeholders, such as clients or service users, carers, advocates, supervisors or managers, other professionals (etc.), in so far as they illuminate your own appreciation of the strengths and limitations of your practice.

- The strengths and limitations of your own skills, professional knowledge, etc. and how this might be changed in future.

- How skills learned in this situation could be used in different ways (or settings) in future.

It also requires that you:

- are open and honestly acknowledge any changes of heart or major shifts in thinking that came about as a result of re-examining assumptions or beliefs because of your placement experiences and the dissonance they may have caused

- acknowledge any failures or mistakes (if they occurred) and show that you recognise how or why this happened and are aware of how to change this in future or provide evidence that the mistake was not repeated in subsequent practice. In other words we know people are not perfect and may on reflection realise they made a mistake, have learned from this and made changes to ensure that errors are not repeated and consistency and competence are achieved by the end of the placement.

Box 9.1 Common pitfalls to avoid when integrating self-reflection

Sometimes students view self-reflection as a separate addition to the analysis and fail to integrate self-reflection throughout their assignments. Sometimes students take a narrow approach to self-reflection, either basing this solely on their personal feelings about practice, or basing this on identifying knowledge and skills they will use in future, rather than encompassing a wide range of issues. For example:

- A few paragraphs are tacked on at the end of the assignment which include self-reflection and self-evaluation, but they constitute a small proportion of the entire assignment, the majority of which discusses theory and/or practice at the expense of including any self-reflection.

- Good attention is paid to identifying influences on practice decisions (e.g. the student identifies how he/she drew on his/her own past bereavement to assist empathy when working with a depressed woman whose husband recently died) but evaluation about practice decisions or the effectiveness of intervention is ignored.

- Reflection and self-evaluation are done to a limited degree, but the discussion ignores issues about the continuum of care and control and professional accountability, and the implications of the student's decisions in terms of continuous professional development, competence and accountability which are central to good self-reflection and evaluation.

- The reflection and self-evaluation which is done is entirely internalised or subjective reflection, without reference to external or objective methods which could assist this process (e.g. supervision by the practice teacher, theoretical models about practice evaluation and reflection applied in analysis about decision-making, clients'/carers' perspectives, alternative opinions from other professionals which led to self-questioning of decisions, etc.).

- Lip-service is paid to reflection through the use of slogans (e.g. 'I reflected on my practice to ensure it was account-able' or 'This is important learning that I will take forward with me to future practice') without really discussing in detail how decisions were made, why, their strengths and limitations and how knowledge and skills could be adapted in future.

Summary and conclusion

Truly reflective practice is not easy to achieve. There is a danger that in producing this kind of guidance, students may be tempted to view self-reflection as something which can be achieved through a cookbook approach. In other words, students may slavishly follow all the steps in the recipe in order so that they achieve competence at reflective practice, without ever really internalising the spirit of the enterprise:

> If a particular social care competence is seen only in terms of a behavioural outcome, this could result simply in the imitation of the desired behaviour and the suppression of the individuals' beliefs and other skills. In contrast integration would involve grafting new skills onto the learner's existing skills, accepting both as valid and helpful to their work. (Horwath and Morrison 1999, p.48)

We would argue that true self-reflection goes beyond this. It is linked to a values commitment to do good (or as the Hippocratic oath would have it, to 'do no harm'). We all want to believe that what we are doing is good and worthwhile work and true self-reflection can involve quite painful self-questioning. Done to excess it could lead to an almost personal sense of insecurity as practitioners question the value of their work. However, done appropriately it ensures practitioners avoid complacency and remain fresh with each piece of practice, so that they continually grow and develop as professionals. It is also one of the main tools that social workers have at their disposal to check out their work to ensure it was effective and ethical.

One of the common errors of students is failing to reflect in integrated assignments. Students can write excellent essays from a purely academic viewpoint, but fail to reflect and evaluate and therefore the assignment does not pass. One of the most difficult things as a tutor is to have to fail an essay which shows a lot of hard work and which meets many of the requirements but does not have any self-reflection and critical analysis of the student's own practice.

That this book has been written is a result of reflective practice on behalf of the authors. As lecturers we examined our previous guidance and teaching, found it needed to be improved, made changes and have reflected on and evaluated our work (getting feedback). This, in turn, led to further changes being made to our guidance and eventually to this book, which includes numerous practical examples of how reflective practice has been evidenced in student assignments. We hope that our guidance about what self-reflection means, and the suggestions (through checklists) about what issues to consider when reflecting on work, will help future students develop good reflective essays and, more importantly, to develop a reflective and self-evaluative approach in all their work.

CHAPTER TEN

Organising and Writing

An integrated assignment can be the equivalent of a bachelor's degree dissertation and (as stated earlier) is often one of the longest (if not the longest) assignment that students complete for their Diplomas in Social Work. All assignments need some forethought and planning if they are to be any good; generally the longer the assignment, the more planning that is needed. This chapter is intended to give students some information about how to organise time effectively when writing. There are also some tips about writing a long assignment as well as a checklist of questions that students may find helpful when revising drafts and proof-reading the final paper. The chapter is organised as chatty answers to frequently asked questions or issues commonly raised by students when completing integrated assignments.

How should I organise my time?

Good time management for a long assignment starts from the moment you decide on the topic. The process of completing an assignment can be broken into three main stages:

- choosing the topic (and getting it approved by your practice teacher and/or tutor if that is required by your programme) – see Chapter 3

- collecting background material – see Chapter 5

- organising and writing – this chapter.

It is important to leave yourself enough time to write the assignment. Different people write at different speeds; it is important to know your own speed of writing and allocate enough time. *Do not underestimate how long it will take you to write the assignment and make sure you leave enough time for revision and proof-reading.* The final essay you submit is expected to be a polished piece of work and will be marked accordingly. Even very experienced academics who have already collected all the information so it is readily at their fingertips cannot write erudite prose in a first draft without any revision. They may take a couple of weeks to write and revise 6000 words. Students who have considerably less experience at writing complex arguments than a published academic certainly need to allocate *more* time, and no shame is attached to this; it is quite normal, positive and healthy (years ago those experienced scholars also took more time to write than they do now).

We usually suggest that people allow themselves approximately one month to write and revise their assignments from first draft through to the final product that is submitted for assessment.

How can I find time to write this while on placement?

Sometimes assignments are due the academic term after the placement is finished. However, quite often they are due while the student is still on placement. Often students say their time management would be easier if the assignments were due after the end of their placements. That may be true. However, it may be that the only way to delay the due date of the final assignments until after the end of placement would be to extend the length of the course (thus affecting the date when the student would qualify and be available for work as a professionally qualified worker).

Taking a few days' leave around the time that assignments are due may be more feasible than changing the assignment due date. Most practice placements have a few days' leeway built in to the usual dates of the placement to allow people to take a few days' holiday, provide allowance for casual illness or personal leave. Many people arrange leave towards the end of their placements to allow themselves the time to write and rewrite their assignments (although not everyone finds this necessary). Usually this will facilitate students completing good assignments while juggling personal and placement responsibilities and still completing the DipSW course on schedule. The key to the issue of finding time is good planning and preparation. You might find it helpful to set goals in order to support this process and the 'SMART' framework for setting objectives suggested in Chapter 11 might help you to do this.

Do other students have to do this?

If there is more than one programme provider in your area, sometimes people may meet DipSW students from other programmes on placement and inevitably students start to compare the different ways in which programmes are organised. Sometimes this leads to the plaintive cry, 'but other students don't have to do this'. Rest assured that you are not unique in having to complete this type of long, complex assignment while on (or shortly after) placement. Many DipSW programmes in the United Kingdom require equivalent types of assignments to be written while on placement, although sometimes the timing of this varies, just as the word limits may be different. It is always tempting to compare courses. However, usually students do not do this systematically and so, by taking one component of the programme out of context and comparing it with one component from another course, they are not really comparing like with like. Each course *as a whole* meets the requirements for professional accreditation – not one aspect on its own. Integrated theory-and-practice assignments are a component of DipSW programmes which CCETSW heartily endorses as an important part of good quality social work education and training. Feeling aggrieved because you think 'only our programme makes us do this' can only interfere with your concentration and take your energy away from your professional studies at a point when it needs most to be tightly focused.

It seems so big! How do I get started writing?

Think back to the first time you wrote an essay. Probably your first essay was quite a short one – 2000 words (perhaps even less). At the time it seemed quite daunting but when you asked for help, you were told to break it down into stages and tackle it a little at a time so it would not seem so hard. The same principle applies to the integrated assignment. First, reread the topic you chose; second, organise the relevant material; third, devise an essay plan.

Why should I reread the topic that I chose?

Go over the plan you developed at the very beginning so that you familiarise yourself with all the issues again. This may seem too obvious for words or even silly, but it is always helpful to go back to the question you set for yourself at the very beginning. You may be surprised at how easily you may have gone off onto a tangent or forgotten what you intended to do. Also, you should review the parameters set for the assignment by your college or university. Does what you plan to do allow you to meet their requirements?

How should I organise the relevant material?

Go over the notes you wrote on each of the books you read. Get out the photocopies of material you collected. Sift through this material making quick easy-to-decipher notes that can be seen easily at first glance. Sticky tabs, Post-it Notes with one or two words on them, highlighter pen on key passages or margin notes are all good methods of noting for quick reference which material applies to which issues you want to discuss.

Once you have done this, start dividing the material into different piles for the different issues or points the assignment will be discussing. It is helpful at this stage to have a work area where materials can be laid out where they will not be disturbed (e.g. all over one table, the bedroom floor, etc.). Make sure each pile is clearly labelled so you can easily tell at a glance which issues/material are in each pile.

How do I devise an essay plan and how do I use it effectively?

Use the rough organisation of material you have already done to help you devise an essay plan. If you had to develop a plan for the assignment back when you were choosing your topic, then you already have a plan half-prepared. Dust it off, read it over, and alter it to fit the way your assignment is now shaping.

An essay plan is another step towards organising your writing. It can be one or two sides of A4 paper with a few notes, or you may prefer to use cue cards – one for each part of the essay or section of the argument you want to make. An essay plan should provide a rough, point-form guide to:

- what points of analysis will be made

- the order in which you plan to make these points – so that it forms a good logical argument

- a rough estimate of how many words (or paragraphs, if that is the way you prefer to think about it) each section will take.

For most people, the process of writing helps to synthesise ideas and in itself is a means of learning. The integrated assignment is intended to facilitate your learning in this way. No assignment asks you for all you know about everything. Writing means sifting through information and sources you have found and discarding those which are less relevant (or relegating them to merely one short sentence and a brief reference), while more words are devoted to analysing and synthesising the sources which are more relevant to your particular area of practice.

One of the best tools to help you achieve this while ensuring you do not miss anything you absolutely must include is to develop an essay plan before you start writing lovely flowing academic prose. Once you have developed an essay plan, check it against the required content, information that your course provides about the standard of work expected and any published marking criteria to see that it matches or could fulfil these expectations. If it does not – change it! If it does, use it as a rough guide while writing the assignment. Once you have written a first draft, check that against the essay plan as well, to see how well you have kept to it, and where you have deviated from it. In some cases the deviations from the essay plan will have only served to improve the essay, but in other cases, checking the first draft against the essay plan and realising how you did something a bit differently will remind you of important points of argument that you left out.

Once you have written your provisional essay plan, you can then compare it with the various piles of material you organised earlier. Perhaps one section ought to be a bit longer than another; if so the plan can be altered to allow for this. However, perhaps the lack of relevant material for one key section has exposed a gap in your research, collection of evidence and material, and background reading. If so, provided you have started the writing process early enough you should still have time to remedy the problem through supplementary reading and research.

How should I structure the assignment? Is there a specific format I must use?

Usually there is no *one* required format which must be used for the integrated assignment. The integrated assignment must follow the general guidelines applicable to all formal academic essays and it is an assignment which requires considerable academic rigour as well as evidence of very good quality professional practice to be demonstrated throughout. However, *all* formal academic essays – and the integrated assignment is one of these – need to follow the basic essay structure common to all academic writing: introduction, middle section and conclusion. Make sure you include this structure in your essay plan and in the assignment you write.

I am always in a muddle about what to put in the introduction and conclusion

An introduction is used to tell the reader what you are going to do in the essay. In an integrated assignment this includes:

- defining the limits of the assignment (i.e. what it is about and what it is not about)
- giving the reasons for choosing this particular question or topic
- informing the reader what argument will be developed in the rest of the essay.

The middle section is used to present your argument supported by the evidence. In an integrated assignment this includes:

- what you did and why

- how you made decisions and how ethics and social work values were embedded in this process

- analysis about the use of theory and research in your practice

- the ways you implemented policy and legislation

- what you brought to practice and what you learned from it

- evaluation of the strengths and limitations of your work

- discussion about success or failure (outcomes)

- analysis about how you practised in anti-discriminatory and antiracist ways.

A conclusion is used to remind the reader what you have done, tie up loose ends and finish off the argument. In an integrated assignment this includes:

- summarising the main analytical points made in the middle section

- pointing out what the essay has and has not proven

- referring back to the question or topic chosen

- giving a sense of ending or completion.

Box 10.1 Tips for assignment structure

Although it may seem artificial to allocate a word limit to each of the sections or sub-sections, nonetheless this is a good discipline to learn, if you do not already know it. There are certain rules of thumb to use about word limits:

- use approximately 10 per cent of the word limit for the introduction

- use approximately 10–15 per cent of the word limit for the conclusion

- this leaves approximately 75 per cent of the word limit for the middle section

- allocate – at least in the essay plan – approximately the same number of words for each sub-section of the middle section of the essay.

This means that if the allocated limit for the assignment is 6000 words, and the middle section has six parts to the analysis, the basic structure should look something like this:

- Introduction – 600 words
- Middle part of argument 1 – 750 words
  - part of argument 2 – 750 words
  - part of argument 3 – 750 words
  - part of argument 4 – 750 words
  - part of argument 5 – 750 words
  - part of argument 6 – 750 words
- Conclusion – 900 words

OK so I have a plan – but how do I actually start writing?

Once you have devised a plan, the next stage is to write a first draft. There is no hard and fast rule for the order of writing. However, many people find it difficult to start with the introduction and prefer to start in the middle of the assignment. It is usually easier if you do not sit down specifically to write the assignment. That tends to feel too big and may lead to anxiety or writer's block. Instead, sit down to try one sub-section of the assignment (not necessarily even the first part of the middle section) – that would only be 750 words, a mere two pages (approximately). *Much* easier! Again, setting goals might help you to break down the task of actually writing into smaller bite-sized chunks.

At this stage, do not be too concerned to make everything read perfectly. The point of a first draft is to get the main ideas and points of argument down on paper and to ensure that most of the pieces of evidence have been slotted in somewhere. Make sure every article, note from the books you read, and example from practice that you sorted into the pile for that section (see the question about 'How should I organise the relevant material?' above) is used in some way in this section.

Box 10.2 Tip for managing your material

Keep all unused material on your right-hand side. As you use it, place it on the 'already used' left-hand side. That way you will always be able to tell which articles, books, practice examples, etc. you have used and which you have not.

Once you have completed the first draft of one sub-section of the essay, clear away all the background material associated with it before bringing forward to your writing area the next pile you have organised for the next sub-section. If you write your first draft one section (sub-section) at a time, it will seem more manageable than trying to write it all in a marathon 24-hour session.

Once you have completed the first rough draft of your assignment, you need to move on to the second stage of writing. This is when you make sure you build in analysis.

Why do I have to analyse?

Many students are better at talking about how and why they practice, making links to theory and ethics, and reflecting and evaluating their work as they speak, than they are at writing about these issues in a formal essay. These students usually pass assignments with solid average marks, but often they do not find their essays very satisfying and feel frustrated that they do not reflect who they are as individuals. They find it frustrating always to receive comments from markers like: 'too descriptive', 'you need to include more analysis' and 'I can tell from this assignment that you learned a lot about this subject, but it is too descriptive and so cannot earn a higher mark'. Essays are supposed to assess how much students have learned. So why, they ask, can they not earn a better mark when the marker has seen they learned a lot?

The reason is because essays are also a tool to assess how well students can critically analyse, reflect, synthesise material, assess the relative merits of argument and develop their own arguments based on evidence. *Once you have completed a rough first draft of the assignment, the next stage is to build in critical analysis.* Analysis will:

- lead to a better mark for the paper

- allow you to develop your own opinions through the argument you choose to support

- make your paper sound original – not just a tired regurgitation of what everybody else has said before

- make your paper interesting for you to write so you enjoy it

- help you to learn more.

Analysis is what makes theory, policy, ethics and so on relevant to practice. It is what helps social workers understand what might be an appropriate response to new practice situations they have not encountered before. Equally importantly, analysis is a good transferable skill that social work employers find highly desirable. People who can write a good convincing analytical argument in an academic assignment have the necessary skills to write a good professional report which serves the purpose. They are also more likely to have the skills to write a report that represents a more accurate picture of the situation and is, therefore, less likely to be discriminatory.

What does good analysis include?

Analysis should include:

- a clearly defined beginning, logical progression of well-organised pieces of evidence and a clearly defined end

- carefully chosen language used with precision and exactitude

- a line of argument running like a thread throughout the entire assignment

- both theory and evidence incorporated throughout the assignment in almost every paragraph, with each related to the other through an explicitly stated argument

- a synthesis of different ideas, theories and research evidence learned from a number of academic and professional sources and/or social science disciplines, all drawn together through your explicitly stated argument

- open acknowledgement of any counter-arguments and contradictory evidence to the argument you are presenting with an explanation why they have been given less credence than the main argument you have adopted

- your own views *only* when supported by evidence or theories/opinions from academic/professional sources (appropriately referenced).

So how do I analyse?

It is difficult to provide step-by-step instructions for you to follow. Analysis in undergraduate social science essays can mean different things depending on the specific topic of each assignment. However, we would suggest that in order to be analytical an integrated assignment should answer the following questions:

- How did I know that fact was significant? What theory, policy, etc. made me aware it was significant?

- Why did I make those decisions? What case law, ethical principle, etc. was satisfied by making those choices?

- How and what did I learn from what I did? How could I improve this in the future?

- How could this be changed to make it applicable to other people or in other settings?

- How does what happened with this person in this situation reflect structural issues (e.g. policy, oppression, values, law) and how might structural issues be affected by this situation?

Box 10.3 Synthesis is such a big word – what does it mean?

Try to think of it this way: In the library there are lots of books on different shelves. You know most of the psychology texts are on those shelves over there. The sociology is in the annexe. The books about social work theory are on the second floor. The material about ethics and values and anti-oppressive practice is on the right-hand side of the philosophy section. And the books about working with domestic violence, women's refuges and criminal justice (related to your specific area of social work practice) are on the left.

Your task, as a student, is to select material from all these different shelves and incorporate bits from all these different disciplines into your assignment. You will *synthesise* by explaining in the essay how they all fit together as different pieces of a whole. In explaining this, you will also show how you used this knowledge in your own work. This illustrates the ways in which a wide range of academic disciplines and knowledge or subject areas inform social work.

A tale of two chairs

This was devised as a teaching exercise to demonstrate to students, through a simple (and extremely silly) essay, the differences frequently found between a descriptive essay and a really good analytical essay. The former type of assignment merely covers the required content, shows that the student learned a lot of facts and may have read the right sources, while the latter uses evidence to support an argument that is developed to a specific purpose.

We start with a typical essay question:

Critically analyse two chairs and assess their strengths and limitations with reference to practice. Your answer should discuss ethical concerns and the implications for anti-discriminatory practice.

In Boxes 10.4 and 10.5 are two example essays which could be written on this topic. The first, a short descriptive essay, would probably fail. The second is analytical in nature, better referenced (*à la* Star Wars!) and would earn a much better mark.

Box 10.4 Essay 1: A very weak descriptive essay

Introduction

This essay will discuss the strengths and limitations of these two chairs for practice.

Middle section

Chair One has four legs and is covered in black material. It is very uncomfortable and it wobbles a bit. It is a bit small. Chair One is old and worn out.

Chair Two has four legs and is covered in blue material. It is also very uncomfortable. It is bigger than Chair One. Chair Two was bought recently and it does not wobble.

It is unethical and discriminatory to give students wobbly chairs to sit on. They do not help us to learn so they are not good practice.

Conclusion

Chair One has four legs and is black, wobbly, old and uncomfortable. Chair Two has four legs and is blue, new and uncomfortable. These chairs are discriminatory and it should not be allowed.

Box 10.5 Essay 2: A good analytical essay

Introduction

The question of which chairs best suit the needs of social work students is central to good practice. Using these two chairs as exemplars, this essay will discuss how the differences between chairs can make a significant contribution to student learning about social work. I will argue that although there are both similarities and differences between these chairs, it is the context in which these chairs operate which lends meaning to them (Windu

1999). It is this which provides students with important messages about their place in a discriminatory and oppressive system.

Middle section

There are several similarities between these chairs. For example, both have four legs and are covered in cloth. Equally, some differences have been noted between these chairs. However, the real issue for concern is not whether mere similarity or difference is identified, but whether or not these factors have a significant effect on the usefulness of these chairs. The fact that one is blue while another is black is not significant. Students can, after all, sit equally well or badly on either blue or black covers. Moreover, the existence of four legs on both chairs is also not a salient point – most chairs have four legs, or the equivalent thereof (Solo 1995). The significant factors for consideration are the way one chair wobbles and both are uncomfortable.

The black chair is typical of the chairs which were bought for classrooms ten years ago. It is uncomfortable because the upholstery is old and wobbles because the legs are worn out. In addition, it was designed for the physical average of students from ten years ago, which exacerbates how uncomfortable it is for the larger students who come to college in the 21st Century (Chewbacca 2000). This discomfort has a significant impact on students' ability to learn. Concentration can lapse from the academic material being presented in class simply through sheer discomfort caused by sitting in the wrong type of chair (Hutt 1996). In addition, the potential long-term physical problems associated with sitting for long periods of time in poorly designed uncomfortable chairs are well documented (Hutt 1996; Maul 2001; Yoda 1998).

The blue chairs were bought last year as replacements for the black chairs; however, they have proven to be of only limited improvement. These larger chairs are too high for many of the mature students who come to college (a significant proportion of social work students); they find their feet dangle off the ground when they sit in them, leading to discomfort and concentration problems in class (as well as potential long-term physical problems). However, it has to be acknowledged that the fact the blue chairs do not wobble is a distinct improvement; health and safety regulations (Ministry of Tatoine 1993) would 'fail' the wobbly chairs due to risk of injury from the collapse of the chair.

Thus it would appear that the blue chairs, although poorly designed, nonetheless are marginally better than the black.

All of this, however, needs to be considered in the light of purpose of social work and social work education. As practitioners we are required to incorporate our ethics and values in all our work (Rebel Alliance Manifesto 1988). We feel deeply the need to empower people and show respect for them as worthwhile individuals. Social work training is supposed to teach us how to do this both through formal teaching and through modelling these values and ethics in action (Skywalker 1998). How well can a course model these principles when it requires students to use substandard chairs as a part of the education programme? We note the style of the new chairs was chosen by a heavily male-dominated management (Leia 1999). Is this an example of structural oppression of predominantly female social work students (Amidala 2001)? Does the fact the choice of size of chairs is more appropriate for younger, larger people reflect common assumptions about who are students (Wan-Kenobi 1994), assumptions that have a discriminatory impact on mature students?

Conclusion

Chairs can have an enormous impact on the practice of education, and through qualifying social work training, on the practice of social workers. The strengths and limitations of these two chairs have been analysed as exemplars of chairs students use at colleges. Various similarities and differences have been noted. What is most noteworthy, however, is the fact that neither chair is very effective in helping students to learn and may even hinder this process. The difficulties with the chairs could be a part of oppressive gender biased and ageist practice. Ultimately, it is evident that these chairs are not good practice. They reflect the low value which is placed on modelling appropriate ethics and standards to students, so that they learn, while still at college, how devalued social work can be.

It is clear that the level of analysis is significantly more developed in the second account and that arguments put forward are well supported by appropriate (if in this example bogus) referencing.

The expected standard of work

An excellent integrated assignment is a carefully written and highly analytical document. This will integrate theory, law, policy, ethics and values, commitment to anti-discrimination and antiracist practice, self-reflection, individual practice evaluation and self-development, and practice experience together throughout the entire assignment. These elements are married into a cohesive whole through good sustained and sophisticated critical analysis. This is not easy to achieve and requires your appreciation of what is required by each of the component parts of the assignment as delineated in the marking criteria/assignment parameters.

The guidance in Chapters 6 to 9 is intended to assist you in understanding the different elements common to all integrated assignments which need to be included. In order to do this, various aspects of the analysis have been discussed under different headings as if they were somehow separate from one another or precluded other issues. However, it must be remembered that a first-class integrated assignment is more than simply a sum of all the parts. More is required than simply ensuring that each assignment has at least one paragraph on each issue. Analysis about the use of theory in practice is not distinct and separate from analysis about ethical issues, any more than self-evaluation is divorced from legal and policy issues, or anti-discriminatory practice is separate from assessment and planning or professional accountability.

Your central task is to write the integrated assignment in such a way that you synthesise many complex and interrelated issues into a compelling analysis about social work practice that convinces the reader of the validity of your argument. As with all assignments, greater weight is placed on complex analysis and critical evaluation and less weight is given to simple description: marks are allocated accordingly. An assignment which simply describes what various authors said about different aspects of theory, law, policy, ethics, anti-discriminatory practice, etc. is likely to earn a low mark. In contrast if your assignment demonstrates good critical analysis of these issues and links them to your own practice, it is likely to earn a higher mark.

Has your course published a general outline of what markers consider the characteristics or qualities associated with each mark classification assignments can earn? Some courses now automatically issue this to students (often in the course handbook). If it is not already provided, you may be able to get one on request. These rank ordering schemes are generally comparable from programme to programme (even while they may differ slightly in detail). The system of initial validation, periodic inspection, ongoing quality assurance systems (of which the external assessors are a part) and revalidation ensures this (CCETSW 1996b). If you have not already seen a general outline of the qualities that are characteristic of assignments earning different mark classifications why not ask to see one? Many students say they find this helpful in understanding why some previous assignments earned disappointing marks, while others, which they did not think quite as good, received a higher mark from the tutor.

What do markers look for?

More is needed than simply stringing together a series of paragraphs. Often assignments have good content, but may nonetheless fail to achieve high marks because core academic writing skills are poor and have let down otherwise good quality work. Why bother, some might ask? If the assignment demonstrates that the student understands and can do, competently, even skilfully, then what is the point of academic prowess? Why bother worrying whether the student's English flows beautifully? Why be concerned about the student's ability to develop an academically sound argument that is supported by a wealth of solid academic and professional references?

This attention to detail can sometimes be considered mere academic pedantry. However, we would argue that this is a debatable point depending on the area of social work practice. The art of developing a good argument in coherent well-crafted English in an academic essay requires good discipline and is a transferable skill to many practice settings. As stated earlier in this chapter, good writing and analytical argument skills used in essay writing may later be put into practice when writing lengthy court reports to present to High Court judges in contested child protection hearings. Equally, if we were seeking funding for a new service or project, putting together a tightly woven argument based on sound understanding of research evidence, policy and funding priorities, we would need very good report writing abilities to support this. These skills should, therefore, be demonstrated through the integrated assignment.

The standard or quality of writing

The assignment should demonstrate a generally good academic ability to write a well-organised and well-argued essay. The general standards of writing and structure which apply to *all* academic essays apply no less to the integrated assignment. Without good writing you will find yourself unable to complete good critical analysis and will struggle to integrate theory with practice, reflect on and evaluate your practice, and analyse ethical and anti-discriminatory issues at the complex level required. We would therefore suggest that you need to be aware of the following criteria when completing your assignment:

- an essay with a clearly defined topic and analytical argument

- a well-written and well-organised essay in which the points flow nicely from one to the other and the logical progression of ideas is clear

- an essay which stays within the word limits.

This requires:

- analytical discussion and a connecting argument which tie together the different points made, evidence discussed and various sections (or sub-sections) of the assignment

- good basic essay structure (introduction, middle section and conclusion)

- good organisation of the middle section of the essay so that it sets out the main points of the argument and supporting evidence in a clear and logical progression

- good quality written English with appropriate attention paid to grammar, punctuation, spelling and academic style

- a careful check on the word count to remain within the required limit.

Box 10.6 Common pitfalls to avoid when writing

Sometimes assignments fail because the quality of basic essay writing is simply too low to permit the kind of complex content and analytical discussion which is required in an integrated assignment. In these situations common problems can include:

- failure to include a clear introduction which defines the parameters of the assignment, gives a brief thumbnail sketch of the practice which will be analysed, and informs the reader about the theme or connecting argument you intend to use

- failure to include a clear conclusion which sums up the main points of the argument and evidence and/or the conclusion fails to complete the argument or provide an answer to the question you set for yourself

- little analysis and no connecting argument (this point is connected to the points raised in Chapters 6 through 9)

- a poorly organised essay which haphazardly jumps from point to point without any logical progression

- colloquial English written in a stream-of-consciousness style

- awkward and seriously ungrammatical English with numerous spelling errors where the poor quality of language impedes reader understanding and the student's ability to develop an argument

- a verbose assignment which is well over the word limit.

The quality of background reading and references

The assignment needs to demonstrate background reading of a wide range of relevant academic and professional good quality sources, and the incorporation of ideas or information from those sources into the body of your essay.

When your assignment is marked, the marker will be looking for:

- breadth *and* depth of reading
- congruence between the sources cited in the body of the essay and those listed in the bibliography
- correct academic referencing.

This requires from you:

- wide reading demonstrated through a bibliography which includes a variety of good relevant academic and professional sources *and* the use of those sources throughout the essay
- good referencing throughout the body of the essay with *all* sources of information and quotations or statistics properly attributed in the correct format, with page references where appropriate.

Box 10.7 Common pitfalls to avoid in referencing and bibliographies

Sometimes assignments are based on too narrow reading or inadequate sources, or the referencing is inadequate. For example:

- an essay which cites only 5 sources in the body of the essay but where 45 sources are listed in the bibliography (if the other sources were read why were they not cited in the body of the assignment?)
- an essay where numerous sources cited in the body of the essay have not been included in the bibliography
- an essay where the bibliography includes far too few sources to support a complex argument in a 6000-word assignment
- a bibliography which includes a lot of class handouts rather than academic or professional sources
- a bibliography which does not include the most relevant academic and professional sources which would usually be included in an essay on this topic – for example: an assignment about work with a vulnerable, frail older person where abuse is suspected which misses *No Secrets* (Department of Health 2000b)

- a bibliography which includes out-of-date sources which have now been superseded (e.g. publications from the 1960s, rather than the 1990s, or an out-of-date *Mental Health Act Code of Practice*)
- bibliographies that are padded with numerous texts that are clearly not relevant to the topic and did not contribute ideas that were used in the body of the essay (e.g. including a source specifically relevant to working with emotionally and behaviourally disturbed adolescents in an essay about social work with a new-born baby)
- paragraphs within the body of the essay which include ideas, evidence, statistics or quotations which were taken from academic or professional books, journal articles, policy documents or legislation but which have not been properly attributed to the source (see also your own college or university regulations about plagiarism)
- the correct system of referencing is not used (e.g. university or departmental regulations require the Harvard system but footnotes are used instead) or serious errors are made in the method of referencing (e.g. use of *ibid.* or *op. cit.* as if they were part of the Harvard system).

Revising your assignment

It is foolhardy to submit the first draft of an assignment for marking – you must revise, redraft and thoroughly proof-read it if you hope to get a decent mark. Good revision is more than simply proof-reading for typographical errors or mistakes in punctuation and grammar (although clearly that needs to be done too). Good revision requires you to take a step back from what you have written and try to look at your assignment through the dispassionate eyes of a marker. Yes, this is the piece of work you poured your heart and soul into and laboured long and hard to deliver! However, now you must consider it coolly, with composure and indifference to all the effort you made, prepared to take the red pen to excise any purple prose that, on sober reflection, you realise is inappropriate. Usually this calm clinical approach is easier to achieve if you start to revise the next day, rather than five minutes after you have finished the first draft and pulled it off the printer.

Many people type their first drafts on a computer, although some people still hand write and then transfer onto a word processor. However, we strongly advise students, if at all possible, not to continue with hand-written documents after the first draft stage. Often revision involves moving paragraphs around on the page or from one section to another, or merging one piece of one paragraph with a bit from another. It is much easier to do this with a word-processed document.

Can I get help with revision?

Most colleges and universities have systems to support students through revision of assignments, although they vary from course to course. In some colleges, social work tutors are prepared to read rough drafts of assignments and discuss them with students. However, increasingly help with revision is done through writing workshops or learner support services organised centrally through the college or university – often through the library or student services.

Some students are reluctant to use these services, feeling somehow they are not meant for them, or that there is a stigma attached to using them. We would encourage *all* students who have ever received comments on previous papers about basic English writing skills, style and essay structure or organisation to use writing workshops or assignment revision tutorial services. They can provide a lot of guidance about how to revise the first (second, third) drafts of assignments. The use of these services in no way reflects badly on students' intelligence, commitment to learn, etc. On the contrary, intelligent, responsible and thoughtful students seek out the help they know is needed. It is foolish to hesitate or be afraid to ask for help. We speak from experience: one of us almost failed her first year of university because of very poor basic essay writing skills. Fortunately she got help through an essay writing workshop, and subsequently went on to earn postgraduate degrees.

Box 10.8 Tips for improving your English quickly

- If you know you have problems with basic writing skills then nothing improves a paper better than writing and rewriting in several drafts, editing to reduce padding and waffle and good proof-reading.

- Use the spell-check and grammar-check applications on your computer (if available) *but* beware of the differences between North American and United Kingdom usage. Remember also that the spell-check facility will not correct misspelled words that are real words (e.g. 'their' and 'there').

- Does your college or university have a support service or writing workshops to help students experiencing writing problems? Often, they can help with editing and redrafting assignments. Usually they have 'tips' sheets for common spelling and grammar errors.

How should I revise my assignment?

Many students find the process of revision baffling. They understand about proof-reading, in order to eliminate typographical errors and mis-spelled words. However, beyond that some students give us mystified and bewildered looks when we reinforce the importance of revision. There are four golden rules of revision:

- It takes time to do it properly – often just as much or more time as writing the first draft.

- It requires you to think analytically about the essay as it is read – not simply to read and reread it as you would a good story.

- You *must* be prepared to make substantial changes as a part of revision.

- The more you revise, the better the paper becomes.

Talk to fellow students who get very high marks for their work. Probably their first drafts were just as dreadful as yours appears to be. The difference is they revised, over and over, and then finally submitted the fifth or sixth version of their paper for assessment.

As you reread and revise what you have written, you should try to critique your own assignment in the same way that the markers will critique your essay when it is assessed. Pretend you are assessing your work, just as a marker would, using the following questions as a guide.

Questions that markers consider when assessing students' work

Here are some of the questions the markers will be considering. Our tips for revision follow each point.

- Do the paragraphs *describe* who did what and what happened when and which author said what or do the paragraphs *analyse* how and why things happened?

  Identify and revise most, if not all, descriptive paragraphs to remove simple description and replace it with critical analysis about how and why that is linked to the chosen question.

- Does the balance between your analysis of theory, practice and self-reflection and evaluation reflect the requirements for content, standards and marking criteria? Approximately how many words are devoted to each?

  If there is too much analysis of one at the expense of discussing the others be prepared to revise by editing and reducing the overly long discussion of the one issue to free enough words to add in more analysis about the other issues.

- How many paragraphs include theory, self-reflection and evaluation and details about your practice *together*?

  If most of your paragraphs contain either one or the other but not two or more elements, you need to plan a major revision so that paragraphs are written to include theory, self-reflection and evaluation and practice married together through analysis about the relevance of each to the other.

- Is sufficient analysis about social work ethics and values and practice dilemmas incorporated throughout?

   If only cursory mention is made, edit and reduce extraneous description about practice and/or theory to free enough words to add in more analysis about ethical issues.

- Have any of the key antiracist and anti-discriminatory issues relevant to this area of practice or chosen topic been missed out?

   If so, edit and reduce extraneous description about practice and/or theory to free enough words to add in analysis about anti-discriminatory practice.

- How many words are devoted to the introduction versus how many words are devoted to each of the sub-sections in the middle section versus how many words are devoted to the conclusion? Is the balance of words per section right or have too many precious words been spent on one section at the expense of words which would be better used elsewhere?

   Be prepared to revise if the balance of words seems wrong by editing and reducing what is too long to free enough words to add in more to the sections which are too short.

- Do the ideas flow logically from one to the other and does the argument seem logical?

   If not, be prepared to revise by juggling the order of paragraphs and adding connecting sentences which help to lead the reader from the idea contained in one paragraph to the idea developed in the next.

- Can you easily identify the central, underpinning argument for the essay?

   If not, alter the wording of paragraphs sufficiently to explicitly link each point back to the intended argument.

- Were any key ideas or points in the argument missed?

Check your draft against the essay plan you developed before you began writing; if you missed something crucial, add it in.

- Is the argument one-sided?

  Always ensure you have accounted for counter-arguments fairly. This can be difficult in a practice-oriented assignment because students feel strongly about their work. Nonetheless, if a bias has crept in, revise to ensure adequate attention is given to the other side of the debate. You do not have to agree with it, just acknowledge it exists and account for why you disagree with it.

- Does the introduction give a short pithy thumbnail sketch of not only the analytical argument being used but also the practice setting/responsibilities and practice examples which will be analysed?

  If either is missing, add it in.

- Does the conclusion include new material or new ideas not discussed earlier?

  If so, remove it and put it in the middle section.

- Does the conclusion sum up the main points of argument and relate them back to the introduction in an answer to the chosen question or topic?

  If not, reread your question again, and paraphrase the line of argument you started in the introduction to rephrase this as an answer to the question.

- Are the spelling, grammar, punctuation and style of language *absolutely perfect?*

  If not, get a good dictionary and grammar guide to aid revision and get someone to help you proof-read. Even if you think they are perfect, ask someone to read the assignment to double-check – particularly for typing errors as we all tend to read over minor errors.

- Are the correct academic sources cited for absolutely every idea used in every paragraph?

  If not, add them. Probably you have forgotten to put in some of those sources you skim read back in the early stages of background reading and research.

- Has every book and article which was used been cited at least once in the body of the essay, and are they all in the bibliography?

  If not, add them. Probably you have forgotten to put in some of those sources you skim read back in the early stages of background reading and research.

- Have some sources been cited too often (e.g. citing one 27 times while each of the rest was cited only once)?

  If yes, add other different sources (and the ideas they contain) so your essay is less dependent on one or two main sources.

- Is the assignment too long or too short?

  Edit and reduce it in length if it is too long; add in more analytical material if it is too short.

We cannot absolutely guarantee that if you follow these suggestions for revision that you will definitely achieve a high mark. However, casting a truly critical eye over your work (being prepared to be ruthless where necessary), revising and proof-reading usually serves to substantially improve an assignment.

A word about word limits

We wish we had a pound for every time a student has said to us: 'But does the word limit really matter?' In a word: YES! Word limits need to be adhered to. There are two main reasons for this.

First, no marker will read on endlessly, long after the required word limit has been exceeded. Either the marker will stop marking after the word limit is exceeded, or a percentage will be deducted from the mark allocated (depending on course regulations). If the marker stops reading and marking after a certain point then those golden words of wisdom on the 55th page will have no bearing on the mark earned. If they do not earn you anything then why bother writing them? Alternatively, marks could be deducted and, if the assignment is seriously over length, this might mean the paper fails.

Second and more importantly, one of the hallmarks of a poor assignment is a seriously over-length essay. Seriously overlong assignments have little structure, are verbose, repetitive and descriptive rather than analytical. Yet the students who write them cannot see what to cut out. They wrote, and as they wrote they realised bits they had left out that were important, so they added them in at the end. Then they reread and realised they had left out something else, so that got added in too. Then they were talking to one of their fellow students and they said they had used this book that was really helpful and so it got added in. And then they had a tutorial and realised they had forgotten something really important, so they had to add it. In fact, they were so concerned to just add in anything that might be important that they forgot one of the most important rules of all – word limits.

Box 10.9 Tips for revision

Use different coloured highlighter pens to draw lines in the margins indicating where the introduction, various sub-sections of the middle part of the essay and conclusion start/finish. That way you can quickly check if you have spent too much time on one section at the expense of another.

Go through the entire essay and write in the margins beside each and every paragraph whether they include examples of:

- theory to practice
- research to practice
- policy to practice
- law to practice
- ethics and values in practice
- anti-discriminatory practice
- antiracist practice

- self-reflection and self-evaluation
- service user/client/carer perspectives
- discussion of professional power and professional accountability.

After you have done this, check back to see if something of each has been done. If not, revise to add in what is missing. Now check it against the marking criteria provided by your programme for this assignment to see if what you have written reflects the balance the programme is seeking. Revise to ensure it does (e.g. if 20% of the mark is weighted for self-reflection, ensure that 20% of the paragraphs include self-reflection).

Box 10.10 More tips for revision

- Go through the essay and place a number in the margins beside each new idea. This is one technique to help you to identify when ideas are split between paragraphs. For example, suppose the paragraph at the top of page 3 discusses how Mr Jones was bereaved and in a crisis so that crisis intervention was appropriate. The next paragraph jumps to discussing Mr Jones's finances and housing policy. Two paragraphs later the ideas of bereavement and crisis intervention are returned to for one paragraph and following that the essay discusses housing policy. The organisation is faulty because the essay jumps back and forth between different ideas and this makes the development of a coherent argument difficult. If the different ideas were numbered (e.g. bereavement/crisis = 1; finances/housing policy = 2) then a quick look at the margins would show what needed to be revised.

- Using a bright coloured pen (e.g. red, green, orange), tick every time a reference has been formally cited in the text of the essay. After this, check every page: if it is awash with pen marks then you know you have put in a lot of references. If there are no tick marks on a page you know you need to find the sources and add in the references.

- Check that all the references you have in the body of the essay are also listed in the bibliography.

Box 10.11 Rules of thumb about references

'How many references should I use?' must be one of the most commonly asked questions from undergraduates. First, you get assignments back with comments about how you used too few sources. Next, after putting in assignments with 30 or more sources in the bibliography you are accused of padding! Then you check with your classmate who wrote a paper that got a 1st and find their essay used only 10 sources while yours got only a bare 3rd, even though you used 30 sources. When you ask, the tutor says, 'Yes but you did not use the right sources.' It all seems very confusing.

The following rules of thumb need to be treated with *extreme* caution. They are intended as crude guides for bewildered beginners and *not* as hard and fast rules. No one ever wrote a superb essay simply by following all these rules. Essay writing is not as simple as that. Moreover, experienced academics will often break the rules, and yet still produce excellent scholarly writing. Nonetheless, these rules of thumb should help beginners to the academic world to make some sense of what seems to be – at first sight – confusing and unclear guidance.

1. Try to ensure you have at least one good academic reference for every paragraph. Long, complex paragraphs probably need two or three different references.

2. Expect to use approximately 30 to 35 good quality different academic or professional sources in the bibliography of an average 6000 word undergraduate essay.

3. Adjust the number of sources up or down depending on:

    (a) the quality of the sources

    (b) the academic level of study – a Master's level programme may expect wider reading

    (c) the way in which you use the sources throughout the assignment

(d) the nature and complexity of your chosen subject

(e) the required word length of your assignment.

4. Do not keep citing the same source over and over and over. Your assignment will be criticised for being 'too dependent on one or two sources'.

5. Do not use lecture notes or class handouts as a source – go to the original book or article that the handouts cite and use that.

Box 10.12 Tips for style

Should I use 'I'?

- As a general rule, purely academic social science disciplines (such as sociology or social policy) frown on students using the personal pronoun, while applied disciplines (such as nursing and social work) sometimes accept it.

- Our recommendation is to check first with your programme tutors before using 'I' in any assignment – even an integrated assignment where you analyse your own practice.

Avoid big sounding words and jargon

- Smaller, simpler words that convey meaning effectively are generally better. For example, explain – do not explicate.

- Try not to use jargon that obscures meaning. For example, do not say:

    I initiated an assessment of need programme through Utopia County Council Policy F755 using form CC521 in accordance both with policy and with social work values of empowerment.

Instead why not try:

    I helped Mrs C to complete her own self-assessment of need; this helped her feel she was being listened to.

How do I make it sound right?

- Avoid stream-of-consciousness style – it works well for creative writing; it will not serve you well in an integrated assignment.

- Avoid convoluted lengthy sentences with several subordinate clauses and brackets that are a paragraph in length.

- A nice mixture of short and long sentences is more interesting to read.

My own words or a quotation?

- Do not use quotations to make your arguments for you. It is better to paraphrase what the book or article says, putting it into your own words to develop your own argument.

- Quotations are used appropriately to illustrate a point or provide an example or piece of supporting evidence.

- If more words are used in quoting what other people have said than saying it in your own words, then probably you have used too many quotations!

Box 10.13 To give opinions or not to give opinions – that is the question

May I give my own opinions?

Opinions *are* acceptable (and welcomed) in student essays when thoroughly supported through academic referencing and a well-developed coherent argument. However, students who are still struggling hard with basic skills of essays and straining to understand how to develop an argument would do well to steer clear of statements like 'in my opinion' or 'I believe' or 'I feel' which act as signals to markers that unsubstantiated polemic may follow.

If I may not give my opinion may I discuss my experience?

The answer in this case is YES – particularly in an integrated assignment which is supposed to marry together your own practice experience with theory. The important thing to remember in this is that you need to ensure your experiences are used to *illustrate* points, not simply as description about what happened. For example, if you were making a point about the limitations of a particular theoretical perspective in practice, you might illustrate this point by indicating how it was of limited benefit in work with a particular client. For example:

> Although my use of a task-centred approach (Doel and Marsh 1992) helped Mr Jones resolve his financial difficulties, his depression over his wife's death continued to deepen. Therefore in my experience with this person, task-centred work was of limited help.

Examples of old assignments

Are there examples of good integrated assignments (which received marks in the range of 2:1 to 1st) submitted in previous years by other DipSW students available through your university or college library? If so, we recommend you take advantage of this opportunity to read them. This should help you to understand the quality of work needed for your own assignment.

Summary and conclusion

This chapter has reviewed various components of organising and writing an integrated assignment. Most of these skills will have already been learned and put to good use by students when completing previous assignments. However, theory-to-practice assignments tend to test students' faith in their own skills, knowledge and academic abilities, which is why they have been discussed here. Good organisation is a critically important skill for good writing. It is important that students allocate enough time to the task of writing and revising and that they use the material they have assembled in an orderly and logical way. Planning is the key to achieving this.

Once the student has decided how and what to say, there remains the sheer hard slog of writing. Tips have been given for tackling this so that it does not feel overwhelming but becomes a manageable process. The process of writing from basic first draft, through the stages of redrafting, and building in cohesive critical analysis throughout has been discussed. In addition, many suggestions have been given for how to revise so that a final polished and refined essay is produced of which the student can feel justifiably very proud.

We cannot promise that every student using this advice will write a fantastically good assignment. However, there are many similarities between what we have mentioned and the suggestions provided by former social work students in the next chapter.

Suggested further reading

Creme, P. and Lea, M. (1997) *Writing at University: A Guide for Students.* Buckingham: Open University Press.

Redman, P. (2001) *Good Essay Writing: A Social Sciences Guide,* 2nd edn. London: Sage.

CHAPTER ELEVEN

The Student's Perspective:
'If It Was Any More Reflective You Could See Your Face in It'

Lee Durrant and Simon Shreeve

We write this chapter as two students who completed the Norfolk DipSW in 1998 and 1999. In completing the integrated assignment, our experiences were quite different. One assignment passed on first submission, and one failed. While the markers acknowledged that the failing assignment was 'academic work of a high standard', it failed because it did not meet the assessment criteria – the writer had gone off topic. This work also failed because there was insufficient evidence of reflection on practice incorporated in the work. Both of these issues are considered in this chapter together with an evaluation of a wider range of issues we believe should be taken into consideration when approaching the integrated assignment. With the rewritten assignment in his hand, the student approached the college tutor with these words: 'If it was any more reflective you could see your face in it.' We are happy to record that on resubmission, the work achieved a pass. The focus of this chapter will be upon our experiences on completing this final, integrated assignment, but clearly much of the information contained within this chapter can be transferred in support of any written assignment. We have used examples from our own assignments in illustration.

We can remember completing the first year of the DipSW, and thinking half-way through, so far so good. We also remember the frequent comments of our tutors, who stressed that the 'easy' part was finished. The first year of our programme was designed to provide us with a wide-ranging core of underpinning skills and knowledge that we would build upon in our final year. Our academic skills were expected to continue to develop so that we could achieve a level of analysis which would reflect the academic status of the course. In our case this was a Diploma in Higher Education, the equivalent to two years of a first degree. The academic standard required of social work students will, of course, vary dependent upon what kind of DipSW programme they are following. On all programmes, however, will be the requirement for the student to demonstrate critical analysis in the integrated assignment. Barnett describes these as:

- evaluation of knowledge, theories, policies and practice
- recognition of multiple perspectives
- different levels of analysis
- ongoing enquiry. (Barnett 1977, p.105)

In addition, we were told that in the forthcoming year we would grow and mature as students and, more importantly, as social work practitioners. Indeed, it became clear to us that there was now a more complex and demanding requirement with regard to both our level of social work practice and our academic studies. It would no longer be enough to be informed about the subject, we were now expected to be able to integrate theory with practice and also to reflect upon our observations. Kolb (1988a) suggests that there is a learning cycle of four stages comprising concrete experience, reflective observation, abstract conceptualisation and active experimentation and within the integrated assignment Kolb's cycle can be seen to apply. As Eby states: 'Kolb's theory of experiential learning clearly suggests that theory and practice flourish and enrich each other in a never ending circle' (Eby 2000a, p.54).

It is easy to recall the anxiety caused by the looming prospect of having to write our integrated assignments as we and other students approached the end of the DipSW course. As the largest assignment on the course, it presents the most comprehensive test of our knowledge as prospective social workers. It is clear that this assignment provides a summative assessment of our learning and development as social work practitioners. According to Walklin, summative assessment can be used to 'determine the overall effectiveness of training and learning outcomes' (Walklin 1990, p.148). However, on a personal level, it wasn't our level of knowledge that was worrying to us. It was more to do with *how* to use and evidence our theoretical understanding in the context of social work. In discussion with other students, it seemed that these concerns were common.

Throughout the previous chapters in this book, advice and guidance have been given to the student on the requirements and expectations of assessors when completing assignments. The first seeds for establishing a topic for this assignment can begin with the student's interactions whilst on placement. All that is then needed is the ability to look deeper into the issues and to ask questions. Linking theory with practice becomes a much less scary proposition when you acknowledge that you are already doing it on a daily basis at work. As Howe (1987) states:

> Social workers should be able to answer the following five questions if they are to establish a practice that is clear, organised and structured:
>
> 1. What is the matter? The worker needs to recognise and identify the problem.
>
> 2. What is going on? The situation has to be assessed, interpreted and explained.
>
> 3. What is to be done? In the light of the assessment, the social worker and client decide on their goals, making plans and clarifying intentions.
>
> 4. How is it to be done? The methods by which the goals are to be achieved have to be chosen.
>
>   Has it been done? The outcome is evaluated.
>
> (Howe 1987, p.7)

In our experience, using the above framework may be helpful to support students in the process of looking deeper and this in turn may help you identify a suitable topic for study as your integrated assignment. In essence, each assignment can be broken down into six parts:

1. the parameters for the assignment

2. the subject or topic chosen

3. the structure of the assignment

4. managing your life to get the work done

5. managing stress

6. meeting the deadline.

The parameters for the assignment

Every piece of work is individual. As a result some students will have a definite idea of their subject material, which may reflect a personal interest. Others will have no idea of what they should focus on and may be alarmed by this. With or without a clear idea of topic, the most important thing to focus upon is the written parameters for the assignment provided by the college or university. After all, most students know that completing assignments successfully is about answering the question fully – hitting the target. It sounds simple, but in order to answer any question, you must understand what is being asked of you and what is required to meet the assessment criteria. In order to do this you will need to consider closely the words used to clarify the parameters.

The assessors will no doubt be searching for a definite link between the parameters given and your chosen subject and how it is presented on paper. It will not be enough to *describe* the situation and your practice. As an accountable professional, you must understand your practice in a wider context. This requires you to draw upon skills of critical analysis. This wider level of analysis needs to incorporate theory, the policy and legal framework, together with professional and personal values. In completing the integrated assignment, therefore, you are required to focus upon a particular issue, demonstrating your ability as an ethical, reflective worker who is also able to integrate theory into practice.

In support of the above, you will find it invaluable to discuss the assignment requirements in some depth with your practice teacher, as well as with your tutor in order to consider *how* your proposed subject area will meet them.

So, what constitutes a good subject? It *must* be linked in some way to your practice on placement. You may have a particular interest in an issue, but unless this can be linked to your practice and evidenced in some way, you are unlikely to meet the criteria. For example:

> …from the report outlining the proposed restructuring of the social services department, I find it difficult to understand how this will more effectively and clearly meet the needs of the service-user. (Example from student paper)

This quotation illustrates that the student had a clear interest in the departmental restructuring and he allocated about half of the assignment to discussion of issues relating to this. As a student on a placement working with adults with disabilities, however, it did not relate directly to the practice, or indeed the parameters of the assessment.

At an early stage, we would advise you to consider some of the practice issues and scenarios that are regularly encountered at your new place of work. It is particularly useful if this is something that you personally find stimulating as you are about to undertake the largest piece of written work for the course, which is going to require significant reading and understanding as well as taking considerable time and energy.

The subject or topic chosen

When identifying a possible subject the practicalities of writing it need to be considered. Is the area too broad? For example, a general analysis of racism in relation to youth offending may offer many issues for discussion, from poverty to structural oppression. However, it is likely that the writer will be unable to focus upon one area in enough depth to cover the parameters of the assignment. In contrast, the subject needs to be comprehensive enough to fill the required word length of the DipSW programme. We have found it helpful to break down the chosen material into subheadings. These could include relevant theories, issues of accountability, ethics and values and the legal and policy framework supported by your own experiences and practice. In addition, you could reflect on how these headings might demonstrate how you have achieved the six core competencies of social work (CCETSW 1996a). For example:

> ...the case [a family of ethnic Albanians] was held by a female social worker...when I took over responsibility for the case...the previous worker advised me that I would have difficulty making eye-contact or holding a conversation with [the husband] and that [the wife] was the person I would have most contact with. As a male worker I soon discovered that the reverse was true. (Example from a student paper)

This extract clearly demonstrates how the student has been able not only to reflect on his own practice, but also to integrate the core competence of Communicate and Engage together with the values requirements and illustrates ethnically sensitive practice. Similarly, the following extract from an assignment illustrates this integration of the competence Assess and Plan with the student's commitment to the 'value and dignity of individuals' (CCETSW 1996a):

> I was able to complete some direct work with [a child of 10 who has ataxic cerebral palsy] who was very upset about the situation at school and said that he was fearful of returning in the new term. Coulshed (1991) states that: 'The child's own views, whether expressed verbally or non-verbally...would be sought to get ideas about the best way to help the child' (Coulshed 1991, p.26). In relation to [this child] I felt that the assessment was not only about matching his eligibility for existing services, but also about identifying the concerns which were important to him and agreeing how best to deal with them. (Example from student paper)

Having assessed the parameters and decided upon a topic that meets them, the next stage is to gather relevant information. As students, this was frequently the part of completing an assignment that we dreaded most. Gathering information and deciding on what material to use would seem, in our experience, to labour on for an eternity. When we look back at our coursework, however, it is easy to identify the assignments which were rushed, in comparison with those which were more carefully planned, researched and structured. We are sure that assessors are also tuned-in to this and, as a result, feel this stage of the process requires a great deal of thought.

At the outset, do some research – is there enough literature about your chosen theme? The student cited above experienced some difficulty in accessing any literature about social work and asylum seekers. As a result, much of the referencing relating to this element of his assignment was sourced from newspapers. Is the literature available broad-ranging and not only limited to social work texts? In addition, if you have a particular standpoint with regard to your topic, try to identify theory that presents an opposing view to offer an opportunity for more balanced and critical analysis. You should also try to identify material from all of the areas of study undertaken as part of the DipSW. In our experience, as the assignment neared completion, it became easy to see links with other modules from earlier in the course, the relevance of which, often questioned at the time, became clearer.

In the extract below, the student identifies links between models of disability which he studied in a module entitled 'Social work with people with physical disability: Practices and policy' with issues faced in his subsequent practice placement working in a children with disabilities team:

> Within this framework [the social model of disability] it is seen as socially constructed, a denial of access to the facilities which non-disabled society takes for granted. Social workers are compelled to recognise the impact of adopting the social model of disability (Oliver and Sapey 1999, p.28). By doing so, their assessment of the disabled child is enabled to focus more upon the needs of the child via the removal of socially imposed restrictions, and less upon supplementing the impairment. (Example from student paper)

In gathering information, it is likely that you will not have access to all of the material when you wish. As suggested in Chapter 5, study skills such as skim reading will be of particular help when you begin to research your subject. At this stage you will be identifying the books that appear relevant. You should try to note down the information and references that you need at this stage – and reserve the appropriate books for the time when you feel you will be into your assignment. This may require some forward planning on your part but could save a great deal of anxiety later on. It is particularly important to keep a record of all references consulted and to compile a complete and accurate bibliography, as we believe that all well-written work can be summed up in one word – *evidence*. In gathering information and researching your subject topic you need to show in the assignment that you are aware of and recognise the factors relevant to your topic.

The structure of the assignment

A useful tool to assist you in writing the integrated assignment is to evaluate the extent to which the content provides evidence of how you have met the CCETSW (1996a, b) values requirements. Demonstration of these values requirements provides evidence of your abilities and growth as a social worker. As a starting point, having them at the forefront of your mind when completing any assignment will ensure that you are motivated to consider the effect of your involvement with individuals and your responsibilities to them. It is likely that you will not have the opportunity to look at each issue in great depth. However, to consider these will support and nurture your 'reflective' capabilities.

The following values requirement, for example, offers a range of interesting issues to be considered: 'Assist people to increase control of and improve the quality of their lives, while recognising that control of behaviour will be required at times in order to protect children and adults from harm' (CCETSW 1996a, p.18).

Recognition of the responsibilities of local authorities can be linked with the issues of care, control and accountability. Considering human rights, for example, in the context of older people who may have Alzheimer's disease, should they have the right to refuse services if their health is likely to be jeopardised? In evaluating this issue, you will need to question your personal views and how this affects your interaction. How might theories of ageism inform your practice balanced against your accountability as a local government officer who is responsible for assessing and managing risk and working within the law? These kinds of analyses are seemingly endless and therefore will not only form an extremely beneficial aid to completing the assignment, but will demonstrate your ethical and reflective practice. For example, Section 47 of the National Assistance Act 1948 provides for:

> securing the necessary care and attentions for persons who:
>
> (a) are suffering from grave chronic disease or, being aged, infirm, or physically incapacitated, are living in insanitary conditions, and
>
> (b) are unable to devote to themselves, and are not receiving from other persons proper care and attention. (Ministry of Health 1948)

In the case of the above legislation, which is currently still in force, you would need to identify how you would reconcile the needs of the individual against your duties to respond to a request for intervention in a situation appearing to meet the above legal criteria.

One of the most important areas to evidence is your knowledge and understanding of anti-oppressive practice and discrimination. This subject caused a high level of anxiety in our particular cohorts. It is clear to us that, in general, they were indeed committed to the principles of anti-discriminatory practice (ADP) which can be defined in broad terms as 'forms of practice that challenge discrimination and oppression' (Thompson 1998, p.77).

However, students often lost marks for being tokenistic in their approach to communicating this in their written work. Do not fall into the trap of making statements such as 'if the client was Black'. These comments are invariably poorly received by assessors. As has been stated earlier, all interactions within social work have a theoretical context, ADP forms a part of this framework. As Dominelli (1989) states in her exploration of racism in social work:

> The subtle dynamics of personal, institutional and cultural racism permeate the routine minutiae of social work policy and practice and these, combined with the strategies white social workers utilise to avoid confronting racism in their work, mean that black people's needs receive short shrift. (Dominelli 1989, p.391)

We write this chapter as white male social workers who undertook our social work training in a predominantly white, rural area. Many of us were aware that on practice placement we might not have an opportunity to work with culturally diverse service users. We recognise, however, that antiracist practice is highly relevant to predominantly white areas:

> Reluctance to accept the existence of racism in rural areas follows from a lack of knowledge and from a misunderstanding of what racism is. Many people are unaware of the extent of ethnic and 'racial' differential in rural areas and they simply assume that there are very few people from ethnic minorities in the countryside. However…there are settled minority groups in every county in England and Wales, and in most counties in Scotland. (Pugh 2000, p.42)

Students will need to be aware that discrimination and oppression manifest themselves in many different guises within society. They will need to be aware of not only race and ethnicity, but also sexuality, religious belief, disability, age, gender, class, poverty and the ways that society fails to recognise and respect diversity. It is important – and is something that students need to get increasingly tuned in to – to recognise the structural factors that affect people's lives. As stressed by Braye and Preston-Shoot (1995, p.43), 'inequality is endemic to the whole fabric of society'.

It may be helpful to include case studies as a method to illustrate your understanding of ADP within an assignment. However, beware of relying too heavily upon these as you may then be cornered into acknowledging the theory purely in relation to the situation given. This could lead to failure to acknowledge or examine certain forms of oppression. Perhaps it would be more appropriate to use a case study to illustrate a variety of different issues. Do not be apprehensive about referring to your experience. This is one of the most valuable sources of your knowledge and understanding. You can go on to place the assignment in a human context, which can reaffirm your statements and arguments whilst illustrating your ability to link theory to practice.

A further method of demonstrating this is the use of research. Giving examples of relevant and up-to-date studies that are relevant to your piece of work will show your appreciation of the importance of research in informing practice. As Stepney states: '…research has the capacity to influence the quality of the policy/practice debate and contribute to more informed programmes of action' (Stepney 2000c, p.11).

The integrated assignment is a relatively large assignment. Consequently, a long endless document with no structure is liable to be confusing for the reader and is also more difficult for the assessor to evaluate. Remember that this piece of work should reflect not only your knowledge as a result of undertaking the DipSW, your previous work experiences in the field of health and social care, but also an entire 80-day placement's worth of experience designed to support you in demonstrating competence in practice as a social worker. This work deserves, therefore, to be presented in a readable and, more importantly, accessible format. For example, in support of this you may consider the use of sections, headings or even chapters: go on – be adventurous!

Managing your life to get the work done

The life of a student social worker can be stressful. Towards the end of the course, the student is faced with completing all allocated academic work as well as passing the 80-day placement, evidencing the core competencies and meeting deadlines. In our experience, the final six months of the course were the most demanding in terms of time, energy, commitment and academic levels of study. Additionally, however, they were, for us, the most rewarding. Much of the study and experience acquired within the previous 18 months came to the fore at this time. At the beginning of the final placement 80 days seemed like a long time. We found, however, with so much going on and the range of demands placed upon us in terms of practice and academic study, it really did pass very quickly. Many students were left with a particularly hectic and stressful last few weeks. Again, careful and clear planning should reduce many of the risks. Make sure that you understand exactly what the requirements of you are, from your university or college tutor, from your placement provider and from your practice teacher. Consideration of issues of leave and ensuring you plan some study time should happen at the learning agreement stage.

Once you have considered the possible case scenarios that you may wish to examine, it is vital to discuss this openly with the client or family concerned. Obviously confidentiality is crucial and permission must be obtained. After all you are discussing very personal facts about people's lives. For one student it was helpful to use an example from practice to illustrate the effects of segregated special education on a child that the student was working with. The student approached both the child and his mother about this and was given permission to use their experiences within the assignment. Indeed as a result of this, the mother expressed interest in the assignment and in this example, the student and the parent were able to discuss the issues associated with segregated education further in relation to her son. Similarly, should you wish to highlight examples of practice other than your own, you will need to consult with colleagues to obtain their consent and also advice. Using the advice and guidance of colleagues was invaluable. We owe an enormous amount to a range of professionals who kept us focused during the placement. They were able to support us in making the link between our experiences and the theoretical component underpinning them.

Managing stress

In our experience as students, anxiety levels with regard to passing and failing assessments tended to be high and this was particularly heightened at the end of the DipSW course when we knew the assignment would produce an overall pass or fail recommendation. This was exacerbated when many of us had already had offers of employment subject to successful completion of the DipSW. Students make a huge commitment financially, personally and practically as well as hope for a successful conclusion – to pass. As we approached the final three or four months of the course, the reality of the possibility of failure became more apparent. Thompson *et al.* (1998) suggest that recognising the range of stressors you face will help you to be better equipped to deal with them. In addition, they advise being able to identify and draw upon a range of potential supports available.

There will be support available to you from both your practice teacher and tutors. Use supervision or tutorials to keep them up to date with the progress of your assignment. In addition, if your caseload or personal life is proving too demanding, you need to be honest with yourself about this.

You also need to share such personal details with your practice teacher and tutors, who will be able to offer some advice and guidance.

Support should also be available from your colleagues. Many social work staff often comment on the benefits of having a student within the team as a source of up-to-date knowledge, refocusing their own theoretical understanding (and of course reducing the unallocated list). Remember that you are part of the team, so don't be afraid to seek appropriate assistance.

Other students are another potential source of support. There are, however, dangers in relying too heavily on discussions on assignments with your peers. Nothing was more guaranteed to send us into a frenzy than to hear what other students stated they had achieved within their assignments. It is important to recognise the individuality inherent in each assignment. Therefore, utilise meetings with other students as a source of valuable discussion, share ideas about linking theory to practice, but *do not* compare your work with that of your fellow students.

With all of the pressures inherent in completing an assignment it is difficult to ensure adequate leisure time. Richards (1999) describes living with pressure as having the following effects:

> Stress puts your body under pressure. It puts a strain on your heart and your digestive system. You become too busy or too tired to exercise or to eat a balanced diet. You haven't got time to relax and you really don't want anyone else to know that you're buckling under the pressure of work. The way you lead your life can make you more resilient to the pressures of work. Or it can make the pressures worse. (Richards 1999, p.54)

Many students not only are faced with writing their assignments and completing their placements, but also have jobs to supplement their income or important family commitments. Despite this, the value of time out cannot be underestimated. Pursue other interests outside of coursework where possible and seek out a range of supports for yourself.

Meeting the deadline

Following many of the tips included here will, we hope, reduce some of the anxiety about meeting the hand-in date. For us this date seemed at one time or other almost artificial – as if it would never come and then, suddenly, it crept up on us from behind. No matter what the level of panic or nerves, most students achieve this deadline with very few exceptions. One of the best ways to ensure that all is going according to plan is to set yourself goals or dates to have completed certain aspects of your work. One way of achieving this is to set and write down 'SMART' objectives (Hayden 1999), which can be seen as stepping stones towards your ultimate goal of completing the integrated assignment. SMART goals involve addressing the following elements:

Specific:	Be clear about what you are trying to achieve. This will ensure greater focus and increase the likelihood of success.
Measurable:	Have some measure of what you are trying to achieve (i.e. How much? Of what?).
Achievable:	To motivate you to action, your goal must be achievable and realistic.
Relevant:	Your goals must be relevant to you and to the assignment. You are more motivated to achieve a goal that you own.
Timed:	When will you achieve this goal? Be specific (i.e. the date/time of completion needs to be specified). (Hayden 1999)

It is a personal thing but these goals could be divided up as follows:

- The outline – what are you going to write about?
- Complete a rough draft – this was a requirement of our particular course in the shape of a preliminary plan. Maybe 400 or 500 words will suffice, as a reference guide for yourself as much as anything.
- Complete your research – this takes ages!
- The final draft.

- Proof-reading – for most people this may be a final read the night before you hand the assignment in; however, reading the document in one go may reveal errors in the flow of the work as well as spelling or grammatical mistakes. You may also spot gaps that can be filled. Allow a week in case of this.

- Hand it in.

Once you have handed in your completed assignment, try not to worry about it. At this stage, it is beyond your control. One of the best ways to help you to move on from this is to treat yourself. An early night, a trip to the cinema or theatre, a day out or a good long soak in the bath and a lie-in in the morning.

Most students pass this assignment and as we said at the start of this chapter – you already know what you need to know – evidencing this is the tricky part. Once your successful assignment is returned after marking, there is a tendency to put it away and move on to the next piece of work. Most tutors will write comments (annoyingly) in the margins of your beautiful dissertation. Despite this, it *is* useful to read these, just to see where you could have improved things.

If you do fail on first submission, initially it is important to deal with your feelings, which can range from shock, surprise, anger, through to feelings of low self-esteem and depression. Use all the supports you have available in order to deal with these feelings – your family, friends and colleagues, your fellow students, your tutor and your practice teacher.

Once you have recovered from the initial disappointing news of failure, spend time reviewing and evaluating the reasons why you did not meet the assessment criteria. It is important to recognise that a powerful way of learning is by reflecting on mistakes. This process of reflection and evaluation can include a careful reading of the assessors' comments about your work. In our experience, these comments provide clear pointers with regard to what needs to be done in order to support the resubmission as a pass. Similarly, if you have access to further tutorial support, use it. Discussion of the issues with a tutor can really help to clarify areas requiring further development and improvement (Creme and Lea 1997). They may also be able to offer advice with regard to accessing appropriate reading and research. Once you have gained clarity concerning what needs to be done in order to meet the assessment criteria, you should then set some new goals and SMART objectives in support of revising and rewriting your assignment.

As comparatively recent graduates of the DipSW, we hope that this chapter will equip you with some additional useful tools in support of achieving the integrated assignment. It is by no means intended as a definitive 'How to do an assignment'. The beauty of any particular piece of work is that it will be unique. An assignment is as much a reflection of your individual experiences, as it is a guide to your knowledge and understanding. We believe that if you use this book, which seeks to promote and enable the student social worker through the integrated assignment, you should be able to avoid having to resubmit your work. The rest is up to you.

CHAPTER TWELVE

The External Assessor's Perspective

Lorraine Agu

Introduction and context

Students are sometimes confused about who external assessors are and what they do. This chapter will explore the role of the external assessor in relation to the requirement for qualifying social workers to demonstrate the integration of theory and practice in order to receive the award of Diploma in Social Work. In doing this, some of the debates concerning theory and practice within social work education are also revisited in the context of current developments and initiatives in the training and education of professional social workers.

The present qualifying award for social work, the DipSW (CCETSW 1989b, 1995a), could still be described as being in its infancy and yet social work education and training is entering another evolutionary phase. The creation of a new national training organisation, the Training Organisation for the Personal Social Services (TOPSS), the abolition of CCETSW, due to be replaced in autumn 2001 by a new regulatory body for social work and social care, the General Social Care Council, England (GSCC), and the commitment to introduce a new qualifying award for social workers represent a major part of the new Labour government agenda to modernise social services and the social care workforce (Department of Health 1998, 2000c). While qualifying social work education and training cannot be blame for all the ills associated with social work as a profession, there have been longstanding critics of the education that social workers receive from within and outside of the profession (Lyons

1999). The inquiry into the death of Victoria (Anna) Climbie, as part of its terms of reference, is paying attention to the training undertaken by those who had worked with Victoria.

There is a near consensus that the education and training required for social workers to work competently and safely with members of the community cannot be satisfactorily achieved within the present two year programme. The review into the DipSW undertaken by JM Consulting (1998, 1999a, 1999b) set out to address some of the issues concerning the content and delivery of social work education and training. The review involved extensive consultation with individuals, academic institutions, employers and professional associations. At present its findings contain a number of proposals regarding the delivery and content of a new award for social worker. Nonetheless there remains uncertainty and debate regarding the proposed structure, and content of qualifying social work training, and the implications for the Post-Qualifying Social Work Award (PQSW) and Advanced Award in Social Work (AASW).

The review confirmed that one of the main problems of the current training is 'related to the length of many of the courses and the amount of learning experience that can be realistically achieved in a two-year programme' (JM Consulting 1999a, p.16). However, the review process identified a wide range of issues concerned with the appropriateness and adequacy of the present curriculum including the inadequate integration of theory and practice. These issues I shall return to later in this chapter.

These criticisms could offer some support to those who have been particularly critical of the anti-intellectualism of some social workers – an anti-intellectualism they feel has been compounded through the emphasis on competency-based social work education since the introduction of the DipSW (Lyons 1999). The review expressed concern with the tendency to the overemphasis of tasks within competency-based education to the detriment of integrated research, knowledge and practice in exercising judgement. However, the competence framework is still going to remain a central tenet of a new award, and is becoming a feature within contemporary higher education particularly for professions which include an experiential component (i.e. assessed practice) to the curriculum (Barkatoolah 1989; Jarvinen 1989). Other proposed changes – such as a national curriculum for social work, or as JM Consulting (1999a) describe it, 'a standard or model curricula', and the possibilities of a 'three plus one' structure, with the first three years in college and a fourth year in practice – raise some serious concerns as to whether a new degree award for social workers will be able to strengthen the relationship and integration of theory and practice in order to produce graduates who are able to analyse and reflect critically upon their practice.

Theory and practice – revisited

Some issues that are being contested as a part of the review process are familiar and represent an articulation of some longstanding debates concerning the relationship between theory and practice within social work education and practice. Theories can provide a framework of understanding, an explanation of the ways things appear to be happening (Stepney 2000a). Theory tends to be associated with thinking and practice with doing, and within social work education and practice, the relationship between theory and practice has tended to become polarised to the extent that 'there is an unacceptable wide gap between theory and practice, a disjuncture between what is taught or learned and what is practised' (Thompson 2000a, p.84). Thus at the risk of overgeneralisation, those in practice are accused of being anti-intellectual and rejecting theory in preference for a theoryless or common-sense approach (Coulshed and Orme 1998). In contrast, those in academia are accused of elitism and blamed for producing theory and research which bears little relevance to the real world of social work that is practised out in agencies. Thompson attributes some of this to the division of labour between those who teach and those who practise and warns that 'theory has come to be seen as the preserve of the academic or educator and practice as being the domain of the practitioner' (Thompson 2000a, p.85).

Though partnership and collaboration between academic institutions and agencies in the provision and management of social work education was heralded as an important feature behind the success of the DipSW (Lyons 1999), the relationship between theory and practice remains as problematic in education as in practice. Employers have been particularly critical of the present education received by social workers, who are perceived as lacking the knowledge and skills required by the workplace. Within social work education the theoretical base is drawn primarily from the social sciences of sociology, psychology and social policy. These have been criticised for being too broad. Stepney qualifies this by stating:

> Sociology, psychology and social policy, whatever their merits and insights they bring, do not offer any neat and consistent theory about human behaviour. The latter derives from an epistemological position that certain truth does not exist. And whilst academics can usefully debate such theoretical dilemmas the practitioner can only afford such luxuries if they bring some tangible benefits and lead to positive outcomes. (Stepney 2000a, p.21)

In the absence of a national curriculum, CCETSW leaves it to individual programme providers 'to decide how best to enable students to achieve a broad understanding of the knowledge base required' (CCETSW 1995a, p.19), though CCETSW also expects that students gain 'a deeper, more extensive understanding of knowledge particularly relevant to the service user group and context of their practice learning opportunities' (CCETSW 1995a, p.19).

Thus, most qualifying courses consist of a hybrid of some of the social sciences subject areas which have been 'subject to a process of professional adaptation and refinement' (Stepney 2000a, p.21). This is taught alongside a body of knowledge which can be referred to as social work studies including theories, methods, values and law. In addressing concerns regarding the present content of the DipSW, the review found that some areas of the curriculum lacked depth, particularly in relation to the social sciences and in understanding of the policy and organisational context of social work. Areas such as social work values, multi-agency working and management skills were expressed as being inadequately covered and there were particular concerns about academics who lacked the latest practice experience and their ability to cover relevant legislation and practices (JM Consulting 1999b).

The review asserted that qualifying education and training should 'develop mature and reflective practitioners who understand the evidence base for their actions; who are able to adapt and develop their practice to challenge poor and inappropriate practice' (JM Consulting 1999a, p.7). Yet it is widely accepted that social work education and practice has consistently lacked a strong research and evidence base for its interventions. The gap between research and practice may be beginning to erode with the activities of the Centre for Evidenced-Based Social Services (Stepney 2000a) and the advent of the Social Care Institute of Excellence (SCIE). The gap between research/theory and practice has to be minimised if social work is to regain some of the respect that has been lost during the high profile failings in recent years (e.g. Bridge Child Care Consultancy Service 1995; Waterhouse, le Fleming and Clough 2000).

The scope and influence of external assessors

External assessment is part of a wider framework of quality assurance of social work education and training, and the creation of a large team of experienced external assessors, drawn from both academic and practice backgrounds, has been a unique feature of the DipSW. There may be some changes to the recruitment and role of external assessors, under the responsibility of the GSCC. However, at the time of writing I will be referring to the role of the external assessor under the present requirements as outlined in the *Manual for External Assessors* (CCETSW 1995b) and *Guidance for New External Assessors* (CCETSW 1998).

The duties of the external assessor are broad and extensive whilst primarily concerned with verifying that the standards achieved for the award are appropriate. External assessors are appointed by CCETSW on the basis of open competition, to play 'an essential role in quality assuring competence by confirming that students who have gone through a DipSW programme's assessment processes have achieved the required standard' (CCETSW 1995b, p.6). They confirm to students, employers, programmes and CCETSW that the results of assessment are 'valid…reliable…and comparable' (CCETSW 1995b, p.6).

Usually two external assessors are appointed to a programme and programmes are advised by CCETSW to appoint an external assessor who is experienced in practice and one who is experienced in teaching. Though CCETSW and, more recently, the Quality Assurance Agency for Higher

Education (QAA 2000) encourage institutions to seek appointments from those in practice, the majority of external assessors and examiners come from academic backgrounds, where the concept of external examining is the norm. QAA in their Code of Practice for external examination suggest encouraging 'staff both to prepare for and undertake external examining, as part of their continuing professional development' (QAA 2000, p.5). Yet assessors who come from practice often complain that their role is not validated as being a legitimate activity for the practitioner and thus relevant to the work of the agency. Encouraging and supporting external assessors from a practice background and also the small proportion of assessors from minority ethnic backgrounds should become one of the primary concerns of the new GSCC if there is to be a true commitment to external assessment and quality assurance.

The role of the external assessor within higher education could be described as being elusive, in particular from the perspective of a student. One could say that higher education has become a more democratic process in recent years. Students are expected to take a more active role in management and quality assurance of their educational experience with participation and representation at course, department, faculty and institutional levels. However, the process of assessment still remains clouded in secrecy under the guise of confidentiality, and many students do not have an understanding of the assessment process and in particular the role of the external assessor. The majority are unlikely to come into contact with an external assessor during the course of their studies. External assessors are sometimes invited (or themselves ask) to meet with a student group. However, from my own experience, I can suggest that the demands placed upon external assessors at times of assessment can result in the work and attention of the assessor being focused solely upon the tasks of reviewing student work and attending the assessment board itself.

As a Diploma in Social Work is awarded alongside an academic qualification, such as a DipHE, BA, BSc or MA, some external assessors may also hold an appointment with the university as an external examiner for the academic award. This requires that the external assessor relates to two different sets of requirements and regulations, one governed by the awarding body for the professional award and one in relation to the validating university. In its guidance to new external assessors, CCETSW warns against being in this position with the following statement:

> If you agree to become an external examiner for the university, in addition to being the CCETSW external assessor, you will be undertaking roles which may conflict where your responsibility will be both for the competence at the Diploma in Social Work level (for CCETSW) and for the standard/level of the University's award. In some instances, the student will achieve a 'pass' in the assessment work, but will be judged not to have fulfilled the items identified at 8.3 in the External Assessors' Manual. (CCETSW 1998, p.4)

The roles in acting as an external assessor for the professional programme and examiner for the academic award nonetheless overlap. They are both concerned with ensuring that the standards set are appropriate, the assessment processes are fair and that the standards and assessment processes for this programme are comparable with those found across institutions around the United Kingdom. This is done through consultations with teaching staff (and occasionally students) and reviewing documentation about module content, teaching methods, reading materials, assignment topics, examination questions, etc. Occasionally an external assessor may observe a class or attend course meetings as an observer, although (as stated earlier) pressures of time do not always permit this.

CCETSW assessors are required to 'verify the programme assessment practice by sampling students' work, assessing all work assessed to be marginal or failing, altering assessment decisions if necessary and certifying all assessment decisions' (CCETSW 1995b, p.9). Completed student work (e.g. formal written essays, case studies, examination scripts) is regularly sampled and reviewed before marks are finally agreed. The extent to which universities provide external examiners with the power to adjust marks set by course tutors or decisions about assessment is determined by the individual institution (QAA 2000: Section 4). A university may defer to the requirements of the professional body. Professional programmes will often include additional course regulations, for example in relation to the number of resubmission attempts and rules of condonement or compensation for marginal or failed work. However, this may not always be the case and external assessors should be aware of their different roles in relation to each body and their potential for conflict. External assessors should not be left alone to struggle with some of these issues, but require clarification and support from CCETSW (in future the GSCC), individual institutions and the QAA.

Ensuring the integration of theory and practice

External assessors are members of the programme's assessment board and should ensure that students who have been recommended for the award of DipSW have met the following requirements:

(i) met the practice requirements of the six core competences;

(ii) met the value requirements through evidence drawn from practice;

(iii) acquired a general understanding of the knowledge base for DipSW and developed and applied aspects of that knowledge in the context of their pathway through DipSW and their related practice learning opportunities;

(iv) demonstrated through formal assessment their understanding and application of law relating to social work;

(v) reflected upon and critically analysed their practice and transferred knowledge, skills and values in practice. (CCETSW 1995a, p.10)

External assessors are required to report annually to CCETSW that students who have been recommended for the award have satisfied these requirements. However, the requirements do not acknowledge the complexities involved in the education and training of social workers, some of which I have discussed earlier in this chapter. Relating theory to practice is not a simple or mechanistic process and is an area in which the most experienced practitioner may struggle. I would agree that there is no such thing as 'theoryless' practice (Coulshed and Orme 1998) and that theory and practice are often integrated with little conscious thought involved (Thompson 2000a). However, the requirements placed upon social workers demand that the relationship between theory and practice becomes more explicit and structured.

The knowledge base for social work is broad and programmes take different approaches to the teaching of some of the broader social science based subjects. For example, some programmes may teach sociology and social policy as separate and discrete subject areas, whereas others may integrate them within a social work module (Lyons 1999). Whatever the merits of the different approaches the challenge for programmes is to provide students with the understanding of key concepts, theories and perspectives in order that they can demonstrate awareness of the sociological and social political context of their practice and achieve professionalism in their work (Rashid 2000).

In order that students are able to meet the practice requirements, programmes need to ensure that students receive effective practice learning opportunities during their practice experience. It has long been accepted that there is a chronic and critical shortage of practice placements but the learning experiences during practice and the role of the practice teacher are crucial in ensuring the integration of theory and practice (CCETSW 1989a). Fisher and Somerton (2000, p.388) recognise this when they state that 'the responsibility for helping students to acquire and use relevant knowledge (including theory in practice) is as much that of the practice teacher as the academic'. They also recognise that some practice teachers, who lack recent educational experience themselves, lack confidence in their ability to facilitate this process. Practice teachers require their own professional development (Walker et al. 1995) either in the form of practice teaching accreditation or through other post-qualifying awards to equip them with more skills to analyse and reflect critically upon their own practice as well as facilitate this development for qualifying students.

It is now usual that practice teachers will be required to mark a practice-based assignment or case study jointly, as part of the student's assessment in integrating theory and practice. Practice teachers may be uncomfortable with this role, never having marked a piece of work (or doing so only on isolated occasions). For an external assessor it is important to identify what provision the programme has made to support practice teachers in this task. If the role of practice teachers in marking is to avoid being seen as tokenistic, it is essential that programmes offer practice teachers guidance and training on marking assignments.

The teaching of values on social work courses has proved controversial and represents some of the discourse surrounding anti-oppressive and antiracist perspectives and requirements within social work education (Penketh 2000). While there are some excellent and innovative approaches to the teaching of values, some students struggle not only with identifying their own personal and professional value base but also in examining this in the context of their own practice. For example, in relation to the first core value requirement ('identify and question their own values and prejudices and their implications for practice'), students may say that they have questioned their own values without exploring the significance of that questioning in relation to the role of social work and their relationship with service users. 'The job of social workers demands we base what we do upon values about the proper way for people to treat fellow citizens' (Parsloe 1996, p.120). *All* students will be unable to accomplish that unless they move beyond internal awareness of what their values, assumptions and prejudices may be to appreciate just how they affect day-to-day tasks students perform at a practical level and their reading at an academic level.

Black students, by virtue of being in a minority in British culture, commonly find themselves in situations which raise their awareness of difference and how people's beliefs, assumptions and prejudices impact in day-to-day life. In this they may be more sensitised than white students in identifying racial discrimination and questioning their response to this. It thus becomes crucially important that white students develop skills at self-questioning about values and prejudices since, as a part of the dominant majority group within Britain, they are less likely to frequently experience situations which raise their awareness, unless they consciously seek them out.

In practice-based assignments and reflective diaries or learning logs it is more common for Black students to reveal their ethnic identity than their white counterparts. This may be a factor of their minority/oppressed position within British culture (Dominelli 1997). White students may thus deal with value issues and anti-discriminatory practice on a less subjective (intuitive/personal) basis. Concerns should be raised about them over-intellectualising these issues or failing to appreciate the emotional base to self-reflection about values, prejudice and anti-discriminatory awareness. It is important that assignments and other assessments clarify the programme's expectations in respect of this, so as to not disadvantage Black students and to encourage more fully critical self-examination by white students. 'White...students and practitioners need to question their internalised, Eurocentric values [while] Black students...need to consolidate a positive sense of identity' (de Gale 1991, p.107). External assessors need to see this evidenced through practice-based assignments, such as the integrated study or case analysis, just as much as through more academic college/university-based work.

CCETSW states 'that it is the clear, consistent and thoughtful integration of values in practice that students must demonstrate and programme providers seek evidence in all assessable work' (CCETSW 1995a, p.18). Thus external assessors need to be satisfied that values are sufficiently integrated within all assessable work and that this is reflected within the assessment criteria. As values should be evidenced in the context of a student's practice, both practice-based assessments and practice teacher reports should provide clear and consistent evidence of all of the value requirements. Good self-reflection and critical self-awareness by students about their practice and developing professional competence should facilitate this; good self-reflection includes an appreciation of how values have impacted on work. Thus a social work student who demonstrates 'permanently reflexive practice' (Husband 1995, p.100) is evidencing how core social work values and anti-discriminatory awareness and antiracism have permeated their work.

Requirements that students demonstrate their understanding of law and its application to practice have proved challenging for programme providers. Some DipSW programmes approach the teaching of law in a more generic way in the first year and as specialist subjects in the second year. Hoad (1998) cites research to state that students and practice teachers feel that students are not always adequately prepared in law before they go into placement and that some of the legal theory as taught in college or university is not sufficiently related to practice. She recognises that there are different perceptions within college and within practice regarding the approaching to teaching of law and that attempts should be made by both tutors and practice teachers to integrate the teaching of law in college and in practice. The involvement of practitioners in the teaching of law in college may serve to remove some of the criticisms regarding the application of law teaching to practice. This could support the needs of students who are placed in the voluntary sector for placements, where there may be limited opportunities to demonstrate understanding of legal issues related to statutory responsibilities associated with local government agencies such as social service departments.

Summary and conclusion

Within this chapter I set out to discuss some of the issues that arise concerning external assessment in DipSW programmes and the requirements for qualifying social workers to demonstrate the integration of theory and practice. Thompson (2000a) has discussed the particular ways in which students can be encouraged to strengthen the relationship between theory and practice, for example through the use of critical incident approaches, learning sets, reflective journals, practice base assignments and direct observation. Some of these I have referred to in the context of the teaching, learning and assessment that occur on qualifying courses. The present DipSW articulates a clear expectation that theoretical perspectives should be integrated and reflected within practice. I have suggested that some of the difficulties that arise for educators, practitioners, students and external assessors lie within the complexity of the task in hand (given the extensive knowledge that qualifying social workers are expected to acquire), the present structure of courses, and the availability of effective practice learning opportunities. To help qualifying social workers to become analytical and reflective practitioners, this expectation about joining theory with practice through reflection must be held firmly as a fundamental philosophy (Moon 1999a) about teaching, learning and assessment for social work education and training.

Thus the integration of theory and practice requires that programmes adopt a holistic approach to the education and training of social workers. The involvement of practice teachers and students is essential to this process. It represents a challenge given the present structures in higher education and movement towards increased flexibility with Accreditation of Prior Learning (and Experiential Learning) systems and modular-based learning. The present shortage of qualified social workers will in all likelihood result in the development of more fast-track routes to qualification. These developments may be necessary but run the risk that they could compromise the quality of the educational and learning experiences of students. Expediency in meeting the demands of the social care workforce need to be balanced against the standards set for qualifying social workers. Meeting those demands cannot be achieved without the integration of theory and practice in educational programmes. The integrated assignment, which demands high quality self-reflection and self-evaluation about how a student has developed as a professional and used theory and values in his/her own work, is an essential component of this.

CHAPTER THIRTEEN

Conclusion – Or 'The Proof of the Pudding...'

This book was written to provide some support to students completing integrated theory-and-practice assignments while on their practice placements. Students sometimes comment that they can feel isolated from colleges and universities when completing these kinds of assignments and confused about what is really needed. Because they have relatively little contact with academic institutions they felt the need for written guidance they could take with them onto placement – hence this book. Students have not been alone in recognising the gap in available guidance. Practice teachers who watch students struggle with these assignments (and who often co-mark assignments along with academic tutors) have also sometimes felt at a loss about how to support students appropriately and help to guide their studies in the right direction.

The integrated assignment is sometimes the longest assignment completed by students on the DipSW and, depending on how a course is structured, it can carry the highest weight of academic credits of any assignment. It requires the student to write a complex, highly analytical essay which integrates both academic theory (research, policy, etc.) and the student's own practice. This takes time and a lot of hard work.

All the stages of work needed to complete an integrated assignment have been discussed in this book. Ideally preparation starts long before students go out on the placement or even think about writing an integrated assignment. Preparation involves students developing analytical thinking skills and some of the preparation for this needs to take place in the classroom months before a practice placement is arranged. Teaching exercises have been discussed in Chapter 2. These exercises support students to learn analytical and reflective skills at relating theory and policy to practice and evaluating their own work.

Once students are on placement they need to devise a topic which will provide a focus for their integrated assignment. This involves identifying the specific pieces of their own practice they will use in the essay and identifying for themselves a theoretical framework, theme or question which they intend to analyse. This is a very important stage since it guides the reading, background research and information gathering which the student will do while on placement. It also helps to make the topic more manageable – a quite important point since students sometimes choose topics which provide the basis for a PhD; steps that should help a student to develop a sufficiently complex yet manageable topic have been discussed in Chapter 3.

By the time students reach their final year and are asked to produce an integrated assignment, most will have developed good study skills. Nonetheless the unique theory-to-practice focus of the integrated assignment, coupled with the pressures of being on placement and managing the personal commitments which are part of a mature student's life, can mean students feel deskilled. They worry about how to find appropriate reading material, how to gather evidence about their practice, organise their time for reading, absorb all the ideas they read about, etc. Thus Chapter 5 focused on providing help with the process of reading and research, so that students can understand the scope of this.

Integrated theory-to-practice assignments require quite a good degree of analysis if they are to be successful. Students are often better at talking about how they used policy, ethics, legislation etc. in their work than they are at writing about this. They stumble at written analysis. These difficulties are related to two main issues:

- not understanding what is meant by 'theory-to-practice', 'ethics-to-practice', 'policy-to-practice', etc.

- not understanding how to write critically in the ways that are demanded in an academic essay.

Understanding the purposes behind theory-to-practice analysis usually helps students to write decent analysis. Some time has been spent discussing this in Chapters 6 to 9. Following this, each chapter discusses the standard of work and types of analyses which are demanded in an integrated assignment. Examples have been given of good analysis drawn from previous students' work; they reflect the range of types of placements students might have on a qualifying social work programme.

Chapter 10 provides guidance to students about what writing skills are involved with analytical essays. Often students have done good background research and have gathered a lot of practice examples. However, they are stymied by the process of getting thoughts and information down on paper. Suggestions for how to organise material and get started writing have been discussed. In addition, Chapter 10 includes guidance on the standard of writing and referencing needed in an analytical essay, and on the difference between 'description' and 'argument and analysis'. The key to writing a superb essay is revision through second, third and fourth drafts. Suggestions for revision have been included as well as a reminder to students about the kinds of things markers look for when assessing essays.

Students are not expected to complete integrated assignments without any guidance whatsoever. Tutors and practice teachers have their own parts to play in supporting the research and writing process. Tutors' support of students will, of course, have predated the start of the integrated assignment, since they will have been the personal tutor and/or taught the student throughout the course. However, the practice teacher's involvement begins from the point where the student starts the placement and starts to choose a topic. The mentoring role of the practice teacher is discussed in Chapter 4. This chapter also discussed how students can use tutorials effectively so that they obtain the kind of help they really need.

Two former students from the Norfolk Diploma in Social Work course, now fully qualified practitioners, contributed Chapter 11, which discusses the student's perspective. They look at the entire process of writing an integrated assignment and discuss frankly the pressures this can create and how to meet these pressures in positive ways that support the development of a good assignment. Stress management and fear of failure are also discussed.

By the end of qualifying training, most students are aware that external assessors' opinions can carry a lot of weight. They know that although their papers are carefully considered by tutors and practice teachers, any provisional mark received might be changed through the moderating and examination board process. They may have read the course regulations or guidance in the student handbook about the role of the external assessor. However, most students never meet an external assessor, and they may find the quality assurance process confusing. Chapter 12 attempts to demystify this process, so that students can understand, from an external assessor, what this role entails and how it affects them as individuals.

We believe that the guidance in this book helps students to pass by ensuring they have sufficient warning about the academic rigour and complexity of analysis so that they are able to seek appropriate levels of support and organise their time in ways which allow good quality study. However, our opinions as tutors may be wrong. The real 'proof of the pudding is in the eating'. We decided to ask students *their* opinions about whether or not this kind of advice was helpful.

Evaluation of guidance booklet

On 17 November 2000 the first cohort of DipSW students to receive a guidance booklet of this type were asked to evaluate its helpfulness. Specifically they were asked: 'Please tell us your views on the strengths and weaknesses of the Guide to the Integrative Assignment (the "Blue Book")' (this was the short name given by students to the guidance booklet, a name based on the bright blue cover we chose which easily distinguished it from the student handbook). Working in small groups they wrote the following comments.

Strengths identified by students

- Generally very good.
- Easy to read.
- Step-by-step guidance – very clear.
- Handy for continual reference – dip in and out.

- It was very helpful to be advised about the 'words' to use (i.e. examine, explore, etc.).

- In particular, examples of titles, etc. helpful.

- Answers any questions clearly.

- Good structure to follow.

- Overall we felt the 'Blue Book' was a good thing!

Weaknesses identified by students

- Very long.

- Too wordy.

Suggestions for improvement made by students

- Examples that are given have too much bias to childcare.

  Amendments have been made to examples in this book and more have been added to correct this imbalance. Examples of good practice have been drawn from the work of students who achieved marks of 2:1 or better and reflect the range of types of practice these students were involved with on placement.

- It would be helpful if there were more information and guidance about how to deal with changes and adaptations as we go along.

  This is difficult since changes and adaptations can be highly individual and alter from assignment to assignment. Concern sometimes arises because of the different perceptions between students of what is a major change and what is minor. One of the difficulties in providing general guidance of this kind is that it is not the most useful way of dealing with this issue. However, one of the appendices includes an example of a pre-liminary plan which the student subsequently changed when completing the assignment. Despite the change the student nonetheless found the plan helpful in completing the assign-ment, which substantially addressed the same practice issues, even though the focus of work had changed somewhat.

- Should be given out earlier to give you time to digest.

- It would be helpful if it was stressed *very* strongly to read and absorb the 'Blue Book' at the beginning of placement – tell the next group we said this!

- As a learning tool could be used for all Year 2 assignments and for the transitional period from Year 1 to Year 2.

- Would be useful at beginning of course to use for all assignments (or beginning of Year 2).

- Perhaps a reduced guide would be useful at start of course, for all assignments.

Clearly, previous students who have used the original guidance booklet, from which this book developed, say it is very helpful.

Further evidence

However, further evidence of its usefulness was found through comparing the standards of student achievement from before and after the guidance.

Students on the Norfolk DipSW programme submit integrated assignments right at the end of their second year. The standard of work expected from students in assignments equates to a bachelor's level dissertation, even though the course is taught at DipHE level. The adjustment for DipHE level of study is made through the overall required length of the assignment (the integrated study required for BSc in Social Studies taught in the same centre is slightly longer). Every year a few students fail their first submissions of the social work integrated study. Typically these are academically weaker students, although occasionally academically very able students might fail because they seriously misunderstood the requirements of the assignment. The students who failed at the first round would usually pass the integrated assignment on resubmission, so they would eventually achieve the professional qualification. However, when they initially failed they would experience hurt and distress and often confusion and puzzlement about why they had failed a piece of work they had put more effort into than anything else done previously.

The guidance that the Norfolk DipSW provided to students up to 1999 consisted of two A4 sheets of paper. The student cohort due to complete the programme in December 1999 had been identified from very early in the first year as being an academically weaker group of students than usual. Within this group, as with all groups of students, there were some people who found academic learning reasonably easy. There were some who found they needed to work that much harder but could nonetheless pass assignments consistently with solidly good marks. And, inevitably, there were some who struggled to understand and achieve passing marks for assignments, although they got there in the end.

However, within this group, there was a larger than usual number of students who were struggling to get there in the end. These are the students who are most at risk of failing a long, complex analytical essay like an integrated assignment. In 1999, there was an unusually high number of failures – 38 per cent of the class, a marked contrast with the more usual 20–21 per cent from the two years previous to this. Following this, the course team revised the guidance provided to students, eventually producing a booklet (the 'Blue Book') for students and practice teachers to refer to while the placement was ongoing. The first cohort to receive this booklet completed their programme in December 2000.

Table 13.1 provides data about student achievement (marks) for their integrated assignments, comparing results from the previous three years with the results from 2000. Three significant findings have emerged:

Table 13.1 Range of marks achieved for integrative assignments by year (1997 to 2000)

(only achievements on first submissions reported)

Marks (%)	Classification	1997 (%)	1998 (%)	1999 (%)	2000 (%)
80 and over	High 1st (Master's level)	0	0	0	3 (14)
70–79	1st (DipHE–BSc level)	3 (13)	0	2 (8)	3 (14)
60–69	2:1	10 (41)	7 (35)	4 (17)	6 (27)
50–59	2:2	3 (13)	6 (30)	2 (8)	3 (14)
43–49	3rd	2 (8)	3 (15)	5 (21)	4 (18)
40–42	Pass (borderline)	1 (4)	0	2 (8)	1 (5)
39 and below	Fail	5* (21)	4* (20)	9** (38)	2* (9)
Total		24 (100)	20 (100)	24 (100)	22 (100)

* all passed on resubmission
** two failed on resubmission

1. The 'usual' failure rate for first attempts at the integrated assignment was 20–21 per cent (1997 and 1998). The student achievement for 2000 indicates the failure rate for first attempts at the integrated assignment was reduced to 9 per cent, a reduction of 12 per cent.

2. The best cohort achievement for the three years previous to 2000 occurred in 1997. In this year 21 per cent of assignments received marks in the low average to average range of 3rd to 2:2. However, in 2000, 32 per cent of assignments received marks in 'low average to average' range, an increase of 11 per cent.

> These two findings considered together are evidence that the revised guidance booklet provided significantly improved support for students who were struggling academically to pass.

3.   In 1997, 54 per cent of the assignments received marks in the 'top' range (i.e. 2:1 to 1st). The achievement of the 2000 cohort is similar in that 55 per cent of the assignments received marks in the top range of 2:1 to 1st. However, within that range, in 1997 13 per cent of student assignments achieved 1st, while in 2000 28 per cent of student assignments achieved 1st (more than double).

> This is evidence that the revised guidance booklet assisted academically more able students to stretch themselves so that they achieved extremely high marks. This was commented on by one external assessor for the programme, who said some of the work being submitted by students in 2000 was Master's degree quality.

Conclusion

Norwich City College students who successfully completed their integrated assignments in 2000 and passed the Diploma in Social Work returned to the college in January 2001 for a celebration luncheon. Anecdotally they told tutors that although they found the experience stressful at the time, they felt they had learned an enormous amount through doing their integrated assignments. They said they found the guidance helpful. They pointed out they benefited from a practical point of view because they understood what we meant by a good standard of work and how to achieve this. However, they also said they felt valued as students through the way the advice had been written and by the fact it was so detailed and acknowledged the way they might feel at the different stages of assignment preparation. This supported them emotionally when they had limited contact with college tutors.

The first class who received the guidance made very positive comments when asked formally to evaluate it. This class also achieved unprecedented high marks as a cohort. We have presented evidence about student achievement at Norwich City College over the past four years. This supports our impression that teaching exercises designed to help students learn and practise analytical theory-to-practice skills before they start their final placements plus clear written guidance about what quality of work is needed and how to achieve this are helpful to all students.

Students said they wished they had had this guidance earlier and that it was more widely available. This struck a chord with us – we remembered how we had wished for this kind of guidance when we were completing our CQSWs all those years ago. We have therefore written this book to help all students completing theory-to-practice types of assignments. It is not a panacea for all ills; it does not substitute for sheer hard work. However, we believe that it can help students to focus their hard work more efficiently and effectively so that they have a better chance of passing. At the same time, we hope that this guidance will also support the enhancement of standards – both academic and professional. We believe that an integrated approach to social work education and practice will also help practitioners to provide services that are ethical and empowering and that facilitate the continued development of social work as a profession.

An Example of a Preliminary Plan

Title

Using task-centred intervention to promote empowerment and user involvement with homeless young people during their transition towards independent living.

Introduction

I am currently based in the Community Support Team (CST). My practice is based around young people (age 15 to 21) who are leaving the care of the local authority or who are homeless, or at risk of becoming so. My practice will involve assessing circumstances and abilities of young people with the view to offering suitable accommodation, attending planning meetings to promote the move towards independent living, and possibly some family work with those requesting support to prevent relationship breakdown.

I have decided to look at the differences in service, opportunities and levels of intervention offered to young people presently looked after compared to those not previously known to social services but who self-refer as homeless. Two cases I have been allocated include:

- a 17-year-old female who asked for help due to her mother's continuing mental health issues. There is a history of being looked after for short periods, but relationships have totally broken down and the young person wants to live independently.

- a 17-year-old male with severe hearing and speech impairments, with communication only possible through an interpreter. He has a history of family abuse and has also asked for help to find independent accommodation.

I plan to compare my interventions with these two cases to those of young people of 15 who are approaching leaving care and need help planning their future pathways.

The CST work closely with other agencies, both statutory, voluntary and charities, in their attempt to provide appropriate services for young people identified under Section 17 of the Children Act 1989 as being 'in need'. I will be analysing my work in relation to task-centred practice, empowerment and user involvement, and to enable this I have identified the following areas of practice as essential in my overall task.

Practice issues

How effective was my task-centred intervention in empowering homeless young people I worked with?

The key to successful planning toward independent living is small, clearly achievable goals which can introduce and build on success, a classic task-centred approach. But how effective is it with sometimes resistant young people? To answer this fully I will be looking at my communications skills with young people and how I build trusting relationships and negotiate contracts to set the wheels of empowerment in motion.

Analyse how I used relevant legislation to encourage user involvement of the individuals I was involved with

Most practitioners talk about user choice and involvement, but how realistic is this in a world of time management and budget constraints? The government has recently produced a document *Me Survive Out There?* which sets out major changes in approach with young people when leaving care at 16. I will be looking at how far my practice is going to be concerned with balancing rights and reality, relating this to issues of care, control, legislation and resources.

Examine how my role within multi-agency work promoted a task-centred model of intervention for young people moving towards independent living

As a member of CST I will be working in partnership with various agencies to provide suitable accommodation and follow up services. Approaches and resources may vary, with different agencies providing short-term answers before moving on. I will examine how far I was able to provide a holistic service, or whether there are gaps in services and resources.

To what extent did the assessment framework enable me to promote empowerment and user involvement when interviewing vulnerable young people?

Much of my practice will centre on assessment of care leavers in relation to their needs and required support levels during their transition into adulthood. There are set guidelines for referral procedures and reviewing. The Children (Leaving Care) Bill introduced 1999/2000 will also have an impact on this process.

Examine my practice in relation to ethical and anti-discriminatory issues throughout my task-centred approach with homeless young people

Much guidance has been written regarding anti-discriminatory policies and procedures. Ethical, effectiveness, efficiency and user-satisfaction arguments suggest practitioners respect and involve users' views as much as possible. I will be looking at how this affects my practice, my awareness of difference and the implications for user involvement of homeless young people.

Specific areas of college-based study
Legislation

CST involves working with the Children Act 1989, specifically Sec. 17 (children in need), Sec. 20 (accommodation), Sec. 24 (after care).

Psychology

Many looked after or homeless young people will have experienced family breakdown. I will be looking at theories of child development, attachment, loss and separation in relationships.

Sociology

Some young people can be hard to place and may be referred from the youth courts for offences such as theft, auto theft, harassment and substance abuse. In this case I would be looking at sociological theories regarding youth offending and deviant behaviour.

Assessment and planning intervention

Using the assessment framework I will be analysing theories of assessment (e.g. Smale *et al.* 1993) in relation to empowerment, user involvement and homelessness.

Care, control and accountability

Throughout social work intervention there are issues of power. I will be aware of these situations and identify anti-discriminatory practice as a possibility and an area that may need addressing.

Social work theory

Although I envisage most of my work to be task centred, referrals that come through when I am duty worker may well initially require crisis intervention.

Ethics and values

Looked after young people can be oppressed because of gender, sexuality, ethnicity, etc. I will reflect, recognise and use my own value base to try to ensure individuals and groups are not discriminated against.

Communication and engagement

Before I can assess a young person I need to be able to engage them and communicate with them, so I will be looking at theories and methods of communicating with young people. I am also aware that not all people will communicate verbally and English may not be their first language.

Mental health

Issues around how the mental health problems of parents can affect the young person's home life and lead to family breakdown.

Methods of inquiry

- Material from City College Library, University of East Anglia (UEA) Library and inter-library loans.

- Internet – specifically Joseph Rowntree Foundation, Barnardo's and National Children's Bureau.

- Social services intranet.

- Handouts and class notes from college modules.

- Networking within the service will also present opportunities to ask advice and opinions from other practitioners.

- In-house training.

- Local charities and specialist groups that provide information and support to homeless young people.

People involved and their roles

- Practice teacher.

- Line manager.

- Team members.

- College tutor.

Preliminary literature search

Alderson, P. (2000) *Young Children's Rights: Exploring Beliefs, Principles and Practice.* London: Jessica Kingsley.

Beresford, P. and Croft, S. (1993) *Citizen Involvement: A Practical Guide for Change.* London: Macmillan.

Broad, B. (1998) *Young People Leaving Care: Life after the Children Act 1989.* London: Jessica Kingsley.

Department of Health (1999) *Me Survive Out There? New Arrangements for Young People Leaving Care.* London: Stationery Office.

Department of Health (2000a) *Assessing Children in Need and their Families.* London: Stationery Office.

Department of Health, Department for Education and Employment and Home Office (2000) *Framework for the Assessment of Children in Need and their Families.* London: Stationery Office.

Doel, M. and Marsh, P. (1992) *Task-Centred Social Work.* Aldershot: Ashgate.

Holmes, J. (1993) *John Bowlby and Attachment Theory.* London: Routledge.

Lynes, D. and Goddard, J. (1995) *The View from the Front: The User View of Child Care in Norfolk.* Norwich: Norfolk County Council Social Services Department.

Marsh, P. and Fisher, M. (1992) *Good Intentions: Partnership in Social Services.* York: Joseph Rowntree Foundation.

Sinclair, R., Garnett, L. and Berridge, D. (1995) *Social Work and Assessment with Adolescents.* London: National Children's Bureau.

Smale, G., Tuson, G., Biehal, N. and Marsh, P. (1993) *Empowerment, Assessment, Care Management and the Skilled Worker.* London: National Children's Bureau.

Stein, M. (1997) *What Works in Leaving Care?* Ilford: Barnardo's.

Stein, M., Rees, G. and Frost, N. (1994) *Running the Risk: Young People on the Streets of Britain Today.* London: Children's Society.

Vostanis, P. and Cumella, S. (eds) (1999) *Homeless Children: Problems and Needs.* London: Jessica Kingsley.

Note

In the final assignment the plan to compare social work with the two 17-year-old service users who were setting up independent living and a 15-year-old who was just at the stage of starting to plan for independence was abandoned. Instead the assignment concentrated on comparing social work with the two 17-year-old service users mentioned in the preliminary plan.

Another Example of a Preliminary Plan

Title

An analysis of the relevance of attachment theory to social work with children for whom the plan is permanence.

Introduction

I have been involved with the assessment and planning of work to prepare a 6-year-old girl for placement with adoptive parents. The main theoretical framework for this work is provided by Vera Fahlberg (1994) and the developing ideas around contemporary attachment theory by David Howe *et al.* (1999) and my integrated assignment will analyse the relevance of these theories and models in my practice.

Lorna (anonymised name) has been looked after by social services continuously for nearly three years and prior to this, she experienced varying levels of neglect and physical abuse by her mother. Numerous attempts have been made to reunify Lorna with her mother and a recent internal review concluded that Lorna has been subjected to unnecessary delay and should have been placed for adoption three years ago. Lorna has been with the same foster carer, Frances (anonymised name), since she was last accommodated in November 1997 and has developed a significant, although not necessarily secure, attachment to Frances.

Lorna is expressing the wish to remain permanently with Frances but this is not an option and the department is applying for a Care Order (Sec. 31, Children Act 1989) and a Freeing Order. The care plan is for Lorna to be placed with a new family for adoption and for her to have indirect contact with her mother. No family has, as yet, been identified.

My role in this case has been to assess Lorna's relationships with her foster carer and mother, to assess her needs in relation to identifying an adoptive family, and jointly to undertake direct work with Lorna to ensure she understands the plans for her and to prepare her for placement.

Practice issues

1. Analyse the importance of planning in preparing children for permanence.

2. Examine my choice of tools and methods in practice.

3. Examine the assessment of attachment in children unable to live with birth family.

4. Investigate how attachment theory relates to outcomes for children.

5. Analyse my promotion of opportunities for learning and development to enable the child to function and participate.

6. Analyse the issues of power and ethics in my interactions and interventions.

Specific areas of college-based study

Anti-discriminatory and antiracist practice is integral to my practice and will therefore be threaded throughout my assignment.

Sociological perspectives

These will be relevant when considering what a new 'family' will mean for Lorna.

Ethics and values

These underpin social work and are particularly pertinent when practice involves a fine balance between care and control. The plan for Lorna goes against her expressed wishes and power issues are therefore very evident in this intervention.

Communication and engagement

These theories are extremely relevant to work with children and attachment theory in particular. Much assessment of attachment is through observing and analysing the complex interactions, verbal and non-verbal, between adults and children.

Legislation

My work whilst on placement is very much tied in with statutory legislation – i.e. the Children Act 1989.

Introduction to research

I will identify pieces of research to inform my arguments and I will therefore be using the knowledge gained in order to be able to critically evaluate this research.

Child protection, children in need and social work practice

Clearly a knowledge and understanding of children's needs will be essential for me to undertake this work. I will need to critically examine my own practice, use of self and the impact of my involvement and interventions.

Communicating with children

As the main focus of the assignment will be the direct work with Lorna, this will be extremely relevant. During the work it will be necessary to reflect, evaluate and review the work according to Lorna's responses, emerging needs, wishes and feelings.

Care, control and accountability

These issues will be constantly coming into play in my work. In this case, it feels as if there is one chance to get it right. The level of success achieved in this piece of work will have a profound effect on Lorna's future and consequences will be far reaching. I am accountable in many ways and conflicting responsibilities which exist have to be balanced.

Assessment and planning

I will be critically evaluating my ongoing assessment of Lorna's needs and how these might best be met. My practice will involve working in partnership not only with Lorna's mother and carer, but also with other professionals both within social services and other organisations.

Methods of inquiry

The two main texts which I will use as a starting point for this assignment will be David Howe *et al.* (1999) *Attachment Theory, Child Maltreatment and Family Support* and Vera Fahlberg (1994) *A Child's Journey through Placement*. Both these books have substantial bibliographies which I can draw on. I have established that my practice teacher and other colleagues have a number of texts which may be useful. One of my colleagues is able to access texts at UEA on my behalf. I have reserved a number of books from my local library and will also use the college library, including the inter-library loan facility as appropriate. I have daily access to the Internet and plan to use this to access Department of Health materials pertinent to my practice in this case. I will also be looking for relevant articles in *Community Care, Professional Social Work* and *Child and Family Social Work*.

People involved and their roles

I will make full use of supervision with my practice teacher and the case supervisor in order to reflect upon the use of attachment theory in practice and relating my practice to theory. In addition, I will draw upon the experience of others as appropriate. It may also be appropriate to share with the service users the relevance of attachment theory to my involvement. Once back at college, I will seek guidance from the most appropriate tutor to check that I am working in the right direction. It may also be that tutors or other students will have texts they can recommend or lend me to further assist my study.

Preliminary literature search

Bee, H. (1995) *The Developing Child.* New York: HarperCollins.

Bowlby, J. (1984) 'The Making and Breaking of Affectional Bonds.' In British Agencies for Adoption and Fostering (BAAF) (eds) *Working with Children.* London: BAAF.

Bowlby, J. (1988) *A Secure Base.* London: Routledge.

Bretherton, I. (1985) 'Attachment Theory: Retrospect and Prospect.' In I. Bretherton and E. Walters (eds) *Growing Points of Attachment Theory and Research*, Monographs of the Society for Research in Child Development Serial 209, vol. 50, pp. 3–35.

Butler, I. and Roberts, G. (1997) *Social Work with Children and Families: Getting into Practice.* London: Jessica Kingsley.

Davie, R., Upton, G. and Varma, V. (eds) (1996) *The Voice of the Child: A Handbook for Professionals.* London: Falmer.

Department of Health (1989) *The Children Act 1989.* London: HMSO.

Department of Health (1990b) *The Care of Children: Principles and Practice in Regulations and Guidance.* London: HMSO.

Department of Health (1991b) *The Children Act 1989 – Guidance and Regulations, Volume 9: Adoption Issues.* London: HMSO.

Department of Health, Home Office and Department for Education and Employment (1999) *Working Together to Safeguard Children: A Guide to Inter-Agency Working to Safeguard and Promote the Welfare of Children.* London: Stationery Office.

Department of Health, Department for Education and Employment and Home Office (2000) *Framework for the Assessment of Children in Need and their Families.* London: Stationery Office.

Fahlberg, V. (1988) *Fitting the Pieces Together.* London: British Agencies for Adoption and Fostering.

Fahlberg, V. (1994) *A Child's Journey through Placement.* London: British Agencies for Adoption and Fostering.

Fonagy, P., Steele, M., Steele, H., Higgit, A. and Target, M. (1994) 'The Emmanuel Miller Memorial Lecture 1992: The Theory and Practice of Resilience.' *Journal of Child Psychology and Psychiatry 35*, 2, 231–257.

Fratter, J., Rowe, J., Sapsford, D. and Thoburn, J. (1991) *Permanent Family Placement: A Decade of Experience.* London: British Agencies for Adoption and Fostering.

Howe, D. (1995) *Attachment Theory for Social Work Practice.* London: Macmillan.

Howe, D. (ed) (1996a) *Attachment and Loss in Child and Family Social Work.* Aldershot: Ashgate.

Howe, D., Brandon, M., Hinings, D. and Schofield, G. (1999) *Attachment Theory, Child Maltreatment and Family Support: A Practice and Assessment Model.* London: Macmillan.

Iwaniec, D. (1995) *The Emotionally Abused and Neglected Child: Identification, Assessment and Intervention.* Chichester: Wiley.

Maluccio, A., Fein, E. and Olmstead, K. (1986) *Permanency Planning for Children: Concepts and Methods.* London: Tavistock.

Mullender, A. (ed) (1991) *Open Adoption: The Philosophy and the Practice.* London: British Agencies for Adoption and Fostering.

Rowe, J. and Lambert, L. (1973) *Children Who Wait: A Study of Children Needing Substitute Families.* London: Association of British Adoption Agencies.

Rutter, M. (1991) 'A Fresh Look at Maternal Deprivation.' In P. Bateson (ed) *The Development and Integration of Behaviour.* Cambridge: Cambridge University Press.

Bibliography

Abbott, A. (1988) *The System of the Professions*. London: Chicago University Press.

Abbott, P. and Meerabeau, L. (eds) (1998) *The Sociology of the Caring Professions*, 2nd edn. London: UCL Press.

Adams, R. (1998) *Quality Social Work*. London: Macmillan.

Adams, R., Dominelli, L. and Payne, M. (eds) (1998) *Social Work: Themes, issues and critical debates*. London: Macmillan.

Aguilera, D. (1998) *Crisis Intervention Theory and Methodology*, 8th edn. St. Louis, MO: Mosby.

Ahmad, B. (1990) *Black Perspectives in Social Work*. Birmingham: Venture Press.

Alcock, P. (1996) *Social Policy in Britain: Themes and issues*. London: Macmillan.

Alderson, P. (2000) *Young Children's Rights: Exploring beliefs, principles and practice*. London: Jessica Kingsley.

Aronfreed, J. (1968) *Conduct and Conscience: The socialization of internalized control over behaviour*. New York: Academic Press.

Atkinson, D. (1999) *Research into Practice: Advocacy – a review*. Brighton: Pavilion Publishing in association with Joseph Rowntree Foundation.

Banks, S. (1995) *Ethics and Values in Social Work*. London: Macmillan.

Banks, S. (2000) 'Social Work Values.' In C. Davies, L. Finlay and A. Bullman (eds) *Changing Practice in Health and Social Care*. London: Sage.

Barkatoolah, A. (1989) 'Some Critical Issues Related to Assessment and Accreditation of Adults' Prior Experiential Learning.' In S. Weil and I. McGill (eds) *Making Sense of Experiential Learning: Diversity in theory and practice*. Milton Keynes: Open University Press.

Barnett, R. (1977) *Higher Education: A critical business*. Buckingham: Society for the Research into Higher Education and Open University Press.

Beauchamp, T. and Childress, J. (1994) *Principles of Biomedical Ethics*, 4th edn. Oxford: Oxford University Press.

Beckett, S. (1999) 'Fostering Siblings Together.' In A. Wheal (ed) *The RHP Companion to Foster Care*. Lyme Regis: Russell House.

Bee, H. (1995) *The Developing Child*. New York: HarperCollins.

Beresford, P. and Croft, S. (1993) *Citizen Involvement: A practical guide for change.* London: Macmillan.

Berne, E. (1961) *Transactional Analysis in Psychotherapy: A systemic and social psychiatry.* New York: Grove.

Berridge, D. and Cleaver, H. (1987) *Foster Home Breakdown.* Oxford: Basil Blackwell.

Best, D. (1998) 'On the Experience of Keeping a Reflective Journal while Training.' In A. Ward and L. MacMahon (eds) *Intuition is Not Enough: Matching learning with practice in therapeutic child care.* London: Routledge.

Bines, H. and Watson, D. (1992) *Developing Professional Education.* Buckingham: Open University and Society for the Research in Higher Education.

Bloom, B. (1965) *Taxonomy and Educational Objective.* London: Longman.

Bornat, J., Johnson, J., Pereira, C., Pilgrim, D. and Williams, F. (eds) (1997) *Community Care: A reader.* London: Macmillan.

Boud, D., Keogh, R. and Walker, D. (1985) 'Promoting Reflection in Learning: A model.' In D. Boud, R. Keogh and D. Walker (eds) *Reflection: Turning experience into learning.* London: Kogan Page.

Bowlby, J. (1984) 'The Making and Breaking of Affectional Bonds.' In British Agencies for Adoption and Fostering (BAAF) (eds) *Working with children.* London: BAAF.

Bowlby, J. (1988) *A Secure Base.* London: Routledge.

Boyd, E. and Fales, A.N. (1983) 'Reflective Learning: Key to learning from experience.' *Journal of Humanistic Psychology 23,* 2, 99–117.

Brandon, D., Brandon, A. and Brandon, T. (1995) *Advocacy: Power to people with disabilities.* Birmingham: Venture Press.

Braye, S. and Preston-Shoot, M. (1995) *Empowering Practice in Social Care.* Buckingham: Open University Press.

Braye, S. and Preston-Shoot, M. (1997) *Practising Social Work Law.* London: Macmillan.

Brayne, H. and Martin, G. (1995) *Law for Social Workers,* 4th edn. London: Blackstone Press.

Brechin, A., Brown, H. and Eby, M. (eds) (2000) *Critical Practice in Health and Social Care.* London: Sage.

Bretherton, I. (1985) 'Attachment Theory: Retrospect and prospect.' In I. Bretherton and E. Walters (eds) *Growing Points of Attachment Theory and Research,* Monographs of the Society for Research in Child Development Serial 209, vol. 50, pp. 3–35.

Bridge Child Care Consultancy Service (1995) *Paul: Death through neglect.* London: Bridge Child Care Consultancy Service.

British Agencies for Adoption and Fostering (BAAF) (2000) *Linking Children with Adoptive Parents.* London: BAAF.

British Association of Social Work (BASW) (1996) *A Code of Ethics for Social Work*. Birmingham: BASW.

Broad, B. (1998) *Young People Leaving Care: Life after the Children Act 1989*. London: Jessica Kingsley.

Butler, I. and Roberts, G. (1997) *Social Work with Children and Families: Getting into practice*. London: Jessica Kingsley.

Butrym, Z.T. (1976) *The Nature of Social Work*. London: Macmillan.

Carew, R. (1979) 'The Place of Knowledge in Social Work Activity.' *British Journal of Social Work 9*, 3, 349–364.

Carter, P., Jeffs, T. and Smith, M. (1995) 'Introduction: Thinking about practice in social work.' In P. Carter, T. Jeffs and M. Smith (eds) *Social Working*. London: Macmillan.

Central Council for Education and Training in Social Work (CCETSW) (1989a) *Improving Standards in Practice Learning*, Paper 26.3. London: CCETSW.

CCETSW (1989b) *Rules and Requirements for the Diploma in Social Work*, Paper 30. London: CCETSW.

CCETSW (1995a) *Assuring Quality in the Diploma in Social Work*. London: CCETSW.

CCETSW (1995b) *External Assessment of the Diploma in Social Work: A manual for external assessors*. London: CCETSW.

CCETSW (1996a) *Assuring Quality in the Diploma in Social Work – 1: Rules and Requirements for the DipSW*, 2nd revision. London: CCETSW.

CCETSW (1996b) *Assuring Quality in the Diploma in Social Work – 2: External Assessment of the Diploma in Social Work*. London: CCETSW.

CCETSW (1998) *Guidance for New External Assessors*. London: CCETSW.

Cigno, K. and Bourn, D. (eds) (1998) *Cognitive-Behavioural Social Work in Practice*. Aldershot: Arena.

Clark, C. (2000) *Social Work Ethics: Politics, principles and practice*. London: Macmillan.

Clay, J. (1996) *R.D. Laing: A divided self*. London: Hodder and Stoughton.

Cleaver, H., Unell, I. and Aldgate, J. (1999) *Children's Needs, Parenting Capacity: The impact of parental mental illness, problem alcohol and drug use and domestic violence on children's development*. London: Stationery Office.

Coles, B. (1995) *Youth and Social Policy*. London: UCL Press.

Corcoran, J. (2000) *Evidence-Based Social Work Practice with Families: A lifespan approach*. New York: Springer.

Cosis Brown, H. (1995) 'The Knowledge Base of Social Work.' In P. Carter, T. Jeffs and M. Smith (eds) *Social Working*. London: Macmillan.

Coulshed, V. (1991) *Social Work Practice*. Basingstoke: Macmillan.

Coulshed, V. and Orme, J. (1998) *Social Work Practice: An introduction*, 3rd edn. London: Macmillan.

Cowen, H. (1999) *Community Care Ideology and Social Policy.* London: Prentice-Hall.

Cree, V. and Davidson, R. (1999) 'Enquiry and Action Learning: A model for transferring learning.' In V. Cree and C. Macauley (eds) *Transfer of Learning in Professional and Vocational Education.* London: Routledge.

Cree, V. and Macauley, C. (eds) (1999) *Transfer of Learning in Professional and Vocational Education.* London: Routledge.

Creme, P. and Lea, M. (1997) *Writing at University: A guide for students.* Buckingham: Open University Press.

Cull, L. and Roche, J. (2001) 'Law and Social Work – Working Together?' In L. Cull and J. Roche (eds) *The Law and Social Work: Contemporary issues for practice.* Basingstoke: Palgrave.

Curzon, L.B. (1985) *Teaching in Further Education: An outline of principles and practice,* 3rd edn. London: Holt Rinehart and Winston.

Dalrymple, J. and Burke, B. (1995) *Anti-Oppressive Practice: Social care and the law.* Buckingham: Open University Press.

Daniel, B., Wassell, S. and Gilligan, R. (1999) *Child Development for Child Care and Protection Workers.* London: Jessica Kingsley.

Davie, R., Upton, G. and Varma, V. (eds) (1996) *The Voice of the Child: A handbook for professionals.* London: Falmer.

Davies, C. (2000) 'Understanding the Policy Process.' In A. Brechin, H. Brown and M. Eby (eds) *Critical Practice in Health and Social Care.* London: Sage.

Davies, C., Finlay, L. and Bullman, A. (eds) (2000) *Changing Practice in Health and Social Care.* London: Sage.

Davies, M. (ed) (1994) *The Sociology of Social Work.* London: Routledge.

Davies, M. (ed) (1997) *The Blackwell Companion to Social Work.* Oxford: Blackwell.

de Gale, H. (1991) 'Black Students' Views of Existing CQSW Courses and CSS Schemes – 2.' In Northern Curriculum Development Project, *Anti-Racist Social Work Education: Setting the context for change.* Leeds: Central Council for Education and Training in Social Work.

Demaine, J. (ed) (1999) *Education Policy and Contemporary Politics.* London: Macmillan.

de Montigny, G. (1995) *Social Working: An ethnography of front-line practice.* Toronto: University of Toronto Press.

Department of Health (1989) *The Children Act 1989.* London: HMSO.

Department of Health (1990a) *Care Programme Approach for People with a Mental Illness,* HC(90)23/LASSL(90)11. London: HMSO.

Department of Health (1990b) *The Care of Children: Principles and practice in regulations and guidance.* London: HMSO.

Department of Health (1991a) *Purchase of Service.* London: HMSO.

Department of Health (1991b) *The Children Act 1989 – Guidance and Regulations, Volume 9: Adoption issues.* London: HMSO.

Department of Health (1995) *Building Bridges: A guide to arrangements for inter-agency working for the care and protection of severely mentally ill people.* London: HMSO.

Department of Health (1997) *Community Care (Direct Payments) Act, 1996: Policy and practice guidance.* London: Stationery Office.

Department of Health (1998) *Modernising Social Services* (White Paper). London: Department of Health.

Department of Health (1999) *Me Survive Out There? New Arrangements for Young People Leaving Care.* London: Stationery Office.

Department of Health (2000a) *Assessing Children in Need and their Families.* London: Stationery Office.

Department of Health (2000b) *No Secrets.* London: Department of Health.

Department of Health (2000c) *Care Standards Act 2000.* London: Stationery Office.

Department of Health, Home office and DfEE (1999) *Working Together to Safeguard Children: A guide to inter-agency working to safeguard and promote the welfare of children.* London: Stationery Office.

Department of Health, Home Office (2000) *Framework for the Assessment of Children in Need and their Families.* London: Stationery Office.

Derezotes, D. (2000) *Advanced Generalist Social Work Practice.* Thousand Oaks, CA: Sage.

Dewey, J. (1933) *How We Think.* Boston, MA: D.C. Heath.

Dewey, J. (1997) *How We Think.* Mineola, NY: Dover (originally published 1910 by D.C Heath, Boston, MA).

Dingwall, R. (1979) *The Social Organization of Health Visiting.* Beckenham: Croom Helm.

Doel, M. (1996) 'Task Centred Work.' In R. Adams, L. Dominelli and M. Payne (eds) *Social Work Themes, Issues and Critical Debates.* London: Macmillan.

Doel, M. and Marsh, P. (1992) *Task-Centred Social Work.* Aldershot: Ashgate.

Dominelli, L. (1989) 'An Uncaring Profession? An Examination of Racism in Social Work.' *New Community 15*, 3, 391–403.

Dominelli, L. (1997) *Anti-Racist Social Work*, 2nd edn. London: Macmillan.

Donnison, D. (1994) 'By What Authority? Ethics and Policy Analysis.' *Social Policy and Administration 28*, 1, 20–32.

Durkin, K. (1995) *Developmental Social Psychology: From infancy to old age.* Oxford: Blackwell.

Dwivedi, K.N. (1996) 'Race and the Child's Perspective.' In R. Davie, G. Upton and V. Varma (eds) *The Voice of the Child: A handbook for professionals.* London: Falmer.

Eby, M. (2000a) 'Understanding Professional Development.' In A. Brechin, H. Brown and M. Eby (eds) *Critical Practice in Health and Social Care.* London: Sage.

Eby, M. (2000b) 'The Challenge of Values and Ethics in Practice.' In A. Brechin, H. Brown and M. Eby (eds) *Critical Practice in Health and Social Care.* London: Sage and the Open University.

Eraut, M. (1994) *Developing Professional Knowledge and Competence.* London: Falmer.

Evans, D. (1999) *Practice Learning in the Caring Professions.* Aldershot: Ashgate.

Fahlberg, V. (1988) *Fitting the Pieces Together.* London: British Agencies for Adoption and Fostering.

Fahlberg, V. (1994) *A Child's Journey through Placement.* London: British Agencies for Adoption and Fostering.

Fairbairn, G. and Fairbairn, S. (2001) *Reading at University: A guide for students.* Buckingham: Open University Press.

Farmer, E. and Owen, M. (1995) *Child Protection Practice – Private Risks and Public Remedies: A study of decision making, intervention and outcome in child protection.* London: HMSO.

Feltham, C. and Dryden, W. (1994) *Developing Counsellor Supervision.* London: Sage.

Finlay, L. (2000) 'The Challenge of Working in Teams.' In A. Brechin, H. Brown and M. Eby (eds) *Critical Practice in Health and Social Care.* London: Sage and the Open University.

Fisher, T. and Somerton, J. (2000) 'Reflection on Action: The process of helping social work students to develop their use of theory in practice.' *Social Work Education 4*, August, 387–401.

Fonagy, P., Steele, M., Steele, H., Higgit, A. and Target, M. (1994) 'The Emmanuel Miller Memorial Lecture 1992: The theory and practice of resilience.' *Journal of Child Psychology and Psychiatry 35*, 2, 231–257.

Fook, J. (1993) *Radical Casework: A theory of practice.* London: Allen and Unwin.

Fook, J. (ed) (1996) *The Reflective Researcher: Social workers' theories of practice research.* Melbourne: Allen and Unwin.

Fortune, A. and Reid, W. (1999) *Research in Social Work,* 3rd edn. New York: Columbia University Press.

Fraser, D. (1984) *The Evolution of the British Welfare State,* 2nd edn. London: Macmillan.

Fratter, J., Rowe, J., Sapsford, D. and Thoburn, J. (1991) *Permanent Family Placement: A decade of experience.* London: British Agencies for Adoption and Fostering.

Fuller, R. and Petch, A. (1995) *Practitioner Research: The reflexive social worker.* Buckingham: Open University Press.

Garnham, A. and Knights, E. (1994) *Putting the Treasury First: The truth about child support.* London: Child Poverty Action Group.

Gibbs, G. (1988) *Learning by Doing: A guide to teaching and learning methods.* Oxford: Further Education Unity, Oxford Polytechnic.

Giddens, A. (1993) *Sociology,* 2nd edn. Cambridge: Polity.

Goffman, E. (1963) *Stigma: Notes on the management of spoiled identity.* Englewood Cliffs, NJ: Prentice-Hall.

Goffman, E. (1967) *Interaction Ritual.* Harmondsworth: Penguin.

Gould, N. and Taylor, I. (eds) (1996) *Reflective Learning for Social Work.* Aldershot: Arena.

Graham, H. (1997) 'Feminist Perspectives on Caring.' In J. Bornat, J. Johnson, C. Pereira, D. Pilgrim and F. Williams (eds) *Community care: A reader.* London: Macmillan.

Gross, R. (1996) *Psychology: The science of mind and behaviour.* London: Hodder and Stoughton.

Hanvey, C. and Philpot, T. (1994) *Practising Social Work.* London: Routledge.

Harding, L. (1997) *Perspectives in Child Care Policy,* 2nd edn. London: Longman.

Hayden, P. (1999) *The Personal Success Pocketbook.* Alresford: Management Pocketbooks.

Hendry, L., Shucksmith, J., Love, J. and Glendinning, A. (1993) *Young People's Leisure and Lifestyles.* London: Routledge.

Hill, J. (1996) 'What Happens to Children when their Parents have Mental Health Problems.' In D. Gregory (ed) *Advanced Professional Practice with Children and Families.* Norwich: University of East Anglia.

Hill, M. (1996) *Social Policy: A comparative analysis.* London: Prentice-Hall.

Hinchliff, S. (ed) (1992) *The Practitioner as Teacher.* London: Scutari.

Hoad, P. (1998) 'Teaching Social Work Law to Students.' In H. Lawson (ed) *Practice Teaching: Changing social work.* London: Jessica Kingsley.

Holmes, J. (1993) *John Bowlby and Attachment Theory.* London: Routledge.

Horwath, J. and Morrison, T. (1999) *Effective Staff Training in Social Care: From theory to practice.* London: Routledge.

Howe, D. (1987) *An Introduction to Social Work Theory: Making sense in practice.* Aldershot: Ashgate.

Howe, D. (1995) *Attachment Theory for Social Work Practice.* London: Macmillan.

Howe, D. (ed) (1996a) *Attachment and Loss in Child and Family Social Work.* Aldershot: Ashgate.

Howe, D. (1996b) 'Relating Theory to Practice.' In M. Davies (ed) *The Blackwell Companion to Social Work.* Oxford: Blackwell.

Howe, D., Brandon, M., Hinings, D. and Schofield, G. (1999) *Attachment Theory, Child Maltreatment and Family Support: A practice and assessment model.* London: Macmillan.

Hugman, R. (1998a) 'Social Work and Deprofessionalization.' In P. Abbott and L. Meerabeau (eds) *The Sociology of the Caring Professions*, 2nd edn. London: UCL Press.

Hugman, R. (1998b) *Social Welfare and Social Value*. London: Macmillan.

Hugman, R. and Smith, D. (eds) (1995a) *Ethical Issues in Social Work*. London: Routledge.

Hugman, R. and Smith, D. (1995b) 'Ethical Issues in Social Work: An overview.' In R. Hugman and D. Smith (eds) *Ethical Issues in Social Work*. London: Routledge.

Hull, R. and Griffin, K. (eds) (1989) *Communication Disorders in Ageing*. London: Sage.

Human Rights Act (1998). London: Stationery Office.

Hunt, G. (ed) (1998) *Whistleblowing in the Social Services: Public accountability and professional practice*. London: Arnold.

Husband, C. (1995) 'The Morally Active Practitioner and the Ethics of Anti-Racist Social Work.' In R. Hugman and D. Smith (eds) *Ethical Issues in Social Work*. London: Routledge.

Huxley, P. (1994) 'The Sociology of Size in Residential Care.' In M. Davies (ed) *The Sociology of Social Work*. London: Routledge.

Inglehart, A. (1995) 'Adolescents in Foster Care: Predicting readiness for independent living.' *Children and Youth Services Review 16*, 314, 159–169.

Iwaniec, D. (1995) *The Emotionally Abused and Neglected Child: Identification, assessment and intervention*. Chichester: Wiley.

James, C.R. and Clarke, B.A. (1994) 'Reflective Practice in Nursing: Issues and implications for nursing education.' *Nurse Education Today 14*, 82–90.

Jarvinen, A. (1989) 'Experiential Learning and Professional Development.' In S. Weil and I. McGill (eds) *Making Sense of Experiential Learning: Diversity in theory and practice*. Milton Keynes: Open University Press.

Jarvis, P. (1992) 'Reflective Practice in Nursing.' *Nurse Education Today 12*, 174–181.

Jarvis, P. (1995) *Adult and Continuing Education Theory and Practice*, 2nd edn. London: Routledge.

JM Consulting (1998) *Review of the Content of the Diploma in Social Work – Discussion Paper*. Bristol: JM Consulting.

JM Consulting (1999a) *Review of the Diploma in Social Work: Report on the content of the DipSW conducted as part of the stage two review of CCETSW*. Bristol: JM Consulting.

JM Consulting (1999b) *Review of the Delivery of the Diploma in Social Work*. Bristol: JM Consulting.

Jones, S. and Joss, R. (1995) 'Models of Professionalism.' In M. Yelloly and M. Henkel (eds) *Learning and Teaching in Social Work: Towards reflective practice.* London: Jessica Kingsley.

Kadushin, A. (1976) *Supervision in Social Work.* New York: Columbia University Press.

Kohlberg, L. (1969) *Stages in the Development of Moral Thought and Action.* New York: Holt Rinehart and Winston.

Kolb, D. (1988a) 'The Process of Experiential Learning.' In D. Kolb (ed) *Experience as a Source of Learning and Development.* London: Prentice-Hall.

Kolb, D. (ed) (1988b) *Experience as a Source of Learning and Development.* London: Prentice-Hall.

Kolb, D. and Fry, R. (1975) 'Towards an Applied Theory of Experimental Learning.' In C.L. Cooper (ed) *Theories of Group Processes.* London: Wiley.

Kuhn, T. (1970) *The Structure of Scientific Revolutions,* 2nd edn. Chicago: University of Chicago Press.

Laing, R.D. (1965) *The Divided Self: An existential study in sanity and madness.* Harmondsworth: Pelican.

Langan, M. (1992) 'Introduction.' In M. Langan and L. Day, *Women, Oppression and Social Work: Issues in anti-discriminatory practice.* London: Routledge.

Langan, M. and Day, L. (1992) *Women, Oppression and Social Work: Issues in anti-discriminatory practice.* London: Routledge.

Langan, M. and Lee, P. (eds) (1989) *Radical Social Work Today.* London: Unwin.

Lazarus, R. (1999) *Stress and Emotion: A new synthesis.* London: Free Association Books.

Leadbetter, D. and Trewartha, R. (1996) *Handling Aggression and Violence at Work: A training manual.* Lyme Regis: Russell House Publishing.

LeGrand, J. (2000) 'Knights, Knaves or Pawns? Human behaviour and social policy.' In C. Davies, L. Finlay and A. Bullman (eds) *Changing Practice in Health and Social Care.* London: Sage.

Lesnik, B. (ed) (1998) *Countering Discrimination in Social Work.* Aldershot: Ashgate.

Lipsky, M. (1980) *Street-Level Bureaucracy: Dilemmas of the individual in public services.* New York: Russell Sage Foundation.

Lishman, J. (1991) 'Introduction.' In J. Lishman (ed) *Handbook of Theory for Practice Teachers in Social Work.* London: Jessica Kingsley.

Lister, P. (1999) 'Mature Students and Transfer of Learning.' In V. Cree and C. Macauley (eds) *Transfer of Learning in Professional and Vocational Education.* London: Routledge.

Lynes, D. and Goddard, J. (1995) *The View from the Front: The user view of child care in Norfolk.* Norwich: Norfolk County Council Social Services Department.

Lyons, K. (1999) *Social Work in Higher Education: Demise or development?* Aldershot: Ashgate.

MacDonald, K. (1995) *The Sociology of the Professions.* London: Sage.

MacDonald, S. (1989) *All Equal Under the Act?* London: Race Equality Unit.

MacIntyre, A. (1985) *After Virtue,* 2nd edn. London: Duckworth.

Maluccio, A., Fein, E. and Olmstead, K. (1986) *Permanency Planning for Children: Concepts and methods.* London: Tavistock.

Marsh, P. (1991) 'Task Centred Practice.' In J. Lishman (ed) *Handbook of Theory for Practice Teachers in Social Work.* London: Jessica Kingsley.

Marsh, P. and Fisher, M. (1992) *Good Intentions: Partnership in Social Services.* York: Joseph Rowntree Foundation.

Ministry of Health (1948) *National Assistance Act.* London: Ministry of Health.

McCurry, P. (2000) 'Adoption Campaign wins boost from research data' *Community Care 1343, October, 10–11.*

Moffatt, K. (1996) 'Teaching Social Work as a Reflective Process.' In N. Gould and I. Taylor (eds) *Reflective Learning for Social Work.* Aldershot: Arena.

Moon, J. (1999a) *Reflection in Learning and Professional Development: Theory and practice.* London: Kogan Page.

Moon, J. (1999b) *Learning Journals: A handbook for academics, students and professional development.* London: Kogan Page.

Morrison, A. (1996) 'Partnership and Collaboration: Rhetoric and reality.' *Child Abuse and Neglect 20,* 127–140.

Mullender, A. (ed) (1991) *Open Adoption: The philosophy and the practice.* London: British Agencies for Adoption and Fostering.

Nash, C. (2000) 'Applying Reflective Practice.' In C. Davies, L. Finlay and A. Bullman (eds) *Changing Practice in Health and Social Care.* London: Sage.

National Organisation for Practice Teaching (NOPT) (2000) *Code of Practice for Practice Teachers.* Stockport: NOPT.

Northern Curriculum Development Project (1991) *Anti-Racist Social Work Education: Setting the context for change.* Leeds: Central Council for Education and Training in Social Work.

O'Hagan, K. (2001) *Cultural Competence in the Caring Professions.* London: Jessica Kingsley.

Oliver, M. and Barnes, C. (1998) *Disabled People and Social Policy: From exclusion to inclusion.* London: Longman.

Oliver, M. and Sapey, B. (1999) *Social Work with Disabled People.* London: Macmillan.

O'Sullivan, T. (1999) *Decision-Making in Social Work.* London: Macmillan.

Ovretveit, J. (1993) *Co-ordinating Community Care: Multidisciplinary teams and care management.* Buckingham: Open University Press.

Parsloe, P. (1996) 'Managing for Reflective Learning.' In N. Gould and I. Taylor (eds) *Reflective Learning for Social Work*. Aldershot: Arena.

Pascall, G. (1986) *Social Policy: A feminist analysis*. London: Tavistock.

Payne, M. (1996) *What is Professional Social Work?* Birmingham: Venture Press.

Payne, M. (1997) *Modern Social Work Theory*, 2nd edn. London: Macmillan.

Penketh, L. (2000) *Tackling Institutional Racism*. Bristol: Policy Press.

Phillipson, J. (1992) *Practising Equality: Women, men and social work*. London: Central Council for Training and Education in Social Work.

Player, C. (1990) *Placement Needs, Resources and Improvements: Report*. Rugby: Central Council for Education and Training in Social Work.

Potier, M. (1993) 'Giving Evidence: Women's lives in Ashworth Maximum Security Psychiatric Hospital.' *Feminism and Psychology 3*, 3, 335–347.

Prince, K. (1996) *Boring Records?* London: Jessica Kingsley.

Pugh, R. (2000) *Rural Social Work*. Lyme Regis: Russell House.

Quality Assurance Agency for Higher Education (QAA) (2000) *Code of Practice for the Assurance of Academic Quality and Standards in Higher Education: Section 4 – External examining*. Gloucestershire: QAA.

Quinn, F.M. (2000) 'Reflection and Reflective Practice.' In C. Davies, L. Finlay and A. Bullman (eds) *Changing Practice in Health and Social Care*. London: Sage.

Rashid, S. (2000) 'Social Work and Professionalization: A legacy of ambivalence.' In C. Davies, L. Finlay and A. Bullman (eds) *Changing Practice in Health and Social Care*. London: Sage.

Redman, P. (2001) *Good Essay Writing: A social sciences guide*, 2nd edn. London: Sage.

Reid, W.J. and Shyne, A.W. (1969) *Breif and Extended Casework*. New York: Columbia University Press.

Rescher, N. (1969) *Introduction to Value Theory*. Englewood Cliffs, NJ: Prentice-Hall.

Richards, M. (1999) *The Stress Pocketbook*. Alresford: Management Pocketbooks.

Richards, S. (2000) 'Bridging the Assessment Divide: Elders and the assessment process.' *British Journal of Social Work 30*, 1, 37–49.

Rogers, C. (1951) *Client Centred Therapy*. London: Constable.

Rogers, C. (1980) *A Way of Being*. Boston, MA: Houghton Mifflin.

Rogers, C., Gendlin, E.T., Kiesler, D.J. and Truax, C.B. (1967) *The Therapeutic Relationship and its Impact: A study of psychotherapy with schizophrenics*. Madison, WI: University of Wisconsin Press.

Rowe, J. and Lambert, L. (1973) *Children Who Wait: A study of children needing substitute families*. London: Association of British Adoption Agencies.

Rowe, J., Hundleby, M. and Garnett, L. (1989) *Childcare Now: A survey of placement patterns*. London: British Agencies for Adoption and Fostering.

Rutter, M. (1991) 'A Fresh Look at Maternal Deprviation.' In P. Bateson (ed) *The Development and Integration of Behaviour.* Cambridge: Cambridge University Press.

Schon, D. (1983) *The Reflective Practitioner: How professionals think in action.* New York: Basic Books.

Schon, D. (1987) *Educating the Reflective Practitioner.* San Francisco, CA: Jossey Bass.

Seden, J. (1999) *Counselling Skills in Social Work Practice.* Buckingham: Open University Press.

Shardlow, S. (1998) 'Values, Ethics and Social Work.' In R. Adams, L. Dominelli and M. Payne (eds) *Social Work: Themes, issues and critical debates.* London: Macmillan.

Shaw, I. (1996) *Evaluating in Practice.* Arena: Aldershot.

Sheldon, B. (1995) *Cognitive-Behavioural Therapy: Research, practice and philosophy.* London: Routledge.

Sheppard, M. (1997) 'The Psychiatric Unit.' In M. Davies (ed) *The Blackwell Companion to Social Work.* Oxford: Blackwell.

Sinclair, R., Garnett, L. and Berridge, D. (1995) *Social Work and Assessment with Adolescents.* London: National Children's Bureau.

Slater, R. (1995) *The Psychology of Growing Old.* Buckingham: Open University Press.

Smail, D. (1993) *The Origins of Unhappiness.* London: Harper Collins.

Smale, G., Tuson, G., Biehal, N. and Marsh, P. (1993) *Empowerment, Assessment, Care Management and the Skilled Worker.* London: National Children's Bureau.

Smale, G., Tuson, G. and Statham, D. (2000) *Social Work and Social Problems.* London: Macmillan.

Social Service Inspectorate/Social Work Services Group (1991) *Care Management and Assessment: A practitioner's guide.* London: HMSO.

Stein, M. (1997) *What Works in Leaving Care?* Ilford: Barnardo's.

Stein, M., Rees, G. and Frost, N. (1994) *Running the Risk: Young people on the streets of Britain today.* London: Children's Society.

Stepney, P. (2000a) 'The Theory to Practice Debate Revisited.' In P. Stepney and D. Ford (eds) *Social Work Models, Methods and Theories: A framework for practice.* Lyme Regis: Russell House.

Stepney, P. (2000b) 'An Overview of the Wider Policy Context.' In P. Stepney and D. Ford (eds) *Social Work Models, Methods and Theories: A framework for practice.* Lyme Regis: Russell House.

Stepney, P. (2000c) 'Implications for Social Work in the New Millennium.' In P. Stepney and D. Ford (eds) *Social Work Models, Methods and Theories: A framework for practice.* Lyme Regis: Russell House.

Stepney, P. and Ford, D. (eds) (2000) *Social Work Models, Methods and Theories: A framework for practice.* Lyme Regis: Russell House.

Strathclyde Social Work Department (1988) 'Temporary Fostering.' Unpublished research paper.

Tait, M. (1999) 'Using a Reflective Diary in Student Supervision.' In V. Cree and C. Macauley (eds) *Transfer of Learning in Professional and Vocational Education.* London: Routledge.

Thoburn, J., Lewis, A. and Shemmings, D. (1993) *Family Participation in Child Protection.* Norwich: University of East Anglia.

Thoburn, J., Lewis, A. and Shemmings, D. (1995) *Paternalism or Partnership? Family involvement in the child protection process.* London: HMSO.

Thomas, M. and Pierson, J. (eds) (1995) *Dictionary of Social Work.* London: Collins.

Thomas, T. (1995) *Privacy and Social Services.* Aldershot: Arena.

Thompson, B. (1990) *Identity and Role.* Milton Keynes: Open University.

Thompson, N. (1991) *Crisis Intervention Revisited.* Birmingham: Pepar Press.

Thompson, N. (1995) *Theory and Practice in Health and Social Welfare.* Buckingham: Open University Press.

Thompson, N. (1997) *Anti-Discriminatory Practice,* 2nd edn. London: Macmillan.

Thompson, N. (1998) *Promoting Equality: Challenging discrimination and oppression in the human services.* London: Macmillan.

Thompson, N. (2000a) *Theory and Practice in Human Services.* Buckingham: Open University Press.

Thompson, N. (2000b) *Understanding Social Work: Preparing for practice.* Basingstoke: Palgrave.

Thompson, N. (2000c) 'Existentialist Practice.' In P. Stepney and D. Ford (eds) *Social Work Models, Methods and Theories: A framework for practice.* Lyme Regis: Russell House.

Thompson, N., Murphy, M., Stradling, S. with O'Neill, P. (1998) *Meeting the Stress Challenge: A training manual for social welfare managers, trainers and practitioners.* Lyme Regis: Russell House.

Thorne, B. (1997) 'Person-centred Counselling.' In M. Davies (ed) *The Blackwell Companion to Social Work.* Oxford: Blackwell.

Timms, N. (1983) *Social Work Values: An enquiry.* London: Routledge and Kegan Paul.

Trevithick, P. (2000) *Social Work Skills: A practice handbook.* Buckingham: Open University Press.

Triseliotis, J., Sellick, C. and Short, R. (1995a) *Foster Care Theory and Practice.* London: Batsford.

Triseliotis, J., Borland, M., Hill, M. and Lambert, L. (1995b) *Teenagers and the Social Work Services.* London: HMSO.

Trotter, C. (1999) *Working with Involuntary Clients.* London: Sage.

United Nations (1989) *Convention on the Rights of the Child.* Geneva: United Nations.

Vostanis, P. and Cumella, S. (eds) (1999) *Homeless Children: Problems and needs.* London: Jessica Kingsley.

Walker, A. (1997) 'Community Care Policy: From consensus to conflict.' In J. Bornat, J. Johnson, A. Pereira, D. Pilgrim and F. Williams (eds) *Community Care: A reader,* 2nd edn. London: Macmillan.

Walker, J., McCarthy, P., Morgan, W. and Timms, N. (1995) *In Pursuit of Quality: Improving practice teaching in social work.* Newcastle upon Tyne: Relate Centre for Family Studies.

Walklin, L. (1990) *Teaching and Learning in Further and Adult Education.* Cheltenham: Stanley Thornes.

Walmsley, J., Reynolds, J., Shakespeare, P. and Wolf, R. (1993a) 'Introduction: Roles and relationships in health and welfare.' In J. Walmsley, J. Reynolds, P. Shakespeare and R. Wolf (eds) *Health Welfare and Practice: Reflecting on roles and relationships.* London: Sage.

Walmsley, J., Reynolds, J., Shakespeare, P. and Wolf, R. (eds) (1993b) *Health Welfare and Practice: Reflecting on roles and relationships.* London: Sage.

Waterhouse, Sir Ronald, le Fleming, M. and Clough, M. (2000) *Lost in Care: Report of the tribunal of inquiry into the abuse of children in care in the former county council areas of Gwynedd and Clwyd since 1974.* London: Stationery Office.

Watson, F. (1998) 'Confidentiality and Risk Assessment: Studies of the professional judgements of nurses, social workers and hospital chaplains.' Unpublished PhD thesis submitted to the University of Leeds, September.

Wetzel, J. (1986) 'A Feminist World View Conceptual Framework.' *Social Casework: Journal of Contemporary Social Work* March, 166–173.

Wheal, A. (ed) (1999) *The RHP Companion to Foster Care.* Lyme Regis: Russell House.

Wheeler, S. and Birtle, J. (1993) *A Handbook for Personal Tutors.* Buckingham: Open University Press.

Whitehead, S. (1992) 'The Social Origins of Normalisation.' In H. Brown and H. Smith (eds) *Normalisation.* London: Routledge.

Williams, F. (1989) *Social Policy: A critical introduction.* London: Polity Press.

Williams, J. and Watson, G. (1996) 'Mental Health Services that Empower Women.' In T. Heller, J. Reynolds, R. Gomm, R. Muston and S. Pattison (eds) *Mental Health Matters: A reader.* London: Macmillan in association with the Open University.

Woods, P. (1996) 'Critical Students: Breakthroughs in learning.' In P. Woods (ed) *Contemporary Issues in Teaching and Learning.* London: Routledge.

Subject Index

Author Index